RECYCLING THE STATE
The Politics of Adaptation
in Ireland

Dedicated to Ireland's emerging scholars
because, as this book testifies,
De réir a chéile a thogtar na caisleáin
(It takes time to build castles)

RECYCLING THE STATE

The Politics of Adaptation in Ireland

Editors
**Katy Hayward and
Muiris MacCarthaigh**

Foreword by
TOM GARVIN

IRISH ACADEMIC PRESS
DUBLIN • PORTLAND, OR

First published in 2007 by
IRISH ACADEMIC PRESS
44, Northumberland Road, Dublin 4, Ireland

and in the United States of America by
IRISH ACADEMIC PRESS
ISBS, Suite 300, 920 NE 58th Avenue
Portland, Oregon 97213-3644

This edition © 2007 Irish Academic Press
Chapters © Individual Authors
Figure 8.3 © Ordnance Survey Ireland/Government of Ireland Copyright
Permit No. MP 000107

www.iap.ie

British Library Cataloguing in Publication Data
An entry can be found on request

ISBN 978 0 7165 2939 2 (cloth)
ISBN 978 0 7165 2940 8 (paper)

Library of Congress Cataloging-in-Publication Data
An entry can be found on request

Cover design by Martin Duggan

Typeset in 11/13pt Sabon by FiSH Books, Enfield, Middx.
Printed by Creative Print and Design (Wales), Ebbw Vale

Contents

List of Figures

List of Tables

List of Boxes

List of Abbreviations

AGIY	Action Group of Irish Youth
AGM	Annual General Meeting
APOCC	All-Party Oireachtas Committee on the Constitution
CDB	City Development Board
COI	Commission on Itinerancy
CORI	Conference of Religious of Ireland
CPG	Corporate Policy Group
CWC	Community Workers Co-operative
DCU	Dublin City University
DoE	Department of Environment
DOHC	Department of Health and Children
DUP	Democratic Unionist Party
DWS	Developmental Welfare State
EC	European Community
EEC	European Economic Community
EU	European Union
FIS	Federation of Irish Societies
GFA	Good Friday Agreement
GLC	Greater London Council
GNP	Gross National Product
GPO	General Post Office
GRO(S)	General Register Office (Scotland)
HC	Human Capital
ICI	Immigrant Council of Ireland
IFB	Intermediary Funding Body
IGC	Inter-Governmental Conference
INES	Irish National Election Study
IPA	Institute of Public Administration
IRA	Irish Revolutionary Army
ITM	Irish Traveller Movement
MRBI	Market Research Bureau of Ireland
NESC	National Economic and Social Council
NGO	Non-Governmental Organisation
NPM	New Public Management

OECD	Organisation for Economic Co-operation and Development
ONS	Office for National Statistics (UK)
PD	Progressive Democrats
PR-STV	Proportional Representation by Single Transferable Vote
PSNI	Police Service of Northern Ireland
R & D	Research and Development
RTÉ	Radio Telefis Éireann
SDLP	Social Democratic and Labour Party
SEUPB	Special European Union Programmes Body
SPC	Strategic Policy Committee
TD	Teachta Dála (member of Dáil Éireann)
UNHCR	United Nations High Commissioner for Refugees
UUP	Ulster Unionist Party

Contributors to this volume

Mark Callanan is a lecturer with the Institute of Public Administration in Dublin, and has a Masters from the College of Europe, Bruges, and a PhD from University College Cork. He has published widely in both domestic and international journals and books, and is co-editor of the standard text on Irish local government, *Local Government in Ireland: Inside Out*. Dr Callanan is a member of the high-level Local Government Customer Service Group and has carried out commissioned research for several Government Departments and the European Commission on issues ranging from EU Structural Funds management to participatory decision-making.

Una Crowley is Government of Ireland (Irish Research Council for the Humanities and Social Sciences) post-doctoral Research Fellow in the Department of Geography, National University of Ireland (NUI), Maynooth, where she also gained her PhD. She is one of Ireland's leading experts on Travellers' citizenship rights. Dr Crowley has recently completed a project on the genealogy of sexuality in Ireland since the nineteenth century.

Bryan Fanning is a senior lecturer in the School of Applied Social Science at UCD. He is the author of *Racism and Social Change in the Republic of Ireland* (Manchester University Press, 2002), *Evil, God the Greater Good and Rights: The philosophical origins of social problems* (Edwin Mellon, 2007) and the forthcoming *Intellectual Politics and Nation-Building: Ireland: 1912–1986* (Irish Academic Press, 2008). He is the editor of *Immigration and Social Change in the Republic of Ireland* (Manchester University Press, 2007), co-editor of *Ireland Develops: Administration and Social Policy 1953–2003* (Institute of Public Administration, 2003), *Theorising Irish Social Policy* (UCD Press, 2004) and *Care and Social Change in the Irish Welfare Economy* (Dublin: UCD Press, 2006).

Katy Hayward is Government of Ireland (Irish Research Council for the Humanities and Social Sciences) post-doctoral Research Fellow at the Institute for British–Irish Studies, UCD, where she is researching the potential of multi-level co-operation for conflict transformation. After completing her PhD on Irish nationalism and European integration in UCD in 2002, she held a research fellowship in the School of Politics and International Studies, Queen's University, Belfast. She is founding convenor of the European Studies Specialist Group of the Political Studies Association of Ireland and has published widely in the fields of European integration, conflict resolution and Irish politics.

Kevin Howard is a lecturer in Dundalk Institute of Technology's Department of Humanities. His PhD on the Irish in Britain was completed in the Institute for British–Irish Studies in UCD in 2003 and he was previously post-doctoral Research Fellow there for the Mapping Frontiers, Plotting Pathways project on cross-border relations in Ireland. His primary research interests are in migration and the politics of transnational ethnicity and he has published in this area, including the article 'Constructing the Irish of Britain' in *Ethnic and Racial Studies* (January 2006).

Adrian Kavanagh is currently a contract lecturer and researcher in the Department of Geography in NUI Maynooth and is a research associate of the National Institute for Regional and Spatial Analysis and the National Centre for Geocomputation. His main research interests lie within the field of electoral geography (in particular, the geography of voter turnout and election boundaries), but interests also include other political geographical topics, such as the geographical background to conflicts. He is currently a committee member of the Geographical Society of Ireland, with responsibility for the editing of the GeoNews newsletter.

Cathal McCall is a lecturer in the School of Politics, International Studies and Philosophy at Queen's University, Belfast. He gained his PhD from the University of Strathclyde, with a thesis that subsequently formed the basis of the book *Identity in Northern Ireland: Communities, Politics and Change* (Macmillan 1999). His research interests address questions of identity in the integrated contexts of Northern Ireland, the island of Ireland, the British Isles and the European Union. His recent research and publications have been focused on issues of social capital and European governance in the Irish border region.

Muiris MacCarthaigh is a Research Officer at the Institute of Public Administration in Dublin. He holds a PhD from the School of Politics and International Relations at University College, Dublin and his most recent publication is *Accountability in Irish Parliamentary Politics* (2005). He also lectures on Irish politics and public administration, and has a strong interest in accountability regimes. He is currently involved with the Comparative Public Organisation Data Base for Research and Analysis network, which is a cross-national research network on the governance of national, regional and local public sector agencies.

Kenneth McKenzie is a postdoctoral researcher in the UCD Geary Institute. He obtained his PhD from Dublin City University (2004), with a thesis on the implications of value shift for political behaviour. He has previously been a lecturer in the Faculty of Health Sciences in Trinity College Dublin. His research interests centre on the analysis of citizens' understanding of the public sphere and he is working on a multidisciplinary project on people's decision-making in health and major life decisions.

Tina MacVeigh is the Education Coordinator with the Fatima Regeneration Board. She is a graduate of UCD and holds an MA in European Social Policy Analysis from NUI Maynooth. Her current research work centres on a community based analysis of the Irish primary education policies aimed at alleviating educational disadvantage. She recently completed a Teaching Fellowship with the School of Applied Social Science in UCD, and in the past has been involved at a local level with community-based projects seeking to raise awareness and develop a rights-based approach to issues of poverty and disadvantage.

Aoileann Ni Éigeartaigh is a Lecturer in the Department of Humanities in Dundalk Institute of Technology (DKIT). Her doctoral thesis (University of Edinburgh 2001) was on consumerism and the mass media in modern literature. She is the vice-chair of the Irish Association for American Studies and a founding researcher at the Centre for the Study of Culture and Society at DKIT. She has published on a variety of topics related to Irish and American culture and literature, including *Borders and Borderlands in Contemporary Culture*, in collaboration with David Getty (Cambridge Scholars Press 2006).

Foreword

So much change has happened in the Republic of Ireland in recent times that it has outrun the capacity of many commentators, whether Irish or foreign, to absorb or understand it in full. One subtle shift is in the realm of popular mentality. The old obsession with moral behaviour, in particular in the areas of sexuality and marriage, has evaporated almost as though it had never existed, even though it had been legislated for by the state in all kinds of strange and wonderful ways. Similarly, attitudes to Northern Ireland and the vexed question of partition and possible reunification of the island have become far more nuanced, calm and amenable to reasoned argument and negotiation. Likewise, attitudes to the United Kingdom have become friendlier and more self-assured.

Yet at the same time old habits persist. In particular, Irish democratic politics is still what it always was: the cleavage in party politics dividing Fianna Fáil on the one hand from Fine Gael, from Labour and the minor parties on the other. The only difference is the admittedly crucial one of Fianna Fáil ceasing to be able to count on a clear majority or near-majority in the Dáil, as was the case up until 1989. Since that vital year, Fianna Fáil has been able to govern only in coalition, either with Labour or with the Progressive Democrats, and clearly de Valera's great pan-nationalist party pines for its old days of glory. The demise of monolithic party government has coincided with a weakening of traditional authoritarian styles in politics. Institutional devices such as the Office of the Ombudsman, Tribunals of Inquiry into the actions of political leaders, the Criminal Assets Bureau and other similar autonomous sources of investigation and even inquisition have left Irish politicians, office-holders and other power-holders more liable than had previously been the case to look over their shoulder and worry about accounting for their behaviour.

Most important perhaps is the fact that the country has become unprecedently rich. Maybe for the first time since the Tudor conquest, the smaller island is possibly richer per head than the bigger island is. This has gone along with an extraordinary and equally unprecedented wave of immigrants into what was traditionally an emigrant country with a well-developed emigrant culture and a huge diaspora in Britain and the United States. To the eastern European immigrants, modern Ireland is the Golden Door, much as America was to generations of Irish work-seekers in previous generations. However, the Irish remain Irish. Perhaps one unchanging facet of Irish culture is its often underestimated ability to adapt. Perhaps the Irish historical ability to fit into other countries' cultures rather easily was combined with a chameleon-like capacity to throw away aspects of Irish culture deemed unnecessary or a hindrance, while adopting new attitudes and habits of behaviour and blandly pretending that nothing has changed. One thing that hasn't changed, in other words, is the Irish ability to deny that things *have* changed.

The present book is a timely analysis of this inherent paradox in the Irish polity. It examines some of the areas of most significant change in recent times – as in the aforementioned relationship with Northern Ireland, emerging challenges for electoral politics, and the new modes of accountability – while highlighting within them those stubborn elements which could actually do with some changing, such as attitudes to traditional minorities or welfare policy. Ultimately it goes to confirm a long-held characteristic of Irish politics: we are uniquely consistent in our inconsistency.

Tom Garvin
Dublin
August 2006

Preface

This book explores the processes of continuity and change that have forged the nature of the state in Ireland. Although recent developments in the Republic of Ireland reflect the impact of global and European social and economic influences, it nonetheless does not conform to the strictures of most academic theories of statehood. The papers collected in this book together fill a vacuum that continues to exist in scholarly research on Irish politics, and they do so in two main ways. First, their use of detailed and original empirical evidence covers various dimensions of the contemporary Irish state from a range of disciplinary perspectives. Secondly, they all demonstrate the usefulness of a 'recycling' model of politics, involving definition, representation and participation, illustrating how the political institutions of the state affect and are affected by the people they purport to represent.

A number of the chapters have their origins as papers presented at the 'Recycling the State' conference held at University College Dublin in April 2002, yet have been extensively expanded and developed in preparation for their inclusion here. The editors wish to thank a number of people for their support and involvement in the conference that formed the genesis of this volume – Jean Brennan, Dr Garret FitzGerald, Jonathan Githens-Mazer, Dermot Hodson, Mr John Hume, Elizabeth Meehan, Stephen Mennell, Eunan O'Halpin and Diane Payne. We are particularly grateful to the staff and graduate students of UCD's School of Politics and International Relations for their (perhaps sometimes unwitting!) participation in the generation of the ideas and themes for inclusion in this book.

Our deepest debt of gratitude is, of course, to all the contributors to this volume, many of whom completed their doctoral theses during the course of the writing of this book. It is through their patient hard work and commitment to the project that this volume uniquely brings together the research of emerging scholars from such a wide range of disciplinary and institutional backgrounds. The fact that the authors' perspectives are refreshingly new and diverse is an appropriate feature of a book addressing the issue of political adaptation in contemporary Ireland.

Katy Hayward
Muiris MacCarthaigh
August 2006

1

Introduction: The politics of adaptation in Ireland

Katy Hayward

From the wooded garden of an ancient land – so the story goes – through storms of invasion, the desert years of oppression, the battles for freedom, and the nurturing of independence, the prophets have foretold the birth of a new Ireland.[1] Now, according to the statesmen of this age, it has come to pass. Lemass' 'new Ireland' of economic liberalisation (Breen et al. 1990: 38);[2] FitzGerald's 'new Ireland' of non-discrimination among 'Irishmen' (1978);[3] the Forum's 'new Ireland' of 'lasting peace and stability' (1984: 5.3); Robinson's 'new Ireland' of 'openness, tolerance and pluralism' (Quinn 1997: 1); Hume's 'new Ireland' of the trinity of strands (1997); Adams' 'new Ireland' of inclusion and equality (2002); McDowell's 'new Ireland' of new opportunities (2007) all point to significant change in the economic, social and political conception of Ireland. Yet reminders of the 'old Ireland' are ever-present; questions of sovereignty, neutrality, territorial unity and cultural integrity abound.

It is possible to argue that these are not merely anachronistic hangovers from bygone times; they remain pillars of Irish political society. In seeking to create the 'new Ireland', the political elite of Ireland have turned not to the future but to the past, reworking what they believe has always been significant. Hence, Lemass' transforming programme of modernisation was to fulfil Ireland's inherent potential (Ahern 2002),[4] EU membership was to be 'a sanctuary for the spiritual values so highly regarded by us' (Haughey 1962),[5] and the 'agreed Ireland' represents a positive development of *traditional* relationships (Hume 1997). For this reason, the 'new Ireland' of today is the product of political adaptation from yesterday in preparation for tomorrow. It is the 'recycling' of what has constituted the political fabric of the Irish state since its inception.

Continuity in change

Snapshots of contemporary Irish society highlight the ambiguities that lie at the heart of the 'new Ireland'. Ireland is the most globalised country in the world, yet it is also close to the bottom of the poverty-table in the EU, with a steady rise in households below the poverty line (Kearney 2004; Nolan et al. 2002).[6] Inequalities also persist between men and women, with the latter earning an average of 82 per cent of their male counterparts' earnings,[7] despite the fact that Ireland has one of the highest levels of female entrepreneurs in Europe.[8] The increase in immigration into Ireland, with applications for asylum rising from 39 in 1992 to a peak of 11,634 in 2002, would suggest that Ireland is an increasingly diverse society (United Nations High Commissioner for Refugees 2005). However, by far the largest proportion (39 per cent) of the total 66,900 immigrants to Ireland in 2002 were of Irish nationality, and the social integration of non-Anglophone migrants is notably poor (ICI 2005; Mac Éinrí 2001). The ambiguities of the moral conscience of the 'new Ireland' are reflected in the fact that Ireland has the highest levels both of binge drinking and of church attendance in Europe (Department of Health and Children 2004; Davis 2003). Concern to increase integrity in Irish society has produced the tightest ever laws against corruption, and yet Ireland's rank in the International Corruption Index is worsening.[9] Such changes in Irish society and, moreover, their complexity point to the need for a model of statehood that is processual rather than static.

'Recycling the state' is about the politics of adaptation in relation to ongoing processes of economic, social and cultural change. Conceptions of how the state has responded to such changes in recent times vary according to the particular dynamics emphasised. Hence, an emphasis upon the significance of European integration leads to focus on the state's new international role; an emphasis on the leap of the Celtic Tiger leads to a focus on the state's economic transformation; an emphasis on the context of globalisation leads to focus on the impact of international communication, trade and technological developments in Ireland. Whether we are looking at global or local processes, the role of the state has altered. This is not a situation unique to Ireland; indeed, the similarity between stimuli for the Irish state's continual adaptation and those of other states is stronger than ever. Nevertheless, the key point of the 'recycling' model is that the Irish state *remains* 'unique': it is addressing issues that transcend national borders in a *national* way. The continuing importance of national difference for modern states relates to the context-based nature of politics, which is directed by a janus-faced vision of past and future and motivated by both pragmatism and ideology. In examining various levels and dimensions of political adaptation in Ireland in recent times, the papers in this volume highlight the central importance of continuity in the Irish state's response to change. To place this approach in context, it is necessary to consider other interpretations of the impact of external and internal change on statehood, and on the Irish state in particular.

The state of change: Alternative interpretations

Comparative political analysis faces a problem when it comes to the Irish case: what to compare Ireland with? Ireland's historically defined resemblance to a spectrum of international actors means that comparisons are at once obvious and tenuous. It is possible, for example, to emphasise the fact that Ireland's economic growth has been assisted by the example of the Asian Tigers and nurtured by the influence of the United States, which also has a deep cultural significance for Irish society. Nevertheless, Ireland's historical links with the United States are barely comparable to those of its nearest neighbour, particularly given the inheritance of various aspects of the 'Westminster model' of parliamentary politics. Yet over eighty years of independence have passed, in which distinctively non-British traits have been self-consciously fostered in Irish state and society. Ireland's increasingly close ties with states and political developments in continental Europe have played an important role in the cultivation of such traits.[10] Indeed, the binding of economic, political and cultural strands in the process of European integration, not to mention the importance of concepts of historical and future development, means that models of the reaction of contemporary *European* states to processes of change are most relevant to the Irish case. It is to such models that we now turn.

Retreating state

Ohmae's neo-liberal vision (1995) has the state retreat in the face of 'globalising forces', as national political structures and cultures are bypassed by those within and beyond the state, for economic gain. Korten (1995) also envisions the state being replaced as the key actor in international and domestic affairs, although he regards this as a negative process, one in which the imperialism of corporations tramples over diversity. In the European context and in light of European integration, these pressures from above and below on the integrity of the state are not just economic but increasingly political. The 'search for salvation' beyond the state, to use Friedman's phrase (1992: 355), is viewed by functionalist theorists as a necessary and inevitable consequence of global change (Haas 1958, 1997). The transcendence of the state is related to the functionalist perception that the logic of transferring sovereignty from the state to the European Union is self-sustaining and self-perpetuating (Dedman 1996: 9). For changes in economic, political and social spheres will lead, it is argued, to the search for integrationist solutions to common problems. When applied to the level of domestic politics, sociological theories of functionalism view social structures (and, subsequently, social relations and conceptions) as adjusting to meet the imperatives of the wider system (Durkheim 1982). Indeed, according to the 'modernist school' of theories of nationalism, the nation–state itself is a product of functionalism, given its development in response to the conditions of modernity, such as industrial development (Gellner 1983) or psychological need (Llobera 1994). As a consequence, some envisage the changing global system as leading towards the eventual replacement of the nation–state by new forms of governance and ideology (Hobsbawm 1990: 164, 1995: 427–431).

Drawing on this interpretation of the modern nation–state in the Irish context have been the 'postnationalist' approaches of those such as Kearney (1997), O'Mahony and Delanty (1998), and Graham (2001). The traditional conceptions of Irish statehood in regard to Europe, Britain and Northern Ireland are, they contend, under increasing pressure (if not obsolete) in the new conditions of postmodernity. Although one uses a philosophical approach and the other applies socio-economic analysis, both Kearney (1997) and Goodman (2000) concur that European integration has significant functional implications for relations between North and South in Ireland. Indeed, Goodman views the Good Friday Agreement (1998) as epitomising the recognition of political forces beyond the state. Significant as the Agreement is, it is nevertheless misleading to present it as an 'about-turn' in the course of Irish political ideology or practice. Indeed, its very success depended on it being 'sellable' to both unionist and nationalist populations as the fulfilment of certain goals that they have traditionally held, whether it be the securing of majority consent in Northern Ireland before constitutional change for unionists or the revocation of the 1920 Government of Ireland Act for nationalists. Indeed, critics of the 'postnational' vision of a new Ireland (as put forward not only by Kearney and Goodman but also by influential politicians such as John Hume and Garret FitzGerald) depict not the retreat but the *restatement* of the nationalist position. As Cunningham (1997: 17) speculates, the neofunctionalist vision of a single Ireland in a single Europe is 'either over-optimistic and naïve or it is deliberately framed to promote *de facto* nationalism'. The fact that old ideas about statehood remain so entrenched and persuasive has led some to argue that the Agreement epitomises the resilience of the Irish state in the twenty-first century.

Resilient state

There are various ways of highlighting the resilience of the modern state in this 'postmodern' era. For example, Cable (1996: 133) contends that the state is responding to – and therefore enduring – the effects of globalisation with increased technologies. From a sociological perspective, Hall (1995: 200) notes that a feature of politics today is the resurgence of ethnic and national identifications rather than their dissipation. In relation to European integration, the resilience of the state is explained through an inter-governmental interpretation of the European Union. For example, Milward (1992) rationalises the existence of the European Union on the basis that its purpose was to 'rescue' modern states in the post-war context. Hoffmann (1966), a realist inter-governmental theorist, also argues that the European Union is the product of governmental elites' awareness of the need for co-operation in order for the nation–state to remain the principal actor in the international system. Thus, European integration is neither cause nor symptom of a retreat of the state, but rather a course of action chosen by member-states as a means of pursuing national interests. As political and economic power is moved beyond the confines of the state, the influence of the national elite is not transferred but increased. For this reason, according to Moravcsik (1999), the success of the European Union can be explained in terms of the success of its member-states and, as even a key figure in the development of the EU itself acknowledged, 'the European project cannot replace the national project' (Delors 1992: 22).

In relation to domestic politics, traditional theories of political sociology such as behaviouralism, elite theory and classical pluralism moved in the twentieth century to sideline the significance of the state as just one out of many forms of dominant power. However, these trends have been challenged by theorists seeking to 'bring the state back in' to our conception of politics and society (Evans et al. 1985). The importance of the state's use of coercive power, its capacity to influence civil society and to affect social divisions, its symbolic significance as the representation of national communities, as well as its continued significance in the international system point to the resilience of the modern state (Giddens 1985 after Weber; Mann 1988; Walby 1990; Anderson 1983). There are various interpretations as to why and how the resilience of the state persists. For example, Jopke (1999) contends that fairly minor changes in the institutional framework of the polity enable the pillars of statehood to remain steadfast. Others see new forces of change at the international level as linked to changes at the local level, with new opportunities being opened for the state to play a defining role (Beck 1997: 99). The unique nature of statehood makes it resilient and facilitates continuity in the midst of pressures for change.

Recycled state

Theories that point to the resilience of the nation–state in the contemporary European context therefore concur with theories of the 'retreating state' on one fundamental principle: the relationship between the state and forces of change is one of antagonism and competition. The approach taken in this volume questions any conceptualisation of the state as a static entity, asserting instead that the endurance of the state arises from its inherently adaptive nature. Our emphasis on the importance of context, the role of the governmental elite and the significance of *processes* rather than institutions or structures in politics places this model in a broadly constructivist framework. In the realm of social science, constructivism holds that social realities exist only by agreement, by human cognitive action and interaction. Hence they are fragile and changeable – shaped, among other factors, by context, influence and (official) discourse. For instance, 'state' is a construct, with the term itself summarising, and even distorting, a complex combination of theoretical and practical elements that vary according to context (see, for example, Berger and Luckmann [1967] and Searle [1995]). Thus, social constructivism recognises that 'knowledge/value systems are continually reshaped as groups react to changing environmental and social conditions' and the meaning and value of the various constituents of statehood are 'interminably negotiated, revised and redefined' (Tilley 1997:511; Özkirimli 2000: 217). Such 'negotiations' happen within the state itself, yet they are necessarily led, expressed and drawn into a coherent whole by official nationalism. They are thus reflected in the discourse or language of the governmental elite, which incorporates elements of the existing political and social situation into a broader vision that constitutes the ideological justification for the projects of the state.

In the context of external pressures, social constructivism highlights the 'symbiotic' relationship between statehood and, for example, European integration. Such symbiosis is necessary because of the 'two-level game' played by governmental elites in making decisions that are viable in both domestic and European bargaining: these elites are under pressure to promote *compatibility* between European and national structures, identities and discourses (Tonra and Dunne 1997: 28). In relation to processes of change, a core tenet of social constructivism is that underlying principles of collective actors change according to experience (Offe and Wiesenthal 1979). What is debated is the depth and form of such change. A standard view among social constructivists (such as that elaborated by Risse and Wiener [1999: 789–790] in relation to European integration) and neo-institutionalists is that new political positions arise from 'critical junctures' of political crisis, which in turn produce change in the underlying discourses, assumptions and identities.[11] The model of 'recycling' proposed here modifies this account by highlighting the continued significance of historical and national context. 'Critical junctures' are important, but they are not the only points at which the underlying discourse changes. Such a view risks reifying the discourse as a 'given' (with the political elite and community remaining faithful to an essential set of discursive norms and principles until a crisis) rather than a 'construct' (with evolving and varied interpretations of these norms and principles at all levels: see below). The need to acknowledge the impact of the actors on the definition and changing of discursive norms and principles is as important a consideration as the one relating to how these factors might influence the actors themselves. Thus, the European Union undoubtedly has a 'transformative impact on the European state system and its constituent units', yet this impact remains for the most part mediated through *national* institutional, structural and discursive realms (Christiansen et al. 1999: 529). Such realms include 'beliefs about the nature of society and country', structural conditions and institutional frameworks which in turn affect the state's vision of the European project itself (Skotnicka-Illasiewicz and Wesolowski 1995: 209; Smith 1992: 76). 'Recycling' old principles and practices for new challenges enables the national political elite to manage not only the progress but also the perception of the state in the continually fluctuating context in which it operates.

Three dimensions of political adaptation

The question of political adaptation to contextual change points to the complex interrelationship of state and society. In focusing on the 'recycling' of the Irish state, the papers in this volume concentrate on the way in which institutional arrangements 'regulate the behaviour of political and societal actors who are both autonomous and interdependent in a democratic polity' (Keman 2002: 7). As Held (1989: 1) notes, the state is 'enmeshed in the political structures of society', which are themselves in turn 'shaped by the state'. Such 'relations of association and appropriation' make simple cause-and-effect analyses of change in a political community insufficient (Schwartz 1988: 145). The fact that these relations are in a constant state of flux, involving not only current dynamics but also influences of history and visions of the future, points to the significance of contextual knowledge (Daalder 2002: 27). A rounded conception of political statehood must include factors other than formal institutionalisation, not least because, as Bentham himself asserted, institutions must themselves 'be suited to the peoples for whom they are made' (Lane and Ersson 2002: 246; Bentham in Plamenatz 1973: 12). Ideal examples to fit the ideal types put forward in political science are hard to find. It is for this reason that the 'recycling' model of political adaptation proposed here is unapologetically inclusive, drawing on the theoretical insights of relevant disciplines as well as on the particular dimensions of the Irish case study examined in this volume. In this model, the state embodies continual processes of 'recycling' in which history, present and future merge in both ideational and pragmatic terms. These

processes encompass three areas of statehood: definition, representation and participation (see Figure 1.1 below).

Definition

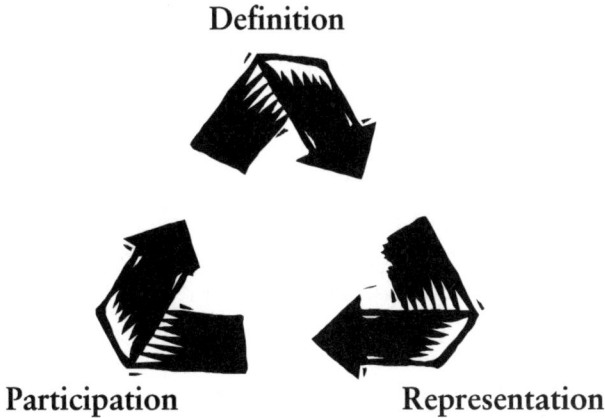

Participation   **Representation**

Figure 1.1 *The model of recycling in political adaptation.*

This model is a development of Andrain and Apter's conception of
the relationship between 'the rulers and the ruled' (1995). According
to these authors, state/society relations have three analytical
dimensions: cultural beliefs (stressing the purposes and interpretations of rule), structural conditions (the organisations through
which political leaders wield power), and behaviour ('how
individuals interpret political messages and operate political
organisations') (p.2). Whereas this model allowed Andrain and
Apter to examine the role of political protest in relation to social
change, the focus on political *adaptation* to change in this volume
requires a stronger focus on the state dimension. Hence the three
types of belief in political life they outline (existential, normative and
imaginative, pp. 15–16) are, far more than different approaches
taken to the state, three dimensions of state ideology itself. For
assumptions of political reality (existential beliefs), goals and policy
priorities (normative beliefs), and utopian visions (imaginative
beliefs) are all central features of official nationalism, which serves
to legitimate and define the state. The definition of the state is the
first dimension of the 'recycling' model of political adaptation.

Definition

The definition of the state has a variety of forms in relation to its range of functions. In identifying this dimension of statehood we are pointing to the 'transcendental' aspect of the political, in which the state is 'more than the aggregate of the interests of its members' (Berki 1979: 2). Transcendentalism is particularly associated with a 'classical' interpretation of politics, in which the assumption of political responsibility by the state leads citizens to identify with it (Schwartz 1988: 7). This identification of citizens with the state is necessary because, to quote Bentham again, 'the community is a *fictitious body* composed of the individual persons who are considered as constituting as it were its *members*' (Bentham in Ricci 1991: 11, emphasis added). One function of the state as the embodiment of a political community is, therefore, to uphold the fundamental, though blurred, distinction between insiders and outsiders. The working-out of this distinction is most clearly seen in the criteria for citizenship – a factor considered in detail in this volume by Crowley and Howard. Citizenship criteria reflect the particular political concepts symbolised in political institutions (Schwartz 1988: 19; Howard 1989: 5). These political concepts 'ascribe meaning to political actions' and thus highlight policy priorities and shape the policy process (Andrain and Apter 1995: 21).

Whereas the political culture of a particular state may be observed through identification of the political ideas and values upheld by individuals through surveys, interviews and the like, this process, as noted at the start of this chapter, can present distorted images when they are viewed as 'snapshots' rather than dimensions of complex processes. This is a criticism made of the behaviouralist approach to politics, where microlevel analysis leads to a functionalist conception of the state as a neutral regulatory institution (Faulks 1999; King 1986). Social constructivists attempt to overcome this problem by emphasising the importance of constructs as opposed to 'givens' in political activity. This is seen in the way political concepts can be variously interpreted. Indeed, the power of elites is maintained in a democracy through their use and (re)interpretation of political language rather than by other means.[12] The hermeneutical dimension of discourse theory allows us to acknowledge that political concepts are necessarily both contextual (which, in the case of most contemporary states, means 'national') and flexible, able to remain relevant in a changing context whilst giving the impression of consistency. This is where the dynamic of recycling comes into play: certain themes, symbols and concepts are significant in the definition of a political community and remain broadly constant, whilst the interpretation of their meaning changes over time. The concepts defining the political community are 'literally thrust' at the citizen in the form of political speeches, symbols, school curricula, public information, and so on (Milbrath and Goel 1977: 146; Billig 1995). Thus the definition of the state is integral to the definition of the position of the citizen within the political community and, more particularly, to citizens' representation by, and participation in, the state.

Representation

Government is authorised and influenced by the engagement of citizens in politics (Barker 1990: 3). For the majority of citizens, this engagement is confined within the strictures of representative democracy; the challenge faced by states today is that the gap between representatives and the represented is widening (Manin 1997: 193). Political representation connects the people to the activity of the governing power in the state (Schwartz 1988: 1). As such, it is the only form of democracy in the contemporary state, the literal absence of citizens from the decision-making of the government being compensated for by their representation in the parliament (Lijphart 1984: 1; Pitkin 1967: 222). Just as the definition of the state and participation in the state involves drawing lines between insiders and outsiders, so representation 'entails the practical exclusion of the mass of people from decision-making' (Judge 1999: 8). Again, structural conditions shape the effectiveness of the representation of the people, with some having political parties that are closely affiliated with their interests and others being on the margins of the political community.

The territorial margins of this community are particularly significant, given that the primary basis of representation remains territorial (Judge 1999: 149). Territory has a particular significance in the case of the Irish state, a fact that is highlighted in this volume in terms of local politics, 'bridge-building' between North and South, and links with the diasporic community. Such dimensions of representation reflect the process of recycling in the Irish state by trying to draw together past, present and future. Nevertheless, new pressures in society are raising new questions as to the effectiveness of political representation. Who is being represented, on what basis

are they being represented, how and in what are they being represented? Over twenty years ago, Hayward and Berki (1979: 264)
proposed the idea that new instrumentalities in European states
would need to counteract the fading significance of traditional forms
of political representation. The fact that new forms of representation
have not been developed has significant implications for the
participation to contemporary politics. This is evidenced by the
recent tendency of official discourse to recognise the importance of
'increasing accountability' as a motivating factor, in apparent obfus-
cation of the many connotations of the term.

Participation

Political participation is integrally related to the definition of the state
because it arises from 'the concepts, ideas, attitudes and institutions
that guide or determine how the development and implementing of
public policy are variously influenced' (Golembiewski et al. 1973: 4).
Thus, at one level, political participation involves the actions of
private citizens that are aimed at influencing the constitution and
actions of a government (Milbrath and Goel 1977: 2; Verba et al.
1978: 1). It is possible to hold a broadly instrumentalist view of this
dimension of political participation, given that reasons for
individuals getting involved in politics are related to perceived
benefits, available resources and time, and pertinent issues as well as
the political environment (Kendrick et al. 1974: 28). However, as
Verba et al. (1978: 19) note, whilst individual motivations and
resources give some a participatory advantage, the role of political
institutions themselves in the mobilisation, affiliation and activity of
such individuals should not be underestimated. Hence, the other
dimension of political participation is the role of the government
itself or, more broadly, the structural conditions of the state, which,
to paraphrase Verba et al. (1978: 6), sets a ceiling and floor on
political activity. Nowhere are the opportunities for political action
more fundamentally defined than in the criteria for citizenship.
Complex distinctions not only between citizens and non-citizens but
also among citizens themselves represent the state-established
hierarchy of involvement in the political community of the state.
However, the papers in this volume draw attention to the fact that the
'hierarchy of political involvement' is also drawn on a daily basis in
the practical inequalities among those resident in and associated with
the state (Kendrick et al. 1974: 20).

Dalton (1996) identifies a number of trends in political participation in liberal democracies. These trends include an increasingly
critical citizenry, a decline in trust in political institutions, declining
voter turnout, a decline in popular involvement in traditional forms
of participation (such as voting or party membership) and a rise in
new forms or participation (such as membership of societal interest-
groups). As the papers in this volume attest, all these trends are
present in contemporary Ireland to various degrees. Different studies
have produced different explanations of the causes of such change
and different prescriptions for its remedy. Although, as Palma (1970:
2) and Milbrath (1973: 282) note, governance would not necessarily
be improved by an increase in political participation, it is apparent
that if they continue unabated, these trends of political disaffection
would have damaging implications for the effectiveness of democracy. The point made in this volume is that the core democratic instruments of Irish statehood are not merely retreating or resilient in the
face of such pressures, but are being recycled (with old elements being
reshaped for new purposes). The chapters collected together here
illustrate these trends and the inclusion of the continuity/change
paradox in virtually every area of contemporary Irish political life.

Acknowledgements

The author gratefully acknowledges funding from the Irish Research
Council for the Humanities and Social Sciences.

NOTES

1   Those who predicted the existence of a 'new Ireland' included Moran (1900), who
    claimed, 'the prospect of such a new Ireland...has already sent a great thrill through the
    land. It is a new and unlooked for situation, full with fate, not only for Ireland but for
    the world', and Morton (1937), writing in celebration of the 1937 Constitution. In more
    recent times, the new European context stimulated Fennell (1972) to call for a new
    Ireland of four provincial regions and Robb (1972) to establish the New Ireland
    Movement for unionist engagement with the Irish state.
2   Lemass was also an important figure in terms of the Irish state's policy towards Northern
    Ireland: 'Lemass sowed the seeds for a new kind of southern nationalism, a positive
    nationalism that was more extrovert, more confident, less threatening and more vibrant
    than anything that had gone before' (O'Malley 2000 page 1).
3   '...recognising that those Irishmen who did not belong in any way to the nationalist
    tradition, as well as those nationalist Irishmen who had sought to achieve Irish freedom
    by a different route from that chosen in 1916 and thereafter, must have equal rights in

the new Ireland; and that there must be no distinction or discrimination between Irishmen, based on past, or continuing, differences of political outlook.'

4 'I was struck by just how far we have come recently, when I came across a speech by Seán Lemass who, in his time as Taoiseach, strongly believed in Ireland's potential and laid the groundwork for our present success.'

5 'I do not therefore fear that we are relaxing our spiritual values and accepting a purely materialistic outlook in joining the Common Market. I think rather that we will be helping to build and strengthen a new Europe which will be a sanctuary for those spiritual values so highly regarded by us.'

6 According to the 2003 EU Survey on Living and Income Conditions, one in five people in Ireland live in poverty (see Central Statistics Office 2005).

7 See European Industrial Relations Observatory (2002).

8 BPW Ireland, News Release August 2002.

9 See Transparency International Corruption Perceptions Index 2002 http://www. transparency.org/cpi/2002/cpi2002.en.html (20/03/2007)

10 This viewpoint was epitomised in an article written by FitzGerald in 1963 on the subject of Ireland's application to the European Economic Community: 'there *is* a danger of our being somewhat swamped by the all-pervasive Anglo-American culture – even at present with all our efforts to isolate ourselves from the world outside – and the more we can reorient ourselves towards Continental influences the more chance we have of resisting Anglo-Americanism' (*Irish Times*, 5 January 1963).

11 As will be elaborated in the section on 'definition' below, social constructivism asserts that collective discourses and identities are significant because they delimit governmental elites' choices in the area of policies, interests and strategies, in the sense that policy-making has to be consistent with the discourses they espouse (Risse and Wiener 1999: 779).

12 Approaches that have variously represented the application of discourse theory to political contexts include those of Barthes, de Saussure, Bourdieu and Habermas.

REFERENCES

Adams, G. 2002. 'Working together for a New Ireland', address by Sinn Féin President at the party's Elected Representatives' conference, Monaghan, 28 October 2002. http://www.csc.tcd.ie/ pipermail/trinity-sinnfein/2002-October/000058.html (12/02/2003).

Ahern, B. 2002. 'Foreword', in *Towards Better Regulation*. Dublin: Government of Ireland, Department of the Taoiseach, February 2002, PN.11153.

Anderson, B. 1983. *Imagined Communities*. London: Verso.

Andrain, C. F. and Apter, D. E. 1995. *Political Protest and Social Change: Analyzing Politics*. Basingstoke: Macmillan.

Barker, R. 1990. *Political Legitimacy and the State*. Oxford: Clarendon.

Beck, U. 1997. *The Reinvention of Politics*. Cambridge: Polity Press.

Berger, P. and T. Luckmann, 1967. *The Social Construction of Reality: A Treatise in the Sociology of Knowledge*. London: Penguin.

Berki, R. N. 1979. 'State and society: An antithesis of modern political thought', in J. Hayward and R. N. Berki (eds), 1–29.

Billig, M. 1995. *Banal Nationalism*. London: Sage.

Business and Professional Women Ireland 2002. News release August 2002, Business and Professional Women, Ireland, http://www.bpw.ie/pdf-files/byotyPressRelease.pdf (10/09/2007).

Breen, R., D. F. Hannon, D. B. Rottman, C. T. and Whelan (eds), 1990. U*nderstanding Contemporary Ireland: State, Class, and Development in the Republic of Ireland*. Dublin: Gill and Macmillan.

Cable, V. 1996. 'Globalisation: Can the state strike back?', *The World Today*, May 1996, 133–7.

Christiansen, T., K. E. Jørgensen and A. Wiener, 1999. 'The social construction of Europe', *Journal of European Public Policy*, 6 (4), 528–44.

Collins, A. 2002. *The Needs of Asylum Seekers in Cork*. Cork: NASC, The Irish Immigrant Support Centre.

CSO 2005. Report on EU Survey on Income and Living Conditions, Dublin: Central Statistics Office, http://www.cso.ie/eusilc/document/eusilc.pdf (20/03/2007).

Cunningham, M. 1997. 'The political language of John Hume', *Irish Political Studies*, 12, 13–22.

Daalder, H. 2002. 'The Development of the Study of Comparative Politics', in H. Keman (ed.), 16–31.

Dalton, R. 1996 [2nd edn]. *Citizen Politics*. New Jersey: Chatham House.

Davis, T. C. 2003. 'The Irish and their nation: A survey of recent attitudes', *The Global Review of Ethnopolitics*, 2 (2), 17–36.

Dedman, M. J. 1996. *The Origins and Development of the European Union, 1945–1995*. London: Routledge.

Delors, J. 1992. *Our Europe: The Community and National Development*. London: Verso.

Department of Health and Children 2004. Second Report of the Strategic Task Force on Alcohol. Dublin: Department of Health and Children, September 2004. http://www.dohc.ie/publications/strategic_task_force_on_alcohol_second.html (26/03/2007)

Durkheim, E. 1982. *The Rules of Sociological Method*. London: Macmillan.

EIRO 2002. *Gender pay equity in Europe*. European Industrial Relations Observatory online, http://www.eiro.eurofound.ie/2002/01/study/TN0201101S.html (20/02/2007).

Evans, P., D. Rueschemeyer and T. Skocpol (eds). 1985. *Bringing the State Back In*. Cambridge: Cambridge University Press.

Faulks, R. 1999. *Political Sociology: A Critical Introduction*. Edinburgh: Edinburgh University Press.

Fennell, D. 1972. *A New Nationalism for the New Ireland*. Belfast: Comhairle Uladh.

FitzGerald, G. 1973. *Towards a New Ireland*. Dublin: Torc Books.

FitzGerald, G. 1978. 'Address by the Leader of Fine Gael at Michael Collins Commemoration', Beal na Blath, 20 August 1978.

Friedman, J. 1992. 'Narcissism, roots and postmodernity: The constitution of selfhood in the global crisis', in S. Lash and J. Friedman (eds), *Modernity and Identity*. Oxford: Blackwell, 331–63.

Gellner, E. 1983. *Nations and Nationalism*. Oxford: Blackwell.

Giddens, A. 1985. *The Nation-State and Violence*. Cambridge: Polity Press.

Golembiewski, R. T., J. M. Moore and J. Rabin (eds), 1973. *Dilemmas of Political Participation: Issues for Thought and Stimulations for Action*. New Jersey: Prentice-Hall.

Goodman, J. 2000. *Single Europe, Single Ireland? Uneven Development in Process*. Dublin: Irish Academic Press.

Graham, C. 2001. *Deconstructing Ireland: Identity, Theory, Culture*. Edinburgh: Edinburgh University Press.

Haas, E. B. 1958. *The Uniting of Europe: Political, Social and Economic Forces 1950–1957*. Stanford, California: Stanford University Press.

Haas, E.B. 1997. *The Rise and Decline of Nationalism*. Ithaca, NY: Cornell University Press.

Hall, S. 1995. 'New Cultures for Old', in D. Massey and P. Jess (eds), *A Place in the World*. Milton Keynes: Open University Press, 175–213.

Haughey, C. J. 1962. 'The Common Market', Speech by Government Minister, University College Galway, 14 December 1962. (Source: M. Mansergh [ed.]). *The Spirit of the Nation. The speeches and statements of Charles J. Haughey [1957–1986]*. Dublin: Mercier Press, 1986, Document 7, 12–13.

Hayward, J. and R. N. Berki, 1979. 'The state of European society', in J. Hayward and R. N. Berki (eds). *State and Society in Contemporary Europe*. Oxford: Martin Robertson, 253–64.

Held, D. 1989. *Political theory and the Modern State. Essays on State, Power and Democracy.* Oxford: Polity.

Hobsbawm, E. J. 1990. *Nations and Nationalism since 1780: Programme, Myth, Reality.* Cambridge: Cambridge University Press.

Hobsbawm, E. J. 1995 [1994]. *Age of Extremes: The Short Twentieth Century 1914–1991.* London: Abacus.

Hoffmann, S. 1966. 'Obstinate or obsolete? The fate of the nation–state and the case of western Europe', *Daedelus*, 95, 863–909.

Howard, D. 1989. *Defining the Political.* Basingstoke: Macmillan.

Hume, J., E. M. Kennedy, T. McEnery and J. van Zandt, 1997 [2nd edn]. *A New Ireland: Politics, Peace and Reconciliation.* Boulder, CO: Roberts Rinehart Publishers.

Immigrant Council of Ireland 2005. *Background Information and Statistics on Immigration to Ireland.* Dublin: Immigrant Council of Ireland, June 2005. http://www.immigrantcouncil.ie/stats.pdf accessed (20/03/07)

Jopke, C. 1999. 'Immigration is changing citizenship: A comparative view', *Ethnic and Racial Studies*, 22 (3), 629–52.

Judge, D. 1999. *Representation: Theory and Practice in Britain.* London: Routledge.

Kearney, A.T. 2004. 'Measuring globalization: economic reversals, forward momentum', *Foreign Policy*, March/April 2004, 54–69.

Kearney, R. 1997. *Postnationalist Ireland: Politics, Culture, Philosophy.* London: Routledge.

Keman, H. 2002. 'The comparative approach to democracy', in H. Keman (ed) *Comparative Democratic Politics.* London: Sage, 3–15.

Kendrick, F., T. Fleming, J. Eisenstein and J. Burkhart, (eds), 1974. *Strategies for Political Participation.* Cambridge MA: Winthrop Publishers.

King, R. 1986. *The State in Modern Society: New Directions in Political Sociology.* London: Macmillan.

Korten, D. 1995. *When Corporations Rule the World.* Connecticut: Kumarian.

Lane, J.-E. and S. Ersson, 2002. 'Democratic performance: Are there institutional effects?', in H. Keman (ed.), 233–56.

Lijphart, A. 1984. *Democracies: Patterns of Majoritarian and Consensus Government in Twenty-One Countries.* New Haven: Yale University Press.

Llobera, J. R. 1994. *The God of Modernity: The Development of Nationalism in Western Europe.* Oxford: Berg Publishers.

Mac Éinrí, P. 2001. *Immigration into Ireland: Trends, Policy Responses, Outlook.* Cork: Irish Centre for Migration Studies. http://migration.ucc.ie/irelandfirstreport.htm (25/02/2003).

Manin, B. 1997. *The Principles of Representative Government.* Cambridge: Cambridge University Press.

Mann, M. 1988. *States, War and Capitalism: Studies in Political Sociology.* Oxford: Blackwell.

McDowell, M. 2007. Statement issued by Tánaiste and Minister for Justice, Equality and Law Reform speaking at the opening of the Progressive Democrats Party conference, 'New Ireland, New Opportunities', Wexford, 16 February 2007. http://progressivedemocratics.ie/press_room/2254/ (19/04/07)

Milbrath, L. 1973. 'Political participation and constitutional democracy', in R. T. Golembiewski, J. M. Moore and J. Rabin (eds), 278–87.

Milbrath, L. W. and M. C. Goel, 1977 [1965]. *Political Participation: How and Why Do People Get Involved In Politics?* Chicago: Rand McNally.

Milward, A. S. 1992. *The European Rescue of the Nation–State.* London: Routledge.

Moran, D. P. 1900. 'The battle of two civilizations', *New Ireland Review*, reproduced in *The Philosophy of Irish Ireland*, 1905, Dublin: James Duffy, 94–114.

Moravcsik, A. 1999. 'Is something rotten in the state of Denmark? Construction and European integration', *Journal of European Public Policy*, 6 (4), 669–81.

Morton, J. B. 1937. *The New Ireland*. London: Sands the Paladin Press.

New Ireland Forum Report. 1984. Dublin: the Stationery Office.

Nolan, B., B. Gannon, R. Layte, D. Watson, C. T. Whelan and J. Williams, 2002. *Monitoring Poverty Trends in Ireland: Results from the 2000 Living in Ireland survey*. Dublin: Economic and Social Research Institute.

Ohmae, K. 1995. *The End of the Nation–State*. New York: Free Press.

Offe, C. and H. Wiesenthal, 1979. 'Two logics of collective action: Theoretical notes on social class and organizational form', *Political Power and Social Theory*, 1, 67–113.

O'Mahony, P. and G. Delanty, 1998. *Rethinking Irish History: Nationalist Identity and Ideology*. Basingstoke: Macmillan.

O'Malley, D. 2000. 'Redefining southern nationalism', speech at the Institute for British–Irish Studies with the Conference of University Rectors, UCD, 20 March 2007. http://www.iol.ie/pd/press releases/200001/omalley001.html accessed 20/03/07

O'Neill, M. (ed.), 1996. *The Politics of European Integration: A Reader*. London: Routledge.

Özkirimli, U. 2000. *Theories of Nationalism: A Critical Introduction*. London: Macmillan.

Palma, G. D. 1970. *Apathy and Participation: Mass Politics in Western Societies*. London: Collier–Macmillan.

Pitkin, H. F. 1967. *The Concept of Representation*. Berkeley: University of California Press.

Plamenatz, J. 1973. *Democracy and Illusion: An Examination of Certain Aspects of Modern Democratic Theory*. London: Longman.

Quinn, D. 1998. 'An Icon for the New Ireland: an assessment of President Robinson', *Studies An Irish Quarterly Review* 86, 343–350, http:// www.jesuit.ie/studies/articles/1998/97090101.htm (12/02/03)

Ricci, D. M. 1991. *Community Power and Democratic Theory: The Logic of Political Analysis*. New York: Random House.

Risse, T. and A. Wiener, 1999. '"Something rotten" and the social construction of social constructivism: A comment on comments', *Journal of European Public Policy*, 6 (5), 775–82.

Robb, J. D. A. 1972. 'New Ireland: Sell-out or opportunity?'. Belfast: New Ireland Movement.

Schmitter, P. C. 1970. 'A revised theory of regional integration', *International Organization*, 24, 232–64.

Schwartz, N. 1988. *The Blue Guitar: Political Representation and Community*. London: University of Chicago Press.

Searle, J. 1995. *The Construction of Social Reality*. New York: The Free Press.

Skotnicka-Illasiewicz, E. and W. Wesolowski, 1995. 'The significance of preconceptions: Europe of civil societies and Europe of nationalities', in S. Periwal (ed.), *Notions of Nationalism*, Budapest: Central European University Press, 20827.

Smith, A. D. 1992. 'National identity and the idea of European Unity', *International Affairs*, 68 (1), 55–76.

TICPI 2002. Transparency International Corruption Perception Index 2002, http://www.transparency.org/cpi/2002/cpi2002.en.html (20/03/2007).

Tilley, V. 1997. 'The terms of the debate: Untangling language about ethnicity and ethnic movements', *Ethnic and Racial Studies*, 20 (3), 497–522.

Tonra, B. and D. Dunne, 1997. *A European Cultural Identity: Myth, Reality or Aspiration?* Dublin: Institute for European Affairs.

United Nations High Commissioner for Refugees 2005. *Asylum Levels and Trends in Industrialized Countries, 2005*. Geneva: United Nations High Commissioner for Refugees.

Verba, S., N. H. Nie and J.-O. Kim, 1978. *Participation and Political Equality*. Cambridge: Cambridge University Press.

Walby, S. 1990. *Theorising Patriarchy*. Oxford: Blackwell.

2

Mise Éire: Recycling nationalist mythologies

Aoileann Ní Éigeartaigh

On 16 April 2006, the Irish state officially commemorated the 1916 Rising for the first time since 1966. The intervention of the Troubles in Northern Ireland and the perceived hijacking of Irish nationalism by the Provisional IRA had made its celebration in the intervening years a political impossibility. In the weeks leading up to the commemoration, Taoiseach Bertie Ahern repeatedly stated that the event and the discussion it inspired would constitute an opportunity for 'remembrance, reconciliation and renewal.'[1] This chapter examines representations of the 1916 Rising, investigating the extent to which they 'recycle' the traditional mythologies and heroes of nationalism on which the ideals of the state and many of its institutions have been based. Central to my argument is the observation that many of the vital tenets of Irish nationalist mythology have persisted into the twenty-first century and can be observed in the attitudes and discourse employed in relation to the 1916 commemoration ceremonies of 1935, 1966 and 2006. What is notable, however, is the facility with which the mythology constantly adapts and assimilates new elements. The recycling of Irish nationalist mythology for the 2006 commemoration thus involves simultaneously its reuse but also, crucially, its reshaping.

Nationalism and nationhood

The relationship between state and nation is at the heart of debates about national identity. In Anderson's seminal text on nationalism and its function in contemporary society (2003: 6), the nation is defined as a kind of metanarrative or ontological framework within which a disparate group of people achieves a sense of unity and commonality:

> it is an imagined political community – and imagined as both inherently limited and sovereign. It is *imagined* because the members of even the smallest nation will never know most of their fellow-members, meet them, or even hear of them, yet in the minds of each lives the image of their communion.

There are two particularly significant elements to Anderson's definition of the nation. First, he emphasises that it is an *imagined* entity: the nation is thus never what limits or excludes outsiders, rather it is the idealised set of values and beliefs that unites a group of people and forms the basis of their support for the institutions of the state. Secondly, it is the ability of the nation to present itself as a *community*, thus providing its members with a sense of belonging and comradeship that is the true source of its power and legitimacy:

> [The nation] is imagined as a *community*, because, regardless of the actual inequality and exploitation that may prevail in each, the nation is always conceived as a deep, horizontal comradeship. Ultimately it is this fraternity that makes it possible, over the past two centuries, for so many millions of people, not so much to kill, as willingly to die for such limited imaginings. (Anderson 2003: 7)

Debates about the role of nationalism in contemporary state-building have tended increasingly to focus on the negative, emphasising its assertion of difference and depicting it as a regressive, limiting and ultimately xenophobic narrative. Hobsbawm (1990: 164), for example, notes that 'the characteristic nationalist movements of the late twentieth century are essentially negative, or rather divisive'. Although a sense of difference and an imposition of limits on the constituents of a nation are crucial to its identity, however, negatives alone cannot explain the extent of the emotional power the nation holds over its members. After all, as Anderson (2003: 141) points out: 'It is useful to remind ourselves that nations inspire love, and often profoundly self-sacrificing love.'

The nation, according to Anderson's formulation, is thus the result of a dynamic exchange of ideas and needs between the state and its citizens. The nation, moreover, does not predate the establishment of the independent political state, but rather is imagined into being in order to explain and justify the institutions and values on which the state is based. Nationalism is the discourse employed by those involved in building the state to harness the support and loyalty of its citizens. What is peculiar about the Irish situation, however, is that the nation – the idealised concept that would legitimate the institutions of the state and unify its citizens – actually predated the foundation of the state. Rather than construct or imagine the nation as a means of legitimising the state and its institutions, therefore, the Irish state found itself from the start in the peculiar position of having to model itself on – in a sense live up to – the ideals and iconography of the nation.

Nationalist narratives are based on the assumption that the Irish nation survived the experience of colonialism and was poised to reawaken once independence had been achieved. This belief was inscribed in nationalist songs such as 'A Nation Once Again', which proclaimed: 'Ireland long a province, be a nation once again'. At the heart of any nationalist endeavour is a demand for the right to self-definition. After all, if the nation, as Anderson states, is an 'imagined community', one of the most important ways in which it can unite its citizens is by providing them with a framework of values and ideals they can believe in and, most importantly, identify with. One of the characteristics of colonialism is that the colonial power denies the colonized subject the right to define itself. In colonial discourse, the colonised subject languishes on the periphery, in the eternal position of a silenced 'other'. The words 'Sinn Féin' – literally 'us ourselves', but used in nationalist discourse in the more assertive sense of 'ourselves alone' – were long associated with the fight for independence, emphasising that the right to define the Irish nation should belong with the Irish people. The primary aim of the Revival movements of the 1890s was to invert the negative stereotypes ascribed by colonial texts to the Irish people and their culture, and to engage in a collective celebration of Ireland's culture and heritage. The importance of re-establishing the Irish nation in cultural terms before seeking political independence is most famously expressed in Yeats' mission statement for the Irish Literary Theatre (1913: 9): 'We will show that Ireland is not the home of buffoonery and easy sentiment as it has been represented, but the home of an ancient idealism'. In other words, it is crucial to re-establish the nation – the imagined, idealized community – before seeking to found an independent political state. This determination to wrest back control of representations of Ireland from the colonising power led to a resurgence of nationalist sentiment, culminating in the 1916 Rising.

Narratives of 1916

The Poet's Rebellion

The Rising is often referred to as the 'Poet's Rebellion'. This is partly because of the presence of a number of poets among the rebels, but also because it was an attempt to rid Ireland of the stigma of mysticism and creativity which had long been used by English rulers as 'proof' that the Irish did not have the practical skills to self-govern. The Rising was a military disaster. It was also, initially at least, extremely unpopular with the public. The execution of the leaders, however, propelled them to the status of martyrs and the Rising quickly became mythologised in the public imagination. As Yeats (1921) succinctly put it:

> I write it out in a verse –
> MacDonagh and MacBride
> And Connolly and Pearse
> Now and in time to be,
> Wherever green is worn,
> Are changed, changed utterly:
> A terrible beauty is born.

What is interesting about the Rising is that it was, in a sense, an unreal event – a spectacle. The rebels had no chance of achieving their aims militarily. They planned the rebellion knowing they were going to be killed. They did not have the support of the public, nor of most of the nationalist politicians. Pádraig Pearse, the poet and revolutionary, provides a valuable insight into his own motivation for rebellion through the volumes of poems and short stories he composed in the years leading up to the Rising. Pearse was acutely aware that the Rising would not be popularly supported. He demonstrates an extraordinary understanding of the struggle he would face, not only against the superior military strength of the British but also for the hearts of the people on whose behalf he was willing to die. Many of his poems take the form of obituaries, justifying the decision he had made to rebel and presuming that his motivations would become clear to future generations. In a sense, he is narrating his martyrdom and subsequent elevation to the status of nationalist hero even before the Rising begins. In one of his best known poems, 'The Mother' (1915), he foresees his elevation into Irish nationalist mythology:

> I do not grudge them: Lord, I do not grudge
> My two strong sons that I have seen go out
> To break their strength and die, they and a few,
> In bloody protest for a glorious thing,
> They shall be spoken of among their people,
> The generations shall remember them,
> And call them blessed.[2]

In order to justify the Rising, Pearse situates it firmly within the unfolding narrative of Irish nationalism. In his writing, he links his military endeavours with that of heroes from Irish mythology, most notably Cúchulainn, Ireland's most famous defender. In Pearse's narration of the Rising, therefore, we see an interesting recycling of Irish mythological heroes, to underline and explain the rebellion.

The recycling of Irish mythology

In 1912, Pearse wrote a poem entitled 'Mise Éire' ('I am Ireland'). As the title clearly demonstrates, this poem represents Pearse's determination to take control of definitions of the Irish nation. The poem is central to our understanding of the mythology of the Irish nation as defined by Pearse and dramatised in the Rising. His vision of the Irish nation inspired generations of politicians and artists, and underlies many of the institutions on which the Irish state was subsequently built.

Pearse's imagining of the Irish nation references two mythological figures which are synonymous with tradition and heroism: the Old Woman of Beare, who was one of many mythological personifications of Ireland; and Cúchulainn, Ireland's greatest mythological hero. Pearse thus conforms to the nationalist tradition of defining the Irish nation as an entity which has its roots in the mythological past. He also demonstrates the extent to which the recycling of these ancient myths is central to his imagining of an independent Ireland:

> I am Ireland:
> I am older than the Old Woman of Beare.
>
> Great my glory:
> I that bore Cúchulainn the valiant.

Pearse's understanding of Irish nationalism is thus based on the relationship he perceives between the land and the ancient mythologies through which it is envisioned. The Rising, for Pearse, embodied the moment during which Irish nationalists, represented by the rebels, would merge with their mythological forebears, thus resurrecting the Irish nation. The Rising, in a sense, thus becomes mythologised even as it is unfolding, and Pearse himself merges with Cúchulainn.

What is fascinating is the extent to which Pearse and the 1916 Rising have retained this element of mythology in the ways they have been represented and treated in official state discourse, and the extent to which they in turn have become recycled as part of the official mythology of the Irish state. In Yeats' poem 'The Statues' (1939), the poet notes the extent to which the figures of Pearse and Cúchulainn almost become synonymous in official retellings of the Rising:

> When Pearse summoned Cúchulainn to his side
> What stalked through the Post Office?

This poem was written in reaction not only to Pearse's own embodiment of the figure of Cúchulainn during the Rising, but also to the decision made by the Irish state to honour those who had fought in 1916 by erecting a statue of Cúchulainn in the General Post Office in 1935.

This event – and in particular the choice of icon – gives an intriguing insight into the extent to which official narratives of history and nationalism had merged with mythology under Eamon de Valera, who became Taoiseach in 1932 and presided over the 1935 commemoration ceremony. The Irish state at this point in its development was thus clearly recycling nationalist mythology in order to construct a relationship with the nation that predated it. Gibbons (1996: 70) points out that the Irish state was at a severe disadvantage from the start, as it tried to compete with the idealised vision of the nation that had resurfaced in the public imagination with the adoption of the 1916 rebels into the official pantheon of heroes. There was, therefore, a huge drive to attain the merger of state and nation through the political and cultural institutions that were established in the early years of the Irish Free State. Referring to debates surrounding the establishment of Ireland's first radio service 2RN in 1926, Gibbons (1996: 71) points out that, whereas most states use their cultural institutions to construct a sense of the nation, in Ireland the position was reversed and the radio service was expected to justify the formation of the state:

> From the beginning, policy formation in Irish broadcasting operated under the assumption that the *nation* was already in place: only the *state* awaited completion as part of the unfinished business of securing a coherent Irish identity. The state derived its legitimacy from the existence of an antecedent nation, and thus the function of broadcasting was not to establish but to revitalize this nation, releasing the cultural energies which, it was believed, had accumulated over the centuries.

Nationalist mythology and statehood

The cyclical process of national mythologising

The incorporation of the discourse and iconography of nationalist mythology into official state discourse provided a useful way to bridge the gap between the idealised nation and the actual state. Bhreathnach-Lynch (1999) notes that the Irish state made a decision very early on to solidify its identity and to begin to unite its citizens in the aftermath of a bitter civil war by investing in its heroes, both real and mythological. Within a decade of independence – and in the shadow of mounting economic problems – a series of statues, plaques and inscriptions had been commissioned to commemorate the heroes on which the values of the new nation were to be built: 'One important reason for the rush to create "new" heroes and revive "old" lies in the need a newly indepe-ndent nation has to quickly establish its own sense of national identity' (Bhreathnach-Lynch 1999: 148).

Bhreathnach-Lynch emphasises that this central role given to nationalist heroes enabled the expression of a number of ideas crucial to the perception of the Irish state as an independent political and cultural entity: it differentiated this state from Britain, it linked the present with the past, and it suggested that the future would be built on the legacy of the present:

> The new Irish State was anxious to establish as soon as possible
> a distinctive national character, one as different as possible from
> that of its erstwhile ruler... A significant aspect of this construct
> of identity was the belief that Ireland's national identity was
> rooted in a Golden Age, that of the ancient Celtic past. Recon-
> necting with and restoring that past would provide the ground
> upon which a sense of national self could take root and flourish.
> The promotion of new heroes suggested not only a positive,
> affirming self-image but also implied that another such age
> would emerge in the near future. (Bhreathnach-Lynch 1999:
> 148).

Here we see a very clear cyclical process being established: the
ancient mythological heroes are used to underpin the philosophy
and identity of the newly formed Irish state; while those involved in
the formation of the state are themselves heroised and, in a sense,
mythologised, in an attempt to build on this heroic legacy and pass
it on to future generations. All of this recycling helps to create the
sense that the Irish state – which came into being in contentious
circumstances – had divided the country during the Civil War but
was now trying to stabilise itself and unite its opposing factions and
was part of a longer and ongoing historical narrative: 'Such
perceptions help sustain the belief among the populace that the
nation is not a transitory construct but rather occupies a distinct
place in a permanent continuum' (Bhreathnach-Lynch 1999: 149).

The advantage of using the mythology and heroes of the ancient
nation to underpin and construct the new Irish state was two-fold.
First, much of the iconography and ideology of the nation was
popularly accepted and thus easy to build on and incorporate into
the identity of the new state. Secondly, by focusing on the heroes of
mythology, the state could avoid addressing and engaging with the
conflict surrounding its foundation.

State power and mythology

It is important to remember that, when we talk about mythologies
in the context of the contemporary state, we are referring not only
to something that links a society to its past, but also to a discourse
that has profound implications for the ways in which that society

develops in the present. At this point it is perhaps useful to reflect briefly on the contemporary meaning of the term 'mythology'. In spite of the fact that mythological tales normally feature super-natural characters and events, they are not the same as fairy tales, fantasies, legends or fables. They reflect and comment on the real situations and problems being experienced by a specific society at a particular moment in time. Mythologies thus give us a significant insight into a society and its ideology. Whenever a society exper-iences turbulence or disorder, its mythologies provide a framework within which the problem can be examined and a solution found. Moreover, as Barthes (1993) has shown, a society's mythologies will always be linked to its dominant ideology and structures of power. In other words, mythologies are created and circulated by those who are dominant within a society, and will necessarily promote beliefs that support their aims and agendas. Because of their status as the products of an ancient and inherited wisdom, however, most mythologies successfully obscure their political and social dimension and attain a taken-for-granted quality. This is what makes them so persuasive and powerful.

Sheehan (1987) helpfully defines the official uses of mythology in contemporary societies in the following terms:

> Myths are normative narratives, setting out a society's history, legitimizing its institutions, codes and values, and envisioning its future development. Myths are synthesizing stories, capturing the Zeitgeist of a time and place, bringing to a focus what forces are at work, highlighting its problem, and crystallizing its values.[3]

It is worth considering this definition in some detail, as it provides a good insight into the role that mythology would play during the early years of the Irish state. Normative narratives set out the expected norms of social behaviour. In other words, they prescribe and encourage certain standards of behaviour and an adherence to designated value and belief systems. Myths also narrate the history of a society, often in parabolic terms. In this way, a myth can rewrite and perhaps reinterpret the story of a society's origins and founding ideals. Many of a society's institutions, such as its legislature and models of governance, are based on the value systems inherent in its mythology. Finally, and perhaps most crucially, a mythology unites a society, linking past with present in a continuum within which the hardships and difficulties of the present can be resolved. A society's mythology, therefore, does not simply bring the past to bear on the present, but allows itself to be reshaped in order to continue to function as a guiding system of beliefs and values for the future. What is crucial is the extent to which having control of a society's mythology enables the imposition of a guiding ideology.

De Valera's use of national mythology

Nationalism, Catholicism and political ideology

Of all the early figures involved in the formation of the Irish state, Eamon de Valera demonstrated by far the greatest insight into the importance – even necessity – of harnessing the mythology of the nation in order to legitimise, and gain popular support for, the development of the state and its institutions. His reign as Taoiseach, which lasted almost without interruption between 1932 and 1959,[4] provides a fascinating example of the political expediency which can be gained from the incorporation of mythological heroes into official state discourse. Although he was often accused of demonstrating an overly simplistic attitude towards the relationship between past and present, what is most interesting about de Valera was his ability to remodel the heroes of the past in order to incorporate the needs of the present.[5] In his continuous referencing of the discourse and iconography of Irish nationalist mythology, which was designed to put forth his blueprint for the future development of the Irish state, he demonstrated a significant facility not only to recycle but also to reshape such narratives in order to include elements of his own personal ideology. In most of the events and institutions he oversaw during his long reign, we can see evidence of this cyclical relationship between past, present and future.

One of the first examples of de Valera's recycling and reshaping of the discourses of nationalist mythology to construct Irish society according to his vision comes from the aforementioned 1935 commemoration of 1916, in which a brass statue of Cúchulainn was placed in the General Post Office, as a symbol of the sacrifice made by those who died there. The use of the mythological figure of Cúchulainn, as noted above, situates Pearse and the rebels within the continuum of nationalist mythology. What is interesting, however, is the image of Cúchulainn that was chosen and the insight it gives us into the specific version of nationalist mythology de Valera was inscribing at the heart of the Irish state. Cúchulainn is depicted at the moment of his death, tied to a boulder, so that he might die upright defending his territory, as was fitting for a hero. Certainly on this narratorial level, the statue was an appropriate memorial to those who had also fought against the odds for the nationalist cause. Several commentators, however, have noted the religious connotations of the figure, depicted in the manner of the *pietà* tradition in religious iconography, to imply an almost Christ-like degree of self-sacrificing. This is an interesting reshaping of the Cúchulainn figure, enabling the merger of the ideologies of nationalism and Catholicism which was at the heart of de Valera's vision for the Irish state:

> The use of such imagery in a monument dedicated to those who had died in the rebellion was significant, juxtaposing as it did the ideals of Christianity with those of revolutionary national-ism to create a potent symbol that would contribute to the visible script of national identity. (Whelan 2001: 139)

As well as incorporating Catholicism into the nationalist discourse, de Valera used the 1935 commemoration as an opportunity to define and delineate the Irish nation officially. His vision was of Ireland becoming a genuinely independent and self-sufficient Republic. As part of this process, he did everything in his power to limit the interaction between Ireland and other countries. He discouraged foreign imports and oversaw a number of stringent censorship laws. His reign can, on the whole, be summarised by referring again to the concept of 'Sinn Féin' ('ourselves alone'): de Valera was determined that having recently achieved independence from the English, the Irish nation would now look into its own past and resist any attempts by outside forces to influence or define it. Murphy notes that de Valera also used the occasion of the 1935 commemoration to impose strict limits on those who could claim to be the inheritors of the Irish nationalist legacy and to marginalise those who did not fit into his narrative. The marginalised included the IRA, whom he had tried, and failed, to co-opt into Fianna Fáil. The contribution made by Irish women during the Rising was also airbrushed out of the official mythology:

> The 1935 commemoration gave de Valera a platform to assume ownership of the Rising's legacy for Fianna Fáil, and to strip the

historical memory of the Rising of those elements which did not fit comfortably with Fianna Fáil's conservative Catholic nationalism. The Rising was rebranded as a Catholic and patriarchal pageant.[6]

What the 'imagining' and performance of the Irish nation by de Valera during the 1935 commemoration demonstrate is the extent to which the narratives of nationalist mythology can be recycled in order to underpin the ethos and ideology of the newly established state. They also show how these narratives were fundamentally reshaped in order to make room for others such as that of Catholicism, which de Valera viewed as a central component of Irish identity, while simultaneously marginalising and effectively rendering invisible contributions by groups who did not fit comfortably within this political and ideological construct. The contradictions and tensions inherent in de Valera's concept of the Irish nation became apparent during the 1966 commemoration ceremony for 1916 (see below), which was significantly undermined by ongoing disagreement about those who were excluded from official narratives of Irish nationalism.

Bunreacht na hÉireann

In 1937, de Valera solidified his vision of the Irish nation in his drafting of Bunreacht na hÉireann, the Constitution of Ireland. From a cultural point of view, this text was de Valera's opportunity to rewrite the mythologies of Irish nationalism in his own terms – to declare, as Pearse had done, 'Mise Éire'. The document he produced is a close reflection of the kind of Ireland he promoted as the legacy of 1916 during the commemoration of 1935. A central focus of this chapter is on the difficulties experienced by the Irish state in bridging the gap between itself and the imagined nation. What is interesting about the 1937 Constitution is that de Valera makes almost no attempt to engage with, or even acknowledge, these difficulties.

The Irish state in 1937 was composed of the twenty-six counties ceded to the Irish Free State by the British Government in 1921. The Constitution of 1937 thus had under its jurisdiction only these twenty-six counties. However, de Valera's Constitution ignores this political reality and addresses itself instead to the nation – the imagined and idealised united Ireland, which had always been at the heart of the nationalist endeavour. In the now infamous Articles 2 and 3, de Valera's Constitution defines the territory of Ireland as follows:

> *Article 2:* The national territory consists of the whole island of Ireland, its islands and the territorial seas.
>
> *Article 3:* Pending the re-integration of the national territory, and without prejudice to the right of the Parliament and Government established by this Constitution to exercise juris-diction over the whole of that territory, the laws enacted by that Parliament shall have the like area and extent of application as the laws of Saorstát Éireann and the extra-territorial effect.[7]

These articles clearly support the nationalist aspiration to reunite the country. While Article 3 acknowledges that the island is divided, its assumption is that reunification will occur. The Preamble to the Constitution also makes reference to the twin pillars of de Valera's ideology, the Catholic religion and the nationalist tradition:

> We, the people of Éire,
> Humbly acknowledging all our obligations to our Divine
> Lord, Jesus Christ,
> Who sustained our fathers through centuries of trial,
> Gratefully remembering their heroic and unremitting
> struggle to regain the rightful independence of our Nation.

De Valera's 1937 Constitution makes a fascinating contribution to debates about the Irish state and its relationship to the imagined Irish nation. In effect, by ignoring the boundaries of the Irish state, de Valera subordinates it to the imagined nation. The Constitution is, therefore, a curious document in the sense that it functions not to legitimate and define the Irish *state*, but rather to render concrete the boundaries of the imagined *nation*. De Valera's 1937 Constitution is perhaps best regarded as a kind of mythological text, in the sense that its main aim was not to legitimise the actual institutions of the Irish state, but rather to mould the realities of the present into a narrative of Irish nationhood firmly inscribed within nationalist ideology. The Ireland defined by Pearse in his poem 'Mise Éire' is clearly still present in de Valera's Constitution.

Hanafin (2000: 148) observes that the writing of any constitution is an anachronistic act, undermined by questions of legitimacy and authority:

> The writing of a constitution is an act that founds a nation ... Strictly speaking, the people do not exist at the moment of founding. It is the founding document that gives them legal effect. Therefore, in order to exist the people must found themselves.

What is significant about de Valera's 1937 text is that the Ireland it 'founds' is the imagined ancient nation rather than the modern nation–state over which it has jurisdiction. Crucial to understanding the development of the Irish state is the extent to which the imagined nation inscribed in the Constitution gained emotional as well as political legitimacy. The Irish people, in other words, began to imagine themselves the inheritors of the ancient nation as recycled in their Constitution:

> This new state was in a very real sense unreal, a mélange of myths and stories projected onto the *de jure* reality of the 26-county state. Yet paradoxically this projection of mythical rhetoric led to the instantiation of a political reality which was to reflect the values of this Gaelic Romantic notion of Ireland. (Hanafin 2000: 155)

Redefining Irish nationhood

The generation of 1966

Many commentators regard the fiftieth anniversary of 1916 as a watershed in the developing narrative of Irish identity and nationhood. The commemoration itself was elaborate. As well as the usual ceremony outside the GPO, Radio Teillifis Éireann had made a mini-television series dramatising the events of the Rising called *Insurrection*, while a pageant entitled *Glorium Eirí Amach na Cásca* was played in Croke Park, Dublin, for the duration of Easter Week. The novelist McAnna notes the effect that such super-charged communal commemorations had on him as a young boy: 'There were big crowds, and cheering, and for me as a 10-year-old, Pádraig Pearse was like Clint Eastwood. It was James Bond stuff.'[8]

It is significant that the 1966 commemoration, apart from pro-viding the focus for nationalist aspirations, also brought to the fore in Irish political and cultural debates what had been a steadily growing disenchantment with official nationalist assumptions. From the early 1960s, a number of groups within Irish society had begun to question the hitherto unchallenged nationalist narratives of Irish history and identity, resenting the limitations or boundaries these imposed on ideas and definitions of Ireland. Gibbons (1991: 561) suggests that the commemoration ironically provided younger generations of Irish people with the opportunity to interrogate nationalist mythologies and question their appropriateness for contemporary society:

> The celebrations attending the golden jubilee of the Easter Rising of 1916 marked a watershed in this process of re-evalu-ation and self-questioning, acting both as an apotheosis and as a purging of the memory of dead generations.

The poet Michael O'Loughlin was one of those for whom the nationalist mythologies were no longer tenable. In a pamphlet written in 1988, he describes his belief that many of the mythologies on which Irish nationalism was based were mere propaganda, designed to preserve a past that was long since gone:

> For my generation the events of Easter 1966 were crucial, so much so that I think it is almost possible to speak of a generation of '66. People from that generation tend to share a number of characteristics. An almost total alienation from the state, a cynicism with regard to national institutions and political life... an unspoken assumption that everything emanating from official sources is a total lie.[9]

Irish women's groups also began to resist their marginalisation from official mythologies of 1916 and to demand that their status within Irish society be readdressed. Many Irish women felt that the constitutional clauses enshrining them in the home limited the possibilities open to them and wrested control of their life and career choices from them. In 1987, Eavan Boland published a poem entitled 'Mise Éire' in which she addresses the repression of women by nationalist mythologies. The title of her poem is clearly a direct challenge both to Pearse's claim to speak on behalf of the Irish nation and to subsequent attempts by Irish politicians and writers to categorise Irish women and thus limit their opportunities. Boland begins her poem with the assertion: 'I won't go back to it'. This is a clear rejection of traditional, nationalist definitions of Ireland. Her primary complaint about nationalist texts is that they obscure the brutality and even criminality of some of the nationalist campaigns for independence. She refers to: '[t]he songs that bandage up the history, the words/ that make a rhythm of the crime'. Her concern appears to be that not dealing honestly with the events of the past can make it difficult for a country to move forward. These lines clearly criticise the degree to which traditional nationalist mythologies have been accepted and never questioned by Irish society. Her particular focus, as a woman, is on the way in which nationalist texts are often complicit with patriarchy in their assumption of control over representations of women.

What begins to emerge during the 1960s, therefore, is a growing body of opposition to the facile incorporation of Irish nationalist mythologies by the Irish state and a demand for a more pluralist attitude towards Irish identity. In a rapidly modernising Ireland, the simplistic binaries of the mythology of the Irish nation as prescribed by Pearse and perpetuated by de Valera were no longer an adequate representation of its citizens.

Constitutional amendments and national change

It is perhaps ironic that it was through the medium of the Constitution – that mythologised text which insisted on a complete merger of nation and state – that the Irish public found the means to begin to express a sense of nationhood more reflective of their reality. Goodrich defines the Constitution as the framing narrative of identity:

> It is the text that establishes our social identity and institutional place, it is the text that provides us with our jurisdiction or right of speech, it is the text in which we are born and in which we die. (quoted in Ryan 2000: 147)

What is crucial about the Constitution – and indeed about any cultural text – is its ability to evolve and assimilate new elements. Fiske (1997: 1) describes the relationship between a cultural text and the society it reflects in terms of an ongoing hegemonic struggle for definition: 'Culture is the constant process of producing meanings of and from our social experience, and such meanings necessarily produce a social identity for the people involved.'

Thus a cultural text both reflects and constructs its social reality, and negotiates between this reality and the expectations of its audience. In order for a cultural text to remain relevant to its audience, it must be prepared to adapt itself to its changing social and political environment. Discussing the role played by the Constitution in reflecting Irish identity in recent decades, Hanafin (2000: 148) suggests that: '[t]he Constitution should act as an enabling mechanism for the development of Irish identities rather than as a means, as it has done in the past, of constricting a more inclusive idea of citizenship'. The definition of the Irish nation inscribed in the Constitution should, therefore, be flexible. The amendments made to the imagining of the Irish nation in the 1998 referendum are a good indication of the degree to which the Constitution can facilitate social and political change. As part of the Belfast Agreement, Articles 2 and 3 of the Constitution were amended in 1999. The emphasis on territory was dropped, in favour of a definition of Irishness that was more inclusive and emphasised a cultural connection with the Irish nation:

> *Article 2:* It is the entitlement and birthright of every person born in the island of Ireland, which includes its islands and seas, to be a part of the Irish Nation. That is also the entitlement of all persons otherwise qualified in accordance with law to be citizens of Ireland. Furthermore, the Irish nation cherishes its special affinity with people of Irish ancestry living abroad who share its cultural identity and heritage.

> *Article 3:* It is the firm will of the Irish Nation, in harmony and friendship, to unite all the people who share the territory of the island of Ireland, in all the diversity of their identities and traditions, recognising that a united Ireland shall be brought about only by peaceful means with the consent of a majority of the people, democratically expressed, in both jurisdictions in the island . . . [10]

These modifications are extremely significant and illustrate a huge change in the signifiers used to define Ireland. Most notably, geography is no longer seen as the main delineator of the nation, and there is no longer an assumption that the Irish nation includes, and has a right to, the territory of Northern Ireland. The amendments were endorsed by over ninety-four per cent of the electorate, which indicates a huge degree of popular support for the new definition of Ireland. It is interesting to note some of the discourse that surrounded the constitutional amendments. The changes to Articles 2 and 3 were a precondition of the Belfast Agreement, and the backing away from claims of jurisdiction over Northern Ireland is often described as a triumph for Northern Unionists. An *Irish Times* editorial, significantly entitled 'Easter 1998', is typical of this summation of the Belfast Agreement and of what it meant for Irish national identity:

> The two great traditions of this island have each yielded on the absolutism of their positions. Nationalists have had to swallow the bitter truth that there will be no united Ireland in the foreseeable future and that, if it comes, it will only do so with the consent of Northern Ireland's majority... And the people of this State will be asked to relinquish the territorial claim to Irish unity which lies at the heart of their political culture and which has been enshrined since 1937 within Articles 2 and 3 of the Constitution.[11]

There is a number of significant inaccuracies in this brief account of the consequences of the Belfast Agreement for the narrative of Irish nationalism. Most significant is the assumption that the claim to Irish unity inscribed in the Constitution was by the 1990s still a significant part of the Irish nation as imagined by its citizens. The size of the majority that endorsed the amendment and the relatively low-key debate it engendered clearly demonstrate that this assumption was false. The use of language in the extract is also interesting: terms such as 'yielded', 'bitter pill' and 'relinquish' suggest that removing the constitutional references to a united Ireland was something the Irish public did reluctantly. In fact, what the 1998 Constitutional amendments symbolised was to a large degree the first accurate alignment of the imagined nation with the political reality of the Irish state. By 'relinquishing' its claim to Northern Ireland, the Irish public was simply expressing in the clearest possible terms that what had become its defining sense of itself was the twenty-six-county modern state. As Ryan (2000: 7) observes, 'one essential component of the republic's self-identity became its independence from the northern state'.

Taoiseach Bertie Ahern reiterates that the 1998 amendment should be regarded as a positive endorsement of the Irish state rather than as a surrendering of nationalist ideals. In a speech made at the 1916 commemoration ceremony in 2006, Ahern stated that:

> The men and women of 1916 gave their lives so that Ireland could gain her freedom... This generation used that freedom to support peace and reconciliation in our own country when, in an overwhelming and historic act of self-determination, we voted for the Good Friday agreement in 1998.[12]

Note here that 'Ireland' refers to the twenty-six county Irish state, and that the 1998 amendments represented not a loss of territory but an act of positive self-determination that involved, above all else, solidifying the division between Ireland and Northern Ireland.

Reclaiming the myth: The 2006 commemoration of 1916

Bertie Ahern's engagement with history

Once it had re-established its boundaries, the Irish state also began to reclaim its mythology for its own use. It is in this context of reclamation that the decision by the Irish government officially to commemorate the 1916 Rising in 2006 is most usefully interpreted. The main instigator of the commemoration ceremony was the Taoiseach, Bertie Ahern. Ahern is an interesting figure to consider in this discussion of an inherited legacy of nationalism, not only because he clearly believes in the ideal of a united Ireland, but because he also retains a deep sense of connection with the past. In his calls for public support in the months leading up to the commemoration, Ahern spoke about history as a cyclical process of engagement and renewal. His emphasis on the need to acknowledge the contributions made by past nationalists in order to build a future gives an interesting insight into what he clearly regards as an ongoing process of self-definition and development. On more than one occasion, he described the commemoration of nationalist heroes of the past as a duty for the contemporary Irish citizen.

Laying a wreathe at Kilmainham Gaol on the morning of the commemoration, Ahern stated that the ceremony was: '[a]bout discharging one generation's debt of honour to another'.[13] This is an interesting phrase, suggesting that, paradoxically, a society must embrace its history in order to move on from it. The depth of Ahern's feelings on the issue is indicated by his use of an almost identical phrase in 2001, on the occasion of the reburial and state funerals of ten IRA volunteers who had been killed in 1916. In a speech on that occasion, Ahern stated that the burial ceremony was an attempt by the Irish state to discharge: '[a] debt of honour that stretches back 80 years'.[14]

Ahern's decision to host the official state funerals was an important moment in the unfolding debates about contemporary Irish nationalism. It symbolised clearly his determination to articulate Irish nationalism as inherently linked both to its mythological past and to the political reality of the Irish state. Many commentators presumed that his motivation was primarily to wrest back control over the narratives and heroes of Irish nationalism from Northern Irish terrorist groups, and thus to exclude these groups from debates about the development of the Irish nation. However, his speeches also indicate a more positive motivation, namely that the Irish state had the right to celebrate its founding mythology without having to apologise for doing so:

> Although we have difficulties of our own time, there is no fair person in this country but thinks that it is good that we bury these men with State honours here today, and indeed that it is time we did so.[15]

The ninetieth anniversary commemoration of the 1916 Rising was described by the Minister for Justice, Michael McDowell, as 'a spectacular success.'[16] Gardaí estimated that 100,000 spectators lined the route of the parade. The event itself incorporated many of the elements traditional to such occasions: the Taoiseach began the day by laying a wreathe in Kilmainham Gaol, where the leaders of the Rising had been executed; 2,500 members of the Defence Forces marched past the GPO; the Tricolour was lowered to half mast during the reading of the Proclamation; the President laid a wreath on behalf of the Irish public; and there was a minute of silence in memory of all those who had died during the Rising. Descendants of the executed rebels were also present at the ceremony, as were the leaders of all the political parties in the Republic (with the exception of Sinn Féin) and the British Ambassador, Stewart Eldon. In short, the commemoration adhered closely to the recognised protocol and formula that had been put in place by de Valera in 1935.

Debating the legacy of 1916

By reinstating 1916 at the heart of official narratives of the found-ation of the Irish state, the commemoration appears to demonstrate a seemingly unbroken link between the past and the present. Certainly, much of the discourse and iconography of traditional nationalism was employed both during the ceremony itself and in some of the discussion surrounding it. However, whereas de Valera had always used the commemoration to inscribe his limited and clearly defined vision of the Irish nation on the public, the 2006 commemoration has generally been regarded as an opportunity to explore and engage with a more pluralistic view of the Irish nation. President Mary McAleese, speaking at a conference organised to debate the legacy of 1916, exhorted the delegates to '[e]njoy the conference and the rows it will surely rise'.[17] Although, there were conflicting opinions about the wisdom of commemorating 1916 given the legacy of violence in Northern Ireland, as the *Letters* pages of several Irish newspapers testify, the contribution to the debate that caused the greatest outrage was in fact McAleese's speech, which airbrushed many of the more contentious elements of 1916 and presented it in simplistic heroic terms:

> There is a tendency for powerful and pitiless elites to dismiss with damning labels those who oppose them. That was probably the source of the accusation that 1916 was an exclusive and sectarian enterprise. It was never that, though ironically it was an accurate description of what the Rising opposed.

Criticism of McAleese's summation of the legacy of the Rising focus-ed mainly on the narrowness of its interpretation and its inability to break away from traditional nationalist discourse. Writing in *The Irish Times* soon afterwards, Raftery noted that:

> Perhaps the most striking aspect of President Mary McAleese's speech on 1916 last month was how old-fashioned it was. Her talk of heroes and sacrifice sound [*sic*] as if the past 30 years of critical historical analysis of the Easter Rising had never happened. In fact, her rhetoric was rooted firmly within the spirit of 1966.[18]

In fact, what most of the rhetoric surrounding the 2006 commemoration illustrates is the extent to which the Rising is increasingly regarded not as the defining, heroic moment when the Irish nation reasserted itself, but rather as part of the ongoing narrative of the development of the Irish state. The following comment from Labour Party Councillor Keith Martin is typical of this more holistic attitude to the legacy of the Rising:

> The Rising is the most important event in Irish history as it was the beginning of the end of an occupation and the spiritual birth of the present Ireland. We should commemorate it with an examination of ourselves as a people and a nation, and of how we relate to other nations and other cultures.[19]

Senator Martin Mansergh (2006), moreover, suggests that there is nothing incompatible in celebrating the achievements of the Rising while simultaneously making room for opposing voices:

> Honouring the Rising is quite compatible with acknowledgement and respect for the contributions of other strands, and with building bridges towards those opposed to the Irish nationalist tradition.

These are very significant statements, which illustrate a huge shift from the narrow, exclusive narrative of nationalism promoted by de Valera and inscribed in previous commemorations. Underlining most of the contributions made to the debate is a sense that Ireland as a nation has moved on from its contentious past and is now in a position to engage with the conflicting legacies of 1916 in a mature and broadminded way:

> [W]hile my reservations about the wisdom of the commemoration itself are strong, the debate sparked by its holding has been healthy. It has been conducted calmly and respectfully. It has also generated much more light, and a lot less heat, than it might have done in the past. This, surely, is a sign of our maturity as a state and as a nation.[20]

What was perhaps most interesting about the reaction to the commemoration was the extent to which the 1916 Rising itself has almost disappeared from the debate. There was relatively little mention of the leaders, the military operation, even the executions. Instead, much of the discussion focused on the contemporary Irish state and the lessons it had learned in the decades since Independence. In fact, underlying many of the remarks from politicians was the sense that the occasion of the ninetieth anniversary of 1916 was less a commemoration of one specific moment of Irish history than an opportunity to take stock of what had been achieved so far and to think about future developments.

Conclusion

The first fifty years of the Irish state, as the examples discussed above clearly demonstrate, constituted an ongoing struggle to merge the mythology of the Irish nation with the continuous development of the Irish state. From the start, the Irish state was clearly subordinated to the nation imagined in official discourse and depended heavily on the recycling of nationalist mythology in order to construct its identity and legitimate its institutions. Over the past two decades, however, we can see a gradual shift in this relationship between nation and state, with the imagined nation gradually being realigned along the political boundaries of the Irish state. The debate surrounding the 2006 commemoration clearly demonstrates that the state and its institutions, rather than the mythological nation of the nationalist imagination, is what commands the loyalty of the citizens of Ireland today. Some of the comments made by Irish politicians are particularly interesting to consider in this context. Trevor Sargent of the Green Party described the parade as a 'symbol of a modern Ireland'. Michael McDowell, Minister for Justice, stated that the success of the commemoration would 'encourage the Irish State to be confident about celebrating 1916'. Taoiseach Bertie Ahern suggested that the hundredth anniversary of the Rising in 2016 would best be celebrated by focusing on its true (if unintended) legacy: the foundation of the Irish state.[21] These remarks demonstrate the extent to which the 1916 Rising and the mythology it both recycled and engendered have, in a sense, become subsumed to the narrative of the Irish state. It is thus appropriate that the 2006 commemoration of the Rising should have resisted the facile assumptions of nationalist mythology and illustrated instead the extent to which the narratives of the imagined nation have been simultaneously recycled and reshaped by the modern Irish state.

NOTES

1 Quoted in *The Irish Times* (17 April 2006: 8).
2 In 2004, the Taoiseach Bertie Ahern cited this poem as his favourite one and recorded a reading of it for *Voices and Poetry in Ireland*.
3 Helena Sheehan. 1987. *Irish Television Drama: A Society and Its Stories.* Available online on: http://www.comms.dcu.ie/sheehan/myth.htm (consulted 22 May 2006).
4 De Valera was Taoiseach from the periods 1932–48, 1951–54, and 1957–59.
5 Bhreathnach-Lynch notes that many of the relatives of the 1916 leaders were very angry with de Valera's attempts to reshape their contributions to Irish nationalism according to his own simplistic narrative (McBride 1999: 155).
6 Colin Murphy, 2006, 'Reconstructing the Easter Rising'. Article available online on: http://www.villagemagazine.ie/article.asp?aid=1280&iid=85&sud=10 (consulted 22 May 2006).
7 The full text of the 1937 Irish Constitution is available on http://www. taoiseach.gov.ie/upload/publications/297.htm.
8 Ferdia McAnna, quoted in, '1916: What does it mean to you?', *The Irish Times* (15 April 2006, Weekend Review, 2).
9 Quoted by Colm Tóibín in 'New Ways of Killing Your Father', London Review of Books online, http://www.colmtoibin.com/essays/lrb/CTLRB 18Nov1993.htm (consulted 22 May 2006).
10 The current text of Bunreacht na hÉireann is available online at http://www. taoiseach.gov.ie/attached_files/Pdf%20files/Constitution%20of%20Ireland.pdf (consulted 22 May 2006).
11 Editorial, *The Irish Times* (11 April 1998).
12 Quoted in *The Irish Times* (17 April 2006).
13 Quoted in *The Irish Times* (17 April 2006).
14 Quoted in *The Irish Times* (15 October 2001).
15 Quoted in *The Irish Times* (15 October 2001).
16 Quoted in *The Irish Times* (17 April 2006).
17 The full text of President McAleese's speech, '1916: A view from 2006', is available online at: http://www. ucc.ie/academic/history/pages/Welcome/1916+McAleese+Speech (consulted 22 May 2006).
18 Mary Raftery, "Dangers of Glorifying the Rising", *The Irish Times* (9 April 2006).
19 Letter to the Editor, *The Irish Times* http://en.wikisource.org/wiki/Constitution-_of_Ireland (7 March 2007).
20 Dan O'Brien, Senior Europe Editor at the Economic Intelligence Unit, quoted in *The Irish Times* (15 April 2006).
21 All quoted in *The Irish Times* (17 April 2006).

REFERENCES

Anderson, B. 2003 [1983]. *Imagined Communities.* London and New York: Verso.
Barthes, R. 1993. *Mythologies.* London: Vintage.
Bhreathnach-Lynch, S. 1999. 'Commemorating the hero in newly independent Ireland: Expressions of nationhood in bronze and stone', in Lawrence W. McBride (ed.), *Images, Icons and the Irish Nationalist Imagination.* Dublin: Four Courts Press Ltd, 148–65.
Boland, E. 1987. 'Mise Éire', in *The Journey.* Reprinted in *Collected Poems.* Manchester: Carcanet Press, 1995, 102.
Bunreacht na hÉireann/The Constitution of Ireland, 2004. Dublin: Stationery Office.

Fiske, J. 1997 [1991]. *Reading the Popular*. London: Routledge.

Gibbons, L. 1991. 'Challenging the canon: Revisionism and cultural criticism', quoted in *The Field Day Anthology of Irish Writing*, Vol. 3. Derry: Field Day, 561–8.

Gibbons, L. 1996. *Transformations in Irish Culture*. Cork: Cork University Press.

Hanafin, P. 2000. 'Legal texts as cultural documents: Interpreting the Irish Constitution', in Ray Ryan (ed.) *Writing in the Irish Republic*. Basingstoke: Macmillan Press Limited, 147–64.

Hobsbawm, E. 1990. *Nations and Nationalism Since 1780: Programme, Myth and Reality*. Cambridge: Cambridge University Press.

McBride, L. W. (ed.), 1999. *Images, Icons and the Irish Nationalist Imagination*. Dublin: Four Courts Press.

Mansergh, M. 2006. 'Rising reinstated claim to full statehood', *The Irish Times*, 11 February 2006.

Murphy, Colin. 2006. 'Reconstructing the Easter Rising'. *Village Magazine*, 16 February 2006. http://www.villagemagazine.ie/ article.asp?aid=1280&iid=85&sud=10 (22/05/2006)

Pearse, P. 1912. 'Mise Éire'. Reprinted in S. Ó Buachalla (ed.). *The Literary Writings of Patrick Pearse*, Dublin: The Mercier Press Limited, 1979, 35.

Pearse, P. 1915. 'The Mother'. Reprinted in Ó Buachalla (ed.) 1979, 27.

Raftery, M. 2006. 'Dangers of glorifying the Rising', *The Irish Times*, 9 February 2006.

Ryan, R. (ed.), 2000. *Writing in the Irish Republic: Literature, Culture, Politics 1949–1999*. Basingstoke: Macmillan Press.

Sheehan, H. 1987. *Irish Television Drama: A Society and Its Stories*. Dublin: RTÉ. http://www.comms.dcu.ie/sheehanh/myth.htm (22/05/2006)

Whelan, Y. 2001. 'Symbolizing the State: The iconography of O'Connell Street and environs after Independence', *Irish Geography*, 34 (2), 135–56.

Yeats, W. B. 1913. 'Mission statement for the Irish Literary Theatre', quoted in Lady Gregory, *Our Irish Theatre: A Chapter of Autobiography*. London: The Knickerbocker Press, 9.

Yeats, W. B. 1921. 'Easter 1916', from *Michael Robartes and the Dancer*. Reprinted in *Yeats Poems*, edited by Peter Washington, 1995, London: Everyman's Library, 1995, 128-131.

Yeats, W. B. 1939. 'The Statues', from *Last Poems (1936–9)*. Reprinted in *Yeats Poems*, 1995, 239–40.

3

Reconfiguring the border
Cathal McCall

If borders define states then an examination of attempts at reconfiguring the Irish border from barrier to bridge is intrinsic to the study of recycling the state. The index of border reconfiguration is the degree of North/South, cross-border co-operation. This chapter asks why North/South co-operation finally became firmly established in the 1990s and 2000s. It thus considers: past failures; the dynamics that encouraged contemporary North/South co-operation; the processes that established the architecture for co-operation; the contemporary manifestation of the border as a bridge; and the prospects for the development of co-operation by the North/South institutions in a political climate that continues to be inter-communally competitive and highly volatile. Also considered is the importance of a recycling of the Irish state in the development of North/South co-operation.

The trajectory of partition

Violence and borders have been integral features of modern states (Poggi 1990; Tilly 1990). In Ireland, effective control of the means of violence after the Irish Civil War (June 1922 to May 1923) and the confirmation and maintenance of the territorial boundary (after 1925) were the two elements that affirmed statehood for the twenty-six county entity. However, the challenge to the Provisional Government's monopoly of violence during the Civil War, and the relative success of anti-Treaty republicans in the general elections of 1923 and 1927, left the legitimacy of the state in doubt until 1932. Irish statehood became finally stabilised only when the electoral success of de Valera's Fianna Fáil party in 1932 was recognised by the first Taoiseach of the Irish Free State, W. T. Cosgrave (Rose 1983: 6).

By 1932, partition had become consolidated. As far as the public sector was concerned, there would be few infringements of partition between the twenty-six county Irish state and the six-county Northern Ireland for many decades to come. According to Dennis Kennedy (1999: 73),

> One of the most remarkable features of the history of the island over the past seventy-five years has been, at government level, the near totality of partition, the replacement of a long established single administrative system by two separate administrative systems, which managed, or contrived, to keep all contact to a minimum, which built no new structures, however modest, to take care of common interests in practical matters and which for many decades had no dialogue at all at political level.

However, sixty years after partition, John Whyte (1983) found a multitude of organisations still operating on an all-island basis in other sectors of organised activity including churches and church-related groups, youth and sporting groups, cultural and scientific organisations, charitable and welfare organisations, professional associations, as well as business, banking, media and arts concerns.[1]

Whyte's extensive inventory of cross-border organisations in the private, business and voluntary sectors stood in stark contrast to the absence of a cross-border dimension to public life on the island in the wake of partition. Nevertheless, periodic efforts were made by some political leaders at bridging the border between North and South from the inception of a two-state Ireland. The Government of Ireland Act (1920) made provision for the cross-border Council of Ireland to act as an institutional bridge between two devolved parliaments in Ireland, one in the North and one in the South. In the event, political aspirations and state-building, North and South, took precedence and the Council of Ireland was still-born. The Craig-Collins pacts of 1922 held out the hope of sustained cross-border political co-operation between Northern Ireland and the Irish Free State.[2] However, the apparent duplicity of Michael Collins, head of the Provisional Government in the South (with Arthur Griffith), and ongoing political and sectarian violence in the North scuttled the pacts (Fitzpatrick 1998; Buckland 2001: 212).[3] Thereafter, the border became an increasingly entrenched political barrier between the Irish state and Northern Ireland.

After the prolonged Cold War between North and South, which lasted from the 1930s to the 1960s and was stimulated in large part by Eamon de Valera's 1937 Bunreacht na hÉireann,[4] rumblings of a renewed attempt at cross-border co-operation were felt in the 1960s, under the auspices of the Lemass/O'Neill *rapprochement*. However, the initiative of the then Taoiseach Seán Lemass and Northern Ireland Prime Minister Captain Terence O'Neill also foundered. Traditionalist unionist forces mustered successfully to stop O'Neill's efforts directed at establishing cross-border co-operation for the socio-economic advancement of Northern Ireland. In 1974, the attempted resuscitation of the Council of Ireland model, to complement the power-sharing Northern Ireland Executive, intensified the Ulster unionist/loyalist backlash against power-sharing with Irish nationalists in Northern Ireland. The backlash, in the form of a general strike, was to scupper the second coming of the Council and terminate the life of the Executive after five months' operation.

These successive attempts at establishing North/South political co-operation proved not only to be unfruitful, they also served to buttress the border so that it acted as an effective barrier between North and South. Therefore, in light of an eighty-year experience of failed attempts at establishing cross-border co-operation and consequent re-enforcement of the border as a barrier, it is remarkable that the Belfast (Good Friday) Agreement (1998) survived the establishment and operation of the North/South Ministerial Council and its Implementation Bodies. Some anti-Agreement unionists argued that these cross-border institutions impugned the integrity of Northern Ireland, an integrity that was further compromised by the continued threat of Irish Republican Army (IRA) violence after the 1994 cease-fire. From this unionist perspective, the threat to the border and the state's monopoly of violence (exacerbated by police reform in Northern Ireland) presented a clear danger for Northern Ireland as a part of a United Kingdom (UK) union state, and for the Ulster unionist identity itself. In light of these threats, it is even more remarkable that the North/South institutions proved to be one of the Agreement's least controversial provisions.

Past failures

The Government of Ireland Act (1920) provided for a Council of Ireland to promote North/South co-operation. At the second reading of the Bill on 29 March 1920, James Macpherson, Chief Secretary for Ireland, claimed that the Council of Ireland could become 'virtually a Parliament for all Ireland, and from that stage to complete union is but a very slight and very easy transition'.[5] Section 2(1) of the 1920 Act outlined the functions of the Council as: the facilitation of harmonious action between the two parliaments; the promotion of a common approach to all-island matters; and the administration of services that were amenable to an all-island approach (Hadfield 1992: 2). However, the Council was paralysed by its vagueness as constituted in the 1920 Act. The dynamics of divergent political aspirations, violence and state-building on both sides of the border conspired to render its paralysis terminal (Tannam 1999). Unionist leaders were preoccupied with having to establish a government and a parliament in the North, which were foisted upon them and for which they had little time to prepare (Buckland 2001: 212). Meanwhile, the Council of Ireland was a non-starter for the Dublin government because participation would symbolise its recognition of the Northern parliament and of a border which excluded six counties from the thirty-two county national territorial ideal.

The Craig-Collins pacts of 1922 represented a more promising initiative for North/South co-operation because of their high-level political nature. The Pacts between Collins and Sir James Craig, the first Prime Minister of Northern Ireland, had the potential to avoid the retreat of Ulster into narrow territorial/cultural confines, since they held out the hope of overcoming the creation of the border as a barrier. One of the terms of the first Pact that Collins and Craig agreed was: 'The two governments to endeavour to devise a more suitable system than the Council of Ireland for dealing with problems affecting all Ireland' (*The Irish Times*, 22 January 1922). Their co-operative objective suggested the possibility of creating the border as a political, economic, cultural and intellectual bridge between Northern Ireland and the Irish Free State. Had it succeeded, an innovative state system may have developed, to the advantage of all the island's communities. Certainly the creation of an intellectual bridge would have been potentially valuable for Ulster unionism, especially when one considers its ensuing decades of political, intellectual and cultural stagnation after the formation of Northern Ireland (Bew 1999: 411). The Irish landed gentry, supplying political reformers like Lord Midleton and Sir Horace Plunkett as well as intellectuals like William Edward Hartpole Leckey and Edward

Dowden at Trinity College, Dublin, were important political and intellectual pillars of unionism. According to Alvin Jackson (2001: 116), 'Irish Toryism supplied much of the organisational infrastructure around which unionism was constructed; and supplied trained advocates to the loyalist cause'. Irish cultural revivalists like Standish O'Grady and George Russell were also sympathetic to the cause of Irish unionism. Therefore, the political, intellectual and cultural remnants of Southern Irish unionism remained valuable and worthy of maintenance. Such maintenance, if undertaken, could have provided the new Ulster unionist identity with a rich source of intellectual and cultural sustenance, as well as political adroitness.

For a time, the Pacts enabled Collins to become the effective representative of Northern Catholics, especially Belfast Catholics (Kennedy 1999: 80). It is possible that, had they succeeded, the Pacts could also have lead to some form of Northern representation for Southern unionists. Craig's practical incentive for co-operation was the possibility of recognition by the Free State government. Craig believed that co-operation would provide the opportunity for securing the principle of consent in North/South relations, that is, that the consent of the unionist community would be required for 'Ulster' to join the Irish Free State (Bew 1999: 407). However, despite the first Pact, Collins continued his pursuit of a non-recognition policy regarding Northern Ireland (p. 408). Simultaneously, the IRA, with help and encouragement from Collins, continued to engage in violence north of the border. In an attempt to end violence and reform the police in Belfast, the two leaders entered into a second Pact. That Pact too foundered, primarily because of the failure of the Northern government to investigate the alleged role of policemen in sectarian murder in Belfast (Farrell 1983: 114–17).

After the death of Collins in the Civil War, continuing disorder in the South and the inability, or reticence, of the Provisional Government in dealing with the IRA challenge to Northern Ireland served to bolster the partitionist resolve of unionist leaders. Consequently, the manifestation of the border as a bulwark against the Irish Free State won out and came to embody the unionist perception of threat emanating from its Irish nationalist 'Other'. The Boundary Commission (1925), which was proposed in the Anglo-Irish Treaty (1921), presented Ulster unionists with the immediate threat of losing territory to the Irish Free State, a threat that failed to materialise (Kennedy 1988: 73). However, other threats proved to be more durable and served to buttress the manifestation of the border as a barrier. The Irish state's constitutional claim to the six counties of Northern Ireland persisted until the 1998 Belfast Agreement and fuelled the sense of territorial siege in the Ulster unionist communal imagination. That the 1937 Bunreacht na hÉireann reasserted the claim and also recognised the special position of the Catholic Church in the Irish state was hardly an inducement for Ulster unionists to reconsider their attitude to Éire and the border (Buckland 2001: 220–21).

The threat from *perfide Albion* also arose periodically. The primary example of British government perfidy occurred in 1940, when Churchill offered de Valera Irish unity as an incentive for granting Allied troops permission to use southern ports. Set against the unionists' self-perception as a loyal wartime subject community and the reaffirmation of Irish nationalist disloyalty through the declaration of Éire neutrality, knowledge of the offer to de Valera served to heighten the sense of threat experienced by the Ulster unionist community (McIntosh 1999: 145). The IRA presented a recrudescent violent threat to the Northern state and to unionists that was intimately associated with the border in ideological and practical terms. Consequently, devoid of political adroitness, the combined effect of these constitutional, perfidious and physical threats, emanating from Dublin, Westminster and the IRA respectively, set Ulster unionism on a course characterised by isolationism, defensiveness, vulnerability and insecurity. The cultural chasm that existed between unionists and Éire, especially after the 1937 Bunreacht na hÉireann, helped to reinforce that sense of threat.

In the post-World War II period, occasional verbal broadsides were fired from the North across the border. In 1949, St John Ervine published his 'semi-official' biography of James Craig, in which he took the liberty of launching vitriolic diatribes directed at the Republic of Ireland and its citizens (McIntosh 1999: 154). According to Gillian McIntosh (p. 156), 'Ervine's biography can be seen as having provided a necessary pressure valve, providing unionists with a high-profile outlet for their feelings towards contemporary events, and an articulation of some of their genuinely held but, at the time, politically sensitive beliefs'. For Basil Brooke, the then Prime Minister of Northern Ireland, the transition of Éire to a republic was 'the last stage of that deplorable journey' (Kennedy 1988: 239).

While overt cross-border contact at a political level had proven to be impossible for four decades after the Craig-Collins pacts, some covert contact did take place. For example, Seán MacBride, the Republic's Minister for External Affairs, met Northern Ireland's Sir Basil Brooke twice (Arthur 2000: 8). More practical low political co-operation was achieved during the 1950s with: the North/South co-operation on the Erne Hydro-Electric Scheme (1950) (Kennedy 2005); the creation of the Foyle Fisheries Commission (1952); and the subsequent establishment of the Great Northern Railway Board (Kennedy 1999: 84). However, high-level political talks resumed eventually with two meetings in the 1960s between Republic of Ireland Taoiseach, Seán Lemass, and Northern Ireland Prime Minister Captain Terence O'Neill.

After becoming Taoiseach in 1958, Seán Lemass embarked on a charm offensive directed at Ulster unionists. His intention was to soften an Irish border that had become a well-fortified barrier after the introduction of the 1937 Bunreacht na hÉireann. A turning point came in July 1963 when, in reference to Northern Ireland, Lemass declared that 'the government and parliament there exists with the support of the majority in the six counties area, artificial though that area is. We see it functioning within its powers... within an all Ireland constitution, for as long as it is desired by them' (quoted in Mulholland 2000: 80). This qualified recognition of Northern Ireland was enough to stir O'Neill's interest in Lemass' call for North/South discussions. However, subsequent anti-partitionist speeches by Lemass in the United States made O'Neill baulk from immediate face-to-face discussions. It wasn't until Brian Faulkner (then a minister in O'Neill's cabinet) offered to meet Jack Lynch (then Faulker's opposite number in the Republic of Ireland) that O'Neill moved to meet Lemass at Stormont on 17 January 1965, with a return visit to Dublin on 9 February (Mulholland 2000: 82). Problematically for O'Neill, he failed to inform most of his cabinet colleagues about the first meeting, leaving traditionalists free to suspect or claim double-dealing. Moreover, Lemass tended to link economic co-operation to political co-operation and the ending of partition. While this linkage in itself may not have been a problem for O'Neill, its timing was. Eventually, pressure from the Reverend Ian Paisley and the threat of revolt from within the ruling ranks of the Unionist Party ran aground the Lemass/O'Neill *rapprochement*. Furthermore, the increase in tension with the 1966 commemoration of the 1916 Easter Rising and the rise to prominence of the Civil Rights campaign effectively halted the attempt at bridge-building (Kennedy 1999: 85). Paisley used his skills as a populist communicator to particular effect when, in reference to the dry and aloof O'Neill, he railed: 'he is a bridge builder he tells us. A traitor and a bridge are very much alike for they both go over to the other side' (quoted in Mulholland 2000: 84).

The Sunningdale Agreement of December 1973 offered renewed hope for the re-creation of the border as a bridge. A new Council of Ireland was proposed as a supplement to a Northern Ireland power-sharing system of government, which had been provided by the Northern Ireland Constitution Act (1973). This Council of Ireland was to comprise of a Council of Ministers with seven members, each drawn from the Northern and Southern governments. The Council was to be invested with an executive and harmonising function as well as a consultative role. Decisions were to be passed by unanimous vote. A Consultative Assembly, comprising thirty members, each from the Northern Ireland Assembly and Dáil Éireann was proposed to perform advisory and review functions (Hadfield 1992: 8, Hennessey 1997: 221). For the Irish government, the proposed Council of Ireland represented a means of dissolving the border and of promoting unification. However, the new cross-border/all-island institution proved to be unpalatable for a majority of unionists. They viewed it much as the Irish government did, though in a totally different light. For most unionists, the Council of Ireland represented a renewed threat to the border with the Irish state, and hence a threat to the existence of Northern Ireland. The Ulster Workers' Council strike of 1974 not only stifled its creation, the strike also collapsed the entire edifice of power-sharing government in Northern Ireland after just five months' operation.

The European Union context

A year previously, the UK and the Republic of Ireland joined the European Economic Community (EEC). From their accession to the EEC, the governments of the Republic of Ireland and UK enjoyed increasing levels of maturity in their relationship. European Community/European Union (EC/EU) membership created the opportunity for the Irish economy to diversify and expand, thus transcending its reliance on UK markets. EC/EU membership also enabled the recycling Irish state to achieve formal equality with the UK state in an international arena. Consequently, the relationship between the two states shifted from one founded on dominance and dependence to one based on equality and interdependence (Arthur 2000: 129; McCall 2001). Furthermore, the neutral arena of the EC/EU enabled British and Irish politicians and diplomats to escape the claustrophobic state confines and a British–Irish relationship forged in antagonism and conflict. Bilateral meetings became commonplace on the fringes of EU meetings, particularly European Council meetings which involved the Irish Taoiseach and the British Prime Minister. The recast relationship that developed was especially valuable for the Northern Ireland problem because it became an international partnership of equals that was beyond the destructive grasp of regionally confined Ulster unionists.

The European context facilitated rounds of Anglo-Irish summitry beginning in 1980 and provided the space for the development of a fledgling Anglo-Irish inter-governmental relationship that involved leading politicians and Cabinet officials. The relationship faltered at times, for example, after the Argentinean invasion of the Falklands/Malvinas on 2 April 1982. However, in December 1984, Mrs Thatcher and Irish Taoiseach Garret FitzGerald met at an EC summit in Dublin. The meeting reopened a line of communication between British and Irish officials responsible for the Anglo-Irish process, a process aided by US political and media interest (Guelke 1988: 217). The subsequent Anglo-Irish Agreement (1985) gave the Irish government a role in Northern Ireland affairs, a role that has been described as being 'more than consultative, but less than executive'.[6] Undoubtedly, Mrs Thatcher's motive for signing the Agreement was heavily influenced by security concerns. However, cabinet colleagues and civil servants impressed upon her the need to place security measures in the context of an overall package that included an Irish dimension (Goodhall 1993). The effect of the Anglo-Irish Agreement was that the Irish government became a minor partner of the British government in the exercise of joint authority over Northern Ireland.[7] Observing its innovative nature, one Irish academic lawyer commented that 'it will be seen by international lawyers as an important new legal model for consideration, adaptation and possible application in other similar international situations of disputed sovereignty over territory' (O'Conner, *The Irish Times*, 21 November 1985). Over sixty years after the efforts of Craig and Collins, innovation in state relations concerning the island of Ireland began to bear fruit, much to the chagrin of most Ulster unionists. Unionist anger at the imposition of the Anglo-Irish Agreement without their consent was compounded by their powerlessness in the face of its international implementation.

At the macro-European level, the Single European Act (1987) provided for the completion of the Single European Market by 1992, and represented a milestone in the recycling of member states generally. The ensuing economic, political and cultural processes of Europeanisation began to pose serious questions for state sovereignty and the manifestation of borders as barriers. The developing EC/EU presented a challenge to the legal sovereignty of the national/nation–state and threatened an increasing challenge to its political sovereignty. Member states either embraced or acquiesced in this transference or 'pooling' of sovereignty in response to the contemporary economic, political and social challenges of globalisation/internationalisation. After 1985, there was a dramatic increase in the frequency of Inter-governmental Conferences (IGCs) which translated into a frenetic bout of EC/EU constitution-building. IGC treaty-making resulted in changing the decision-making rules that enabled the EU to increase its policy-making capacity. Consequently, the entrepreneurial Commission, driven by its federalist President, Jacques Delors, moved the EC/EU into key areas of state activity and highlighted the fact that Europeanisation was reconfiguring west European borders (Caporaso 1996).

The antipathy of unionist leaders to these European developments was compounded by the general Euro-enthusiasm of Irish nationalists. In particular, unionist leaders viewed the articulation of 'post-nationalism' and a 'Europe of the Regions', by the then Social Democratic and Labour Party (SDLP) leader, John Hume, as a Jesuitical ploy used to disguise Irish nationalist irredentist ambition. Consequently, Europeanisation was regarded by Ulster unionist elites as little more that a supplementary weapon in the Irish nationalist anti-partitionist canon. Furthermore, the Anglo-Irish Agreement (1985), which brought an infringement of the political and cultural substance of sovereignty directly to the Irish border, had traceable Euro-roots which could only further strengthen unionist antipathy to the development of the EC/EU.

By the end of the 1980s, Ulster unionists were thus presented with a burgeoning array of inter-related features of contemporary dynamics which militated against their traditional ideological position, which was one of exclusion regarding Irish nationalists/republicans in the governance of Northern Ireland and of territorialism regarding state borders, especially the border between Northern Ireland and the Republic of Ireland. These features included: the loss of state power in 1972, after fifty years of unionist hegemonic rule in Northern Ireland; the transformed British–Irish inter-governmental relationship after 1973; the development of Europeanisation and regionalisation, directly affecting borders in the British Isles; and a further modification in unionist–nationalist power relations after the signing of the Anglo-Irish Agreement in 1985. These dynamics determined that a unionist strategy based on exclusion and on a border that functioned as a barrier to North/South co-operation and common action was no longer tenable. Eventually, unionist anger, coupled with the failure of subsequent extra-parliamentary 'Ulster Says No' boycotts, gave way to active engagement in political dialogue and political process during the early 1990s, an engagement that held out the prospect of reconfiguring the Irish border in the context of a recycling Irish state.

Political process and the Belfast Agreement

After 1991, political talks aimed at resolving the Northern Ireland conflict had a three-strand structure, featuring Northern Ireland, North/South and British-Irish dimensions. Again, North/South co-operation and the transformation of the Irish border from barrier to bridge was on the political agenda. Leaders of both the Ulster Unionist Party (UUP) and Reverend Ian Paisley's Democratic Unionist Party (DUP) participated in these talks, which also involved the Irish government in a central coordinating role. The limitations of boycott and the importance of engagement in the political process were lessons learned by leaders from across the unionist political spectrum. However, the idea of political *process* clashes with the traditional unionist ideological preference for the status quo (Harris 1995). Therefore, acceptance of the three-strand structure for talks did not necessarily translate into the acceptance of a political process leading to a three-strand structure for the governance of Northern Ireland that included formal North/South co-operation. Paisley was not about to do what he had accused O'Neill of trying to do twenty-five years earlier, namely 'go over to the other side'. He and his party colleagues staged numerous walkouts during the talks process of the 1990s, exiting permanently on the arrival of Sinn Féin representatives into negotiations leading to the Agreement (1998).[8] Nevertheless, leading representatives from the UUP and the smaller loyalist parties remained in the multi-party negotiations.

The Agreement reflected the three-strand framework of the negotiations that preceded it. The framework encompassed the North/South (cross-border, island of Ireland) relationship, the east-west (or British–Irish) relationship, as well as the relationship between the Irish nationalist and Ulster unionist ethno-national communities within Northern Ireland. The complementary institutions provided by the Agreement included a Northern Ireland Executive, Assembly and Civic Forum, a North/South (cross-border, island of Ireland) Ministerial Council and its Implementation Bodies, and a British-Irish Council and British–Irish Intergovernmental Conference. The Agreement nominally reaffirmed United Kingdom sovereignty over Northern Ireland in the formal–legal sense. However, these multifarious territorial and cross-border institutions were instrumental in recycling the state because they helped to spread the political and cultural substance of sovereignty across a British, Northern Ireland, North/South, British–Irish and EU axis, each having autonomy, or potential autonomy, in policy-making and administration (Ruane and Todd 2001: 936). Henry Patterson (2001: 182) astutely described these arrangements as a 'constitutional triumph for unionism, combined with a certain political and ideological retreat'.

Throughout the crises in the implementation of the Agreement, cross-border co-operation remained relatively free from controversy. This is remarkable, given the legacy of failed cross-border initiatives and the fact that a fleet of black Mercedes cars, in slow cavalcade, rolled over the border at Middletown, County Armagh, in December 1999, and delivered the ministerial cabinet of the Irish government to the inaugural meeting of the North/South Ministerial Council in Armagh city. The spectacle caused moderate northern nationalist representatives to blush because, in a region where symbolism has the potential to wreck painstakingly constructed initiatives, the implication of attendance at the funeral of the UK union state was inescapable.

On occasion, Peter Robinson (DUP, Deputy Leader) attempted to inject a note of controversy on the issue of post-Agreement North/South co-operation. For example, in remarks to the 2002 annual conference of the Young Democrats, the DUP's youth wing, he claimed that the North/South bodies posed the 'greatest long-term threat' to the Union (*The Irish Times*, 18 February 2002). However, the cross-border institutions stirred little controversy in the unionist community because issues of police reform and IRA decommissioning were more pressing concerns; that is, the means of violence rather than the border took precedence in the state concerns of most unionists. The active involvement of leading Sinn Féin figures in the post-Agreement (1998) administration of Northern Ireland precluded a comparison with Collins' non-recognition policy. However, the IRA's retention of its arsenal and its continued intelligence gathering and training, as well as violent acts by dissident republicans, invited unionists to infer some acquiescence by Sinn Féin in post-Agreement IRA activity – an activity which was reminiscent of Collins' support for an ongoing IRA violent campaign north of the border while he simultaneously agreed to Pacts with Craig.

Pro-Agreement unionists may also have had some success in their presentation of the North/South institutions as being strictly under the control of the Northern Ireland Assembly and limited to practical low-level cross-border matters. Somewhat contrary to the pro-Agreement unionist interpretation, the North/South Ministerial Council was allocated a measure of autonomy in pursuit of its goals of co-operation and coordination, providing that agreement was reached among participants who included Ulster unionist representatives. However, decisions reached in the Council that were 'beyond the authority of those attending' required the consent of both the Oireachtas (Irish Parliament) and the Northern Ireland Assembly (*The Agreement*, Strand 2, para.6). Moreover, the refusal of UUP ministers to attend any North/South Ministerial Council meeting that included Sinn Féin members, which was announced on 21 September 2002, highlighted the power of veto exercised by UUP elites over the re-creation of the border as a bridge.[9]

The border as a bridge

The North/South Ministerial Council represents the main 'architectural' feature of the bridge between Northern Ireland and the Republic of Ireland. When not suspended on account of crises in the implementation of the Agreement, the Council provided a forum for functional co-operation on aspects of transport, agriculture, education, health, the environment and tourism. In the Northern Ireland Programme for Government (2001) some of these aspects were identified; for example, in the area of education, under-achievement, the mobility of teachers and university co-operation were highlighted; in the area of health, cancer research, cross-border emergency planning and rapid response schemes were specified (6.3, Sub-priority 1).

European Structural Funds were singled out as a particularly important area for cross-border co-operation. Overtly, Euro-federalist language was used in support of this co-operation; Section 6.4, sub-priority 2 of the Agreement states: 'borders should not be barriers to balanced development across the European Territory'. In this regard, a 'Common Chapter' focusing on the development of North/South co-operation was agreed, which was common to both the Structural Funds Plan for Northern Ireland and the National Development Plan for the Republic of Ireland.[10]

Prior to prolonged suspension of the Agreement's main institutions in 2002,[11] the North/South Ministerial Council began to address the potentially important issue of opening a vertical line of communication to the European Commission regarding North/South interests. While the Northern Ireland Assembly was prevented by its devolved status from entering into international relations, the Northern Ireland Act (1998) did not withhold 'the exercise of legislative powers so far as required for giving effect to any agreement or arrangement entered into' in the North/South Ministerial Council (Section 55), or by, or in relation to, the North/South Implementation Bodies (Hadfield 2001: 97). Thus the North/South institutions were free to conduct their transnational operations on an all-island and EU-wide basis. Such an exercise begins to address the ambiguous article in the Agreement (1998), which states: 'Arrangements to be made to ensure that the views of the [North/South Ministerial] Council are taken into account and represented appropriately at relevant EU meetings' (Strand 2, para. 17).

The North/South Implementation Bodies concentrated on the specifics of co-operation regarding trade and business development, inland waterways, food safety, the Irish and Ulster Scots languages, agriculture and marine matters, and special EU programmes. Despite the 2002 suspension of the Assembly and North/South Ministerial Council, the Implementation Bodies continued functioning, on a 'care and maintenance' basis. Some or all of the Implementation Bodies had the potential to become important nodes for cross-border and island of Ireland co-operation. However, mindful of the emphasis placed by the Northern Ireland Programme of

Government on EU Structural Funds as an important area for North/South co-operation, special consideration is given below to this area and to the role of the Special EU Programmes Body (SEUPB). As one of the North/South Implementation Bodies, SEUPB was charged with responsibility for the management of the EU PEACE II (2000–6) programme[12] and Community Initiatives such as INTERREG III (2000–6).[13] It was also responsible for the monitoring, promoting and implementation of the Common Chapter on cross-border co-operation.[14]

With its wide-ranging and complex mandate regarding Structural Funds and Community Initiatives, as well as limited staff and resources, SEUPB faced a number of challenges regarding its ability to balance management and development, all-island and cross-border aspects, as well as its novel transnational position in a multi-level network stretching from the local, grassroots level to the supranational level (Laffan and Payne 2001: 14–15). Perhaps because of administrative difficulties and structural complexity, SEUPB initially relied on the Northern Ireland Department of Finance and Personnel for support in the exercise of its managerial authority, which suggested that an innovative transnational body like SEUPB is more suited to a development role in the context of cross-border co-operation.

There is no doubt that crises in the implementation of the Belfast Agreement seriously impeded innovation and development regarding North/South relations. Indeed, the North/South Ministerial Council emerged as a first port of call for the exercise of the UUP veto when difficulties were to be experienced. There were also predictable problems involving staff and resource transfer and the shift of responsibility from central administrations to the novel Implementation Bodies (Pollak 2001). These problems were a factor in determining the gap in funding which emerged with the delayed implementation of PEACE II and INTERREG III. Although a bridging support in the region of five million sterling was provided by a number of Northern Ireland departments, this support did not avert a crisis in the voluntary sector, including in the sustainability of many of the voluntary networks and local groups funded through the IFBs under PEACE I.[15] Consequently, political and institutional change and a shortage of funds posed a major challenge to the future role of the voluntary sector in cross-border development.

Despite these substantial problems, 'live' North/South institutions remained key to the progress of reconfiguring the border, given that there were ministers and civil servants engaging in the North/South Ministerial Council for the promotion of cross-border co-operation. Consensual decision-making involving North and South, nationalists and unionists, was understood to be the underlying principle for transforming the border, from a political, economic, social and cultural barrier into a bridge. One practical application of this principle involved the attendance of two Northern Ministers, one being invested with sectoral responsibility and the other being a 'shadow minister' from the other (nationalist or unionist) community, at every sectoral North/South Ministerial Council meeting (Pollak 2001: 16). Of course, most Irish nationalists still understood the North/South structures to be important institutional nodes which provided the basis for a fledging all-Ireland structural framework. Meanwhile, the low-key practical operation of North/South institutions, relatively free from political symbolism, enabled pro-Agreement unionists to accept cross-border bodies as useful institutions for political, economic, social and cultural well-being in Northern Ireland, as well as for improved relations between unionists and the Republic of Ireland. A sufficient easing of the conflict between unionist and nationalist 'truths', resulting from ideological shift on the part of nationalist/republican and pro-Agreement unionist elites, remains the fundamental feature of the process of reconfiguring the border between North and South.

Unionist politics and the Irish state

When past failures and the ongoing unionist–nationalist conflict are considered, it is something of an achievement that the complicated architecture for cross-border co-operation was established and operated successfully, even if sometimes in a state of partial suspension. However, the ongoing unionist–nationalist political and cultural conflict weakens the architecture fundamentally, and it is, in particular, elements of the unionist political elite that threaten to re-establish the border as a barrier. Prospects of developments are also affected by the mundane politics of centre–periphery (Belfast/Dublin–North/South institutions) bureaucratic machinations. Another important factor, which should not be underestimated in any consideration of such prospects, is the relationship between Ulster unionists and the recycling Irish state.

The Ulster unionists' approach to cross-border co-operation is intimately linked to their political, economic, social and cultural understanding of the Irish state. The yardstick of this interpretation is the perceived sense of threat emanating from the South. In 1995, the then UUP MP John D. Taylor (subsequently Lord Kilclooney) embarked on a campaign to secure the leadership of his party. Although defeated in the leadership by David Trimble, Taylor's campaign marked a significant turning point in the relationship between the Ulster unionist community and the Republic of Ireland. Significantly, Taylor talked at venues throughout the Republic, as well as in Northern Ireland. In his speeches he concentrated on the remit of proposed North/South institutions. Drawing a distinction between 'cross-border' and 'all-Ireland' references in this context,[16] Taylor argued that the former were acceptable whereas the latter were anathema to unionists (Cash 1996: 216). He also emphasised the need for unionists to embark upon a co-operative relationship with the SDLP and the Dublin government. Significantly, Taylor sought to challenge the unionist interpretation of the Republic of Ireland as exclusively Catholic and Gaelic when he noted 'significant progress towards the creation of a pluralist society free from Church control' (*The Irish Times*, 28 March 1995). Such a challenge signalled the possibility of downgrading the perceived cultural threat emanating from the Irish state.

The 1998 amendment of Articles 2 and 3 of Bunreacht na hÉireann had the effect of neutralising the complementary territorial threat for the Ulster unionist community. While unity remains 'the firm will of the Irish nation', 'respect for diversity of . . . identities and traditions' (revised Article 3.1) suggests that unity does not necessarily imply a unitary state, should consent for a 'united Ireland' be forthcoming in the North and the South (O'Leary 2001: 67).[17] David Trimble appeared to recognise the concessions to unionism implicit in these consitutional changes when he endorsed a co-operative North/South approach with the Agreement (1998). However, in political speeches, Trimble displayed regressive tendencies in his perception of the Republic of Ireland. For example, in March 2002, at the annual meeting of the UUP's ruling council in Belfast, he exclaimed: 'Contrast the United Kingdom state – a vibrant multi-ethnic, multinational liberal democracy, the fourth largest economy in the world, the most reliable ally of the United States in the fight against international terrorism – with the pathetic sectarian, mono-ethnic, mono-cultural state to our south.'[18] With their cultural references and supremacist overtones, Trimble's remarks suggested that the Catholic, Gaelic–Irish, barbarous and backward stereotype of Ireland and Irishness, as well as the Protestant, reformist, civil and progressive stereotype of the UK and Britishness, still have some currency among pro-Agreement unionists.

Ironically, the leading ex-UUP (subsequently DUP) MP Jeffery Donaldson was more in tune with the shifting perceptions of Taylor when, in December 2001, he commented:

> You will find today, more so than in 1974 with Sunningdale and the Council of Ireland, that there is less resistance to North/ South institutionalised co-operation. That is heavily influenced by changes that have taken place in the Irish Republic. It is seen today as being much less dominated by the Roman Catholic Church, with changes to the constitution that reflect this. It has become a more open society; a more modern society; econo- mically, it is doing very well: all of those things have had an impact here in Northern Ireland and amongst unionists. [We], therefore, feel that perhaps we can do business with the Irish Republic in a manner that will be mutually beneficial. So long as there is recognition of the principle of consent, then the border is going to be there as long as that is the wish of the majority of the population here, but that should not prevent co- operation between two areas that are part of the European Union. It is true that Europe has had an influence here in creating a context within which greater co-operation can take place without people feeling that their sovereignty and identity is being threatened. There is a very delicate balance. If the North/South Ministerial Council and the Implementation Bodies are about co-operation between both parts of this island then I think unionists rest easy. (extract from interview with author, 3 December 2001)

Donaldson's new DUP colleagues, meanwhile, continued to pay ideological observance to the traditional unionist principles of exclusion regarding Irish nationalists and republicans in governance and of the manifestation of the border as a barrier. While this did not preclude their practical involvement in some of the institutions of the Agreement, notably the Northern Ireland Assembly and Executive, they maintained their boycott of North/South institutions and their objection to any infringement of the border between the Northern

Ireland and the Republic of Ireland (Wilford 2001: 120). However, with Donaldson's decampment to the DUP and that party's annihilation of the UUP in the 2005 UK General Election, leading DUP members led by Peter Robinson began to 'go over to the other side'.[19] Their stated purpose was to 'present the unionist case', but this also entailed exploring possibilities for a form of North/South co-operation that they could accept. The long-term success of this shift depends on a number of factors, not least the absence of political and violent threat from Irish nationalism/republicanism and the reinforcement of unionist perceptions of a recycling Irish state.

Conclusion

Before the 1998 Belfast Agreement, all efforts directed at reconfiguring the border through increased North/South co-operation were in vain. After the early failures, unionists were anxious to maintain the border as a barrier between Northern Ireland and the Irish state. Constitutional, perfidious and violent threats emanating from the Irish government, the British government and the IRA respectively were largely responsible for this preference. The cultural chasm that existed between Ulster unionists and the Irish state also played a significant underlying role. However, contemporary changes in the European state-system, in the British–Irish inter-governmental relationship and in the power relationship with Irish nationalists in Northern Ireland were contemporary dynamic forces that determined a shift in the ideological position of pro-Agreement unionists. This shift entailed the inclusion of nationalists and republicans in the governance of Northern Ireland. It also resulted in the acquiescence of pro-Agreement unionists in institutionalised North/South co-operation and in the transformation of the border from barrier to bridge. In no small part, constitutional and cultural changes in the Irish state made possible this cross-border co-operation involving pro-Agreement unionists, and to some degree neutralised general unionist opposition to such co-operation. Nevertheless, for years after the signing of the Agreement, the unionist ideological shift remained partial and tenuous, threatened as it was by a preoccupation with the capacity of the IRA to challenge the monopoly of violence in the North. Consequently, the success in establishing a contemporary political and institutional bridge between North and South was tempered by the debilitating turbulence that marked the border's fledgling years.

After the formal ending of the IRA's armed campaign in July 2005, the role of the Irish state in future North/South bridge-building cannot be underestimated. The removal of the constitutional threat, the ebbing influence of the Catholic Church, as well as the Republic's Celtic Tiger prosperity have already posed a significant challenge to unionist attitudes to North/South co-operation. Reconfiguring the border as a bridge is also integral to recycling the Irish state. In this respect the EU has had a profound effect, as has the maturation of the twenty-year British–Irish inter-governmental partnership. In strategic terms alone, this partnership has yielded an all-island infrastructural vision for the new century which potentially strengthens the hand of public, private and Third sector organisations that help to bridge the border.[20]

NOTES

1   Whyte also noted that many organisations, particularly charitable and welfare organisations and professional associations, are structured on an East–West (British–Irish) basis, e.g. the Royal National Lifeboat Institution and the Association of Certified Accountants.

2   The Irish state has existed in different forms and under different names. The Irish Free State was changed to 'Éire' (Ireland) in de Valera's 1937 Constitution, which also ended dominion status. Éire became a republic in 1949 with the enactment of the Republic of Ireland Act (1949) and the symbolic declaration of a republic on Easter Monday 1949. More recently, the Republic of Ireland has been referred to simply as 'Ireland', for example, in the Belfast Good Friday Agreement (1998), suggesting a twenty-six county statist conception of Ireland.

3   Between December 1921 and May 1922 there were 236 fatalities.

4   The 1937 Irish Constitution not only ended the Free State's dominion status, it also gave special position to the Catholic Church in Éire and reiterated its territorial claim over the whole island.

5   *House of Commons Debate*, 127, Cols 928–30, 29 March 1920.

6   This description belongs to the then Taoiseach, Garret FitzGerald.

7   However, the UK government retained sovereignty over Northern Ireland in a formal–legal sense.

8   Sinn Féin joined the multi-party negotiations in September 1994, after the IRA cease-fire.

9   David Trimble had imposed a previous ban on the participation of Sinn Féin ministers in North/South Ministerial Council meetings.

10   www.northernireland.gov.uk/press/dfp/010620g-dfp.htm (29/01/2003).

11   Prolonged suspension was a direct result of 'Stormontgate', which began with a Police Service of Northern Ireland (police) raid on the Sinn Féin offices at Parliament Buildings, Stormont in October 2002. Documents and computers were seized and three workers were arrested on suspicion of subversive activity. Charges against them were dropped in December 2005 and one of the three, Denis Donaldson, Head of Sinn Féin offices at

Parliament Buildings, subsequently admitted to being a British spy. He was shot dead in April 2006.

12 PEACE II aimed to build upon the cross-community, cross-border approaches to funding adopted under PEACE I. PEACE II allocated approximately €740m to Northern Ireland and the border counties of the Republic of Ireland. The EU allocated €530m between 2000 and 2004, with a further €176m coming from public sector funds and €33m from the private sector (www.cec.org.uk). PEACE II had five priority areas namely economic renewal, social inclusion, locally based regeneration, the creation of an outward and forward-looking region, and cross-border co-operation. The cross-border co-operation priority was allocated €39.72m (stg£24.45m) or 9.3 per cent of the total package in Northern Ireland and €39.72m in the border region of the Republic of Ireland. Between 2000 and 2006, at least €400m (stg£240m) was envisaged for cross-border co-operation from the Northern Ireland and Republic of Ireland Community Support Frameworks (Northern Ireland Programme for Government 2001). Intermediary Funding Bodies (IFBs), which are voluntary and community sector-based, continued to play a key role under PEACE II and were made responsible for the allocation of 34 per cent (approximately stg£100m) of the total funds (www.cec.org.uk/ni/funding.pdf [13/01/2005]).

13 INTERREG III, which is an EU-wide Community Initiative aimed at encouraging indigenous cross-border co-operation in an attempt to off-set the negative effects of EU economic integration for peripheral regions, made €170m (approximately stg£104m) of funding available for Northern Ireland and the border region of the Republic of Ireland.

14 www.northernireland.gov.uk/press/dfp/010620g-dfp.htm (13/01/2005).

15 www.niassembly.gov.uk/finance/reports/report3-99rl.htm (13/01/2005).

16 The Northern Ireland Programme for Government (2001) settled for the term 'all-island' and used it in conjunction with 'cross-border' to describe the work of the North/South Ministerial Council and Implementation Bodies (www.pfgni.gov.uk/dec2001pfg/ch6.htm [13/01/2005]). Here, 'cross-border' may refer solely to 'the border region'.

17 For Dennis Kennedy, the 2001 census figures on religious affiliation in Northern Ireland, which revealed that Catholics made up 44 per cent of the population while Protestants accounted for 53 per cent, indicated that a 'united Ireland' was not a realistic proposition (*The Irish Times*, 28 December 2002).

18 *Observer*, 10 March 2002. Lord Laird of Artigarvan, then joint chair of the languages Implementation Body, supported Trimble's assertion, claiming: 'There are 25,000 Ulster-Scots people in the Republic who have not had their cultural identity recognized' (*Irish News*, 11 March 2002).

19 For example, in April 2006, Peter Robinson led a DUP delegation to Killarney where he addressed the British-Irish Inter-Parliamentary Body (http://cain.ulst.ac.uk/issues/politics/docs/dup/pr240406.htm) (16/06/2006).

20 An Taoiseach Bertie Ahern announced that 'over €100 billion will be spent on infrastructure on this island over the next 10 years...I think it shows...what the extraordinary potential is of the peace process and the peace dividend' (www.times online.co.uk/taoiseach) (20/12/2005).

REFERENCES

Agreement between the Government of the United Kingdom of Great Britain and Northern Ireland and the Government of Ireland Belfast, 10 April 1998. Belfast: HMSO.

Arthur, P. 2000. *Special Relationships: Britain, Ireland and the Northern Ireland Problem*. Belfast: Blackstaff.

Bew, P. 1999. 'The Political History of Northern Ireland since Partition: The prospects for

North-South co-operation', in A. F. Heath, R. Breen and C. T. Whelan (eds), *Ireland North and South*. Oxford: Oxford University Press, 401–8.

Buckland, P. 2001. 'A Protestant state: Unionists in government, 1921–39', in D. G. Boyce and A. O'Day (eds), *Defenders of the Union: A Survey of British and Irish Unionism Since 1801*. London: Routledge, 211–26.

Caporaso, J. 1996. 'The European Union and forms of state: Westphalian, regulatory and post-modern', *Journal of Common Market Studies*, 34 (1), 29–52.

Cash, J. D. 1996. *Identity, Ideology and Conflict: The Structuration of Politics in Northern Ireland*. Cambridge: Cambridge University Press.

Donaldson, J. Interview with author, Lisburn, 3 December 2001.

Farrell, M. 1983. *Arming the Protestants: The Formation of the Ulster Special Constabulary and the Royal Ulster Constabulary 1920–27*. London: Pluto.

Fitzpatrick, D. 1998. *The Two Irelands*. Oxford: Oxford University Press.

Goodhall, D. 1993. 'The Irish question', *Ampleforth Journal*, 98 (1) (Spring).

Guelke, A. 1988. *Northern Ireland: The International Perspective*. Dublin: Gill & Macmillan.

Hadfield, B. 1992. 'The Northern Ireland Constitution', in B. Hadfield (ed.), *Northern Ireland: Politics and the Constitution*. Buckingham: Open University Press, 1–12.

Hadfield, B. 2001. 'Seeing it through? The multifaceted implementation of the Belfast Agreement', in R. Wilford (ed.), *Aspects of the Belfast Agreement*. Oxford: Oxford University Press, 84–106.

Harris, E. 1995. 'Why unionists are not understood', in A. Aughey, D. Burnside, E. Harris, G. Adams and J. Donaldson (eds), *Selling Unionism*. Belfast: Ulster Young Unionist Council, 27–47.

Hennessey, T. 1997. *A History of Northern Ireland, 1920–1996*. Dublin: Gill & Macmillan.

Jackson, A. 2001. 'Irish Unionism, 1879–1922', in D. G. Boyce and A. O'Day (eds), *Defenders of the Union: A Survey of British and Irish Unionism Since 1801*. London: Routledge, 115–36.

Kennedy, D. 1988. *The Widening Gulf: Northern Attitudes to the Independent Irish State*. Belfast: Blackstaff.

Kennedy, D. 1999. 'Politics of North-South relations in post-Partition Ireland', in P. J. Roche and B. Barton (eds), *The Northern Ireland Question: Nationalism, Unionism and Partition*. Aldershot: Ashgate, 71–96.

Kennedy, Michael, 2005. 'The realms of practical politics: North–South co-operation on the Erne Hydro-Electric Scheme', Discussion Paper for the research project, *Mapping Frontiers, Plotting Pathways: Routes to North–South Co-operation in a Divided Island*. www.mappingfrontiers.ie (accessed 15/03/07).

Laffan, B. and D. Payne, 2001. *Creating Living Institutions: EU Cross-Border Co-operation after the Good Friday Agreement*. Armagh: Centre for Cross-Border Studies.

McCall, C. 2001. 'The production of space and the realignment of identity in Northern Ireland', *Regional and Federal Studies*, 11 (2), 1–24.

McIntosh, G. 1999. *The Force of Culture: Unionist Identities in Twentieth-Century Ireland*. Cork: Cork University Press.

Mulholland, M. 2000. *Northern Ireland at the Crossroads: Ulster Unionism in the O'Neill Years, 1960–9*. Basingstoke: Macmillan.

O'Leary, B. 2001. 'The Character of the 1998 Agreement: Results and prospects', in R. Wilford (ed.), *Aspects of the Belfast Agreement*. Oxford: Oxford University Press, 47–83.

Patterson, H. 2001. 'From Insulation to Appeasement: The Major and Blair Governments Reconsidered', in R. Wilford (ed.), *Aspects of the Belfast Agreement*. Oxford: Oxford University Press, 166–83.

Poggi, G. 1990. *The State: Its Nature, Development and Prospects*. Oxford: Polity.

Pollak, A. 2001. 'The policy agenda for cross-border co-operation: A view from the centre for cross-border studies', *Administration*, 49 (2), 15–22.

Rose, R. 1983. *Is the United Kingdom a State?* Glasgow: University of Strathclyde.

Ruane, J. and J. Todd, 2001. 'The politics of transition? Explaining political crises in the implementation of the Belfast Good Friday Agreement', *Political Studies*, 49, 923–40.

Tannam, E. 1999. *Cross-Border Co-operation in the Republic of Ireland and Northern Ireland*. Basingstoke: Macmillan.

Tilly, C. 1990. *Coercion, Capital and European States AD 900–1990*. Oxford: Basil Blackwell.

Whyte, J. 1983. 'The permeability of the United Kingdom–Irish border: A preliminary reconnaissance', *Administration*, 31 (3), 330–45.

Wilford, R. 2001. 'The Assembly and the Executive', in R. Wilford (ed.), *Aspects of the Belfast Agreement*. Oxford: Oxford University Press, 107–28.

4

Recycled connections: The Irish state and its diaspora

Kevin Howard

The two decades between 1984 and 2004 witnessed a remarkable recycling of the relationship between Ireland and the ethnic Irish abroad – the Irish in Britain in particular. Across this time scale, the Irish state's attitude and engagement with its expatriates in the UK has moved from *laissez-faire* to 'pro-active' engagement (Council of Europe 1999). This chapter explores three aspects of this politics of adaptation, beginning with the state's conceptual redefinition of the Irish in Britain and the dramatic growth in state patronage for the British-based approved representatives of the ethnic Irish community. These two aspects are complementary, thus mutually reinforcing both the idea and the institutionalisation of a transnational Irish community. However, this recycling has only gone so far. The logic of de-territorialisation, i.e. the reconfiguring of the Irish nation's parameters to include citizens *outside* the state, could be seen to require some mechanism for their political participation *within* the state. This hasn't happened. Moreover, when proposals are made to grant expatriates political rights in the state, they are rejected, which indicates clear limits to the state's recycled transnationalism. It is an analysis of the debate over the political rights of the external citizenry that constitutes the third aspect of this chapter's exploration of the politics of adaptation.

These three aspects of adaptation with regard to state-diaspora relations correspond to the three main themes of this book: definition, representation and participation. First, there has been a conceptual *redefinition* of the external Irish from emigrants to transnational diasporans.[1] The notion of an Irish diaspora has become part of modern Ireland's discourse. Emigration itself, the key sociological factor that has shaped modern Ireland, is recycled. Emigrants and their descendants, redefined as a global Irish diaspora, recast Ireland as the bio-territorial epicentre of a global network numbering in the tens of millions. In relation to the Irish in Britain the prevailing consensus was that the second-generation rapidly assimilated into British society displaying little or no interest in maintaining an Irish identity – nor was there any encouragement on the part of the Irish state for them to do so. The descriptor 'Irish in Britain' reflects this. The Irish community was *in* Britain; not *of* Britain. Redefined in diasporic terms however, these emigrants and their descendants were conceptualised as a multigenerational ethnic community similar to Irish-Americans, thus challenging the consensus of rapid assimilation.

In addition to fostering a conceptual redefinition of the Irish in Britain, the Irish state has come to play a role in shaping the activity and representation of this particular Irish community in civil society. Comparative studies show that antagonisms can exist between the kin-state and diasporic actors (Anderson-Paul 2001; Shain and Bristman 2002). When it comes to financial support, harmonious state/diaspora relations may be best served by state funding directed at putatively non-political organisations. In the Irish case, the largest single recipient of Irish exchequer funding is the civil umbrella group, the Federation of Irish Societies (FIS), which has subsequently become in effect the Irish government's link to the Irish community in Britain. It may be argued that, through increasing such financial support in recent years, and through its official endorsement of the FIS, the Irish state has had an immense influence on the orientation of ethnic Irish civil society activity in Britain.

Thirdly, while the practical value of political rights can be questioned, it remains the case that the holding of these rights is at the core of what it is to be a citizen (Soysal 1994; Turner 2001). The denial of such rights is a diminution of citizenship. Irish citizens outside the state have no political rights, nor substantive political voice within the state. Thus, despite the radical transformation in state–diaspora relationships, there is a hierarchy in the category of the Irish citizen based on territorial residency in the twenty-six county state. Those who find themselves outside the state, either through emigration or through partition, are certainly nationals; their citizenship is, however, a 'second-order citizenship', as it is ranked on the basis of territorial residence.

Ireland's laissez-faire approach to emigration

Irish migration to Great Britain has been substantial for centuries
(Fitzgerald 1992). Figure 4.1 is a simplified representation of the
numbers of the Irish-born recorded in Great Britain from 1841, the
first time a place of birth question was included in British censuses,
up until 2001. Despite the necessary simplicity of the graph below,
it must be agreed that it provides an easily grasped impression of the
numerical and temporal scale of migration from the island of Ireland
to Great Britain, which continued without cessation before and after
Independence.

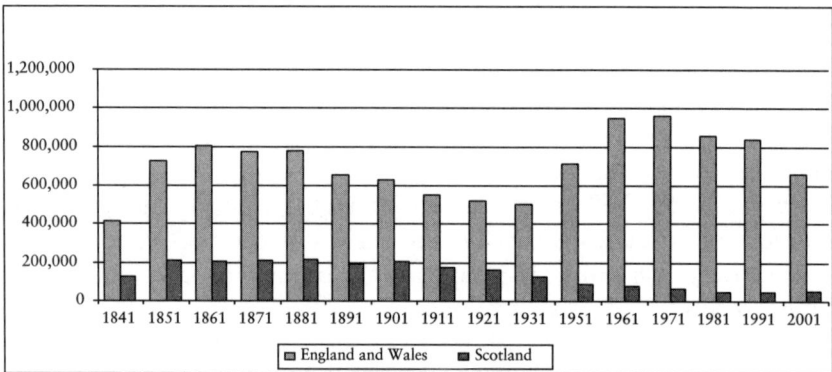

Figure 4.1 Pattern of the Irish-born recorded in Great Britain
Censuses, 1840–2001.[55]

Source: Jackson (1963), Office for National Statistics (2002), General Registrar's
Office (Scotland) (2002)

Despite its profound impact on Ireland, emigration has received
very little official analysis. Since the Second World War, only three
major reports have been produced:

- *Emigration and other Population Problems* (Commission on
  Emigration, 1954);
- *The Economic and Social Implications of Emigration*
  (National Economic and Social Council, 1991);
- *Ireland and the Irish Abroad* (Task Force on Emigration,
  2002).

Yet these three reports profoundly reflect the contexts within which they were produced. They map the conceptual transition in how state–emigrant relationships are understood. For most of independent Ireland's history, the causes and implications of emigration for the state and for Irish society have been largely regarded as facts of life about which little could be done. As for the emigrants themselves, while their hard currency remittances were very welcome (if not taken for granted), the kin-state did not concern itself in any tangible way with their welfare in their sites of settlement (Lee 1989; MacLaughlin 1997).

This indifference is clear in the first major report on emigration referred to above. The post-war economic boom amongst first world countries engendered massive labour migration. In addition to inter-state migration, the period was characterised by increased urbanisation within states, as people migrated from rural areas to the expanding towns and cities (Panayi 2000). Ireland was no exception to this general trend. In 1954, the *Commission on Emigration and other Population Problems,* established in 1948 under the auspices of John A Costello's coalition government, published its report. The context in which the research was compiled was a period of massive out-migration from Ireland. However, the report noted an unusual feature:

> In the case of Ireland, as a rule, the towns to which the rural Irish migrated were in Great Britain and America...Our demographic history has been unique...this is a striking feature of our population problem – the country loses through emigration each year a number of people roughly equivalent to one-third of the annual number of births. (Report of the Commission on Emigration, 1954, para. 461)

In other words, while Ireland's experience of migration fitted the general trend of industrialising Europe, the towns to which the rural Irish migrated were outside the country, principally in Britain.

Despite the sophistication of analysis in this report, its assumptions are conventional. Apart from the moral dangers posed by Britain, it had little to say regarding the emigrants once outside Ireland. The report did concede that:

> There is much support for the view that some type of social bureau should be established in Great Britain to look after the

welfare of our emigrants there...We are of the opinion that the suggestion is a good one and...if it were then considered necessary that there should be a reasonable amount to help to establish a bureau, we think it should be provided out of State funds. (Report of the Commission on Emigration 1954, para. 328)

This was rejected. Indeed, as Delaney (2000) has shown, successive Irish governments were indifferent towards Irish emigrants in their sites of settlement. In 1965, in response to the clergy's appeal for government state aid in supporting Irish welfare initiatives in Great Britain, Seán Lemass declared that:

The government remains of the opinion that the diversion of Irish State revenue to the support of Irish centres in England would be unsound from the point of view of State finance and would, in practice, be incapable of being kept within fixed limits. (cited in Delaney 2000: 259)

Forty years after Independence, emigration remained a central feature of Irish life. What also remained a central feature of Irish political life was an attitude of indifference to Irish citizens outside the state. It was assumed that Irish emigrants assimilated rapidly into British society. This orthodoxy was given one of its most influential expressions in 1978 by the Maynooth sociologist Liam Ryan (1978: 61):

Irish assimilation into British society is among the fastest that occurs [sic] among immigrant groups anywhere in the world. Assimilation is practically complete in a single generation. The children of Irish immigrants, sometimes to the distress of their parents, grow up seeing themselves as English or Scots; they may acknowledge their Irish ancestry and exhibit a few inherited traits, but for all practical purposes they are indistinguishable from their British peers whether in respect of dress or in social, cultural, or religious behaviour .

The Irish in 'multicultural' Britain

The unexpected return of mass emigration from Ireland in the 1980s stimulated an intense debate concerning the nature of the relationship between the Irish state and the Irish abroad. The debate was given greater poignancy through being set against the immediate backdrop of the 1970s, a period when, for the first time since the 1840s, the numbers of Irish people 'coming home' exceeded those leaving. Despite fifteen years of EEC membership, by the late 1980s it looked as if migration had resumed its traditional pattern, i.e. outwards. Across the decade the average annual rate of emigration was 35,000 persons, with an officially estimated peak of 70,600 in 1988–9. The scale of people leaving the country reached that of 1950s, a period aptly described as the 'Lost Decade' (Keogh et al. 2004). As in the 1950s, the most important destination for 1980s emigrants was Great Britain, particularly London. Of the estimated 130,000 who went to Britain, the majority were between 20 and 34 years of age (Courtney 2000: 303).

However, the ethnic makeup of the host-country had changed radically in the intervening three decades. Britain's post-war economic expansion had drawn immigrants from Ireland and from the non-white former colonies of the British Empire. By the 1980s the British-born descendants of those earlier immigrants were staking their claims to distinctive places in British society. Hesitantly, Britain was being redefined as a multicultural society (Spencer 1997; Parekh et al. 2000). It was no longer assumed that migrants and their descendants could, would and should assimilate into British society, thereby losing their ethnic distinctiveness. In short, the 1980s was the decade in which multiculturalism in Britain was becoming mainstream. This was the context into which Ireland's new wave of emigrants arrived.

Mobilisation of the Irish community

The British state's implementation of multiculturalism created an opportunity structure for ethnic activism; ethnic Irish community activists (both British and Irish-born) mobilised to secure a place for their community in this framework (Howard 2006). The 1980s saw a mushrooming of Irish community mobilisation on the part of recently arrived immigrants and of British-born descendants of the Irish who had arrived in the 1950s and 1960s. Quite unlike the other significant minority ethnic groups emerging in Britain, Irish ethnic activists had an external support on which they sought to draw – namely Ireland, their kin-state. Initially, however, the Irish state, through the offices of the Embassy in London, was not at all interested in supporting or endorsing any Irish community activism in England. Support for the recognition of the Irish as a substantial minority ethnic community that experienced discrimination and disadvantage comparable to that of non-white groups came from the Greater London Council (GLC). It was the GLC that, in 1983, appointed Great Britain's first local government Irish liaison officer and which convened a conference aimed at evaluating the needs of the ethnic Irish community. A year later, the Strategic Policy Unit of the GLC produced a report on the Irish community in London, which showed:

> a community poorly housed, and suffering from a dispropor-
> tionately high incidence of mental illness in relation to its size. It
> is a community baited by the media, suffering constant attacks
> on its cultural and social identity and deterred from political
> mobilisation by the threat of imprisonment and exile under the
> Prevention of Terrorism Act. The root of these problems lies in
> racism against the Irish, a factor yet to be acknowledged as a
> major problem in British society. (GLC 1984: 11)

This document highlighted the key issues upon which the Irish case for inclusion in the multicultural framework was built: (a) relative socio-economic disadvantage exacerbated by (b) anti-Irish racism, with the latter being 'whitewashed' out of the picture. As a consequence, the report recommended to the GLC's Ethnic Minority Committee that:

> the Committee recognise the Irish as an Ethnic Minority Group
> and to adopt the following definition of the Irish for such
> purposes: persons who come from, or whose forbears originate
> in, Ireland and who consider themselves Irish [and that] London
> Boroughs be requested to adopt the definition of Irish given
> above for the purposes of ethnic monitoring (GLC 1984: 11)

One of the most effective of the activist groups that emerged in the mid-1980s was the Action Group for Irish Youth (AGIY). In October 1986 AGIY convened its first Annual General Meeting (AGM) and set out what it saw as the particular problems facing 'new-wave' immigrants and the strategy it aimed to adopt. Crucially, this meeting rejected the hitherto apolitical low-profile approach of previous Irish emigrant cohorts. In short, as with the group identities emerging amongst the descendants of non-whites, who articulated their British space with another place, it was clear to AGIY that the Irish *in* Britain had to become the Irish *of* Britain:

> If the Irish in Britain are to develop into a full maturity as an ethnic community, with important contributions to make to both Ireland and Britain they need to accept their dual status as being neither fully in one society or culture nor out of the other and make some sense of that position by creating their own emigrant culture (AGIY, 14 October 1986)

So, increasingly from the mid-1980s onwards, new voices were added to the perennial debate about emigration. In addition to the claims being made from *within* Ireland that the state had an obligation to end emigration, new demands were being made from *outside* Ireland that the state had an obligation to communities made up of Irish citizens and their foreign-born descendants; that the borders of Irishness were not co-terminous with the state.

Response within Ireland

In the late 1980s, as had happened in the immediate post-war period, mass emigration prompted the commissioning of research. In 1991, the National Economic and Social Council (NESC) published the second major report on emigration, *The Economic and Social Implications on Emigration* (NESC 1991). However, this report was sensitive to the changed British context and had listened to the views of ethnic Irish community activists. It observed that the conditions now existed within which an Irish–British ethnic community could emerge, similar to that of Irish-America. Pro-active engagement by Irish governments would aid this:

> With many new immigrant groups, and now an integral part of Europe, the new Britain being constructed today offers many positive possibilities for the development of an Irish–British culture and identity, which could act in much the same way as the Irish-American experience. A positive Irish emigration policy, which would help develop such a positive immigrant absorption model in Britain, would help repay the debt we owe our emigrants and the hurt which our previous neglect might have occasioned. (NESC 1991: 271)

The 1991 NESC report signifies a radical shift in thinking on the nature of the relationship between Irish governments and the Irish in Britain. In addition to the changed British context, the report emphasised the obligation the Irish state had to its emigrants.

The clearest expression of the conceptual recycling of the external Irish is given in the third of the major reports on emigration: *Ireland and the Irish Abroad*. In December 2001, Ireland's Department of Foreign Affairs initiated its Task Force on Policy regarding Emigrants. As its name implies, the focus of the report was entirely on the impact of emigration on the emigrants themselves and on the difficulties they faced in their sites of settlement, and its emphasis was transnational. The task force published its report in August 2002. It symbolises the conceptual recycling of expatriate Irish, from emigrants to diasporans. Indeed, the report concluded with the observation that:

> A key thread running through this report has been a conviction that the Irish Abroad are an integral part of the Irish Nation and must be recognised and treated as such. As the Constitution recognises, nationality is essentially about identity not territory. Those who have left this country remain part of what we are as a Nation. It is not enough to remember them; we must value them, as they do us. (Task Force on Policy regarding Emigrants 2002: 53)

Ireland and the Irish Abroad, as the above quotation exemplifies, asserts the de-coupling of territory and identity implicit in the revised Article 2 of the Irish Constitution. The Irish nation was not, nor ever had been, co-terminous with the either the Irish state or the island of Ireland. This was the homeland of a multi-million strong Irish diaspora, who looked to the Irish state to endorse the diaspora's identity and to support its members materially.

Nationals and citizens

The Irish constitution and Irish citizenship

We can conceptualise citizenship regimes as being arranged along a spectrum: at one end, *ius soli* – entitlement to citizenship through birth on a particular territory; at the other, *ius sanguinis,* entitlement to citizenship through descent. If one conceptualises *ius soli* and *ius sanguinis* as the two 'ideal-type' opposite ends of this spectrum, the British citizenship regime has moved along it away from *ius soli* towards *ius sanguinis*. Britain, however, is just one in a range of states where the impact of recent (that is, post-World War II) immigration has engendered changes to citizenship regimes (Brubaker 1996; Jopke 1999). Under the impact of immigration, the citizenship regimes of France and Germany, too, have been restructured. The UK and France have become more exclusive and Germany more inclusive – evidence, according to some commentators, of the convergence of citizenship regimes (Weil 2004).

The perceived impact of immigration also underpins the removal of Ireland's automatic *ius soli* provision. Up until 2004, a child born on the island of Ireland was automatically an Irish, and hence a citizen of the EU, irrespective of the citizenship status of the child's parents. Ireland's *ius soli* dimension of its citizenship regime became the subject of widespread public debate through the issue of so-called 'asylum babies'. The government purported that maternity services, particularly in Dublin, were being intolerably strained due to women showing up to give birth solely in order to gain Irish, and hence EU, citizenship for the child. It was further purported that our EU neighbours were expressing concerns about the exploitation of this back door into Europe. When pushed for substantiation of these claims, the government changed tack and stressed the need to protect the integrity of Ireland's citizenship laws, 'threatened' as they were by unscrupulous immigrants.

The putative 'threat' arose as a consequence of the amended Article 2 of the Constitution, endorsed by referendum following the Good Friday Agreement (GFA). The revised Article 2 reads:

> It is the entitlement and birthright of every person born in the island of Ireland, which includes its islands and seas, to be part of the Irish nation. That is also the entitlement of all persons otherwise qualified in accordance with law to be citizens of Ireland. Furthermore, the Irish nation cherishes its special affinity with people of Irish ancestry living abroad who share its cultural identity and heritage (Article 2, Constitution of Ireland)

This was interpreted to mean that *ius soli* was a constitutional right. In other words membership of the nation and entitlement to citizenship were interpreted as one and the same thing. Given this, any restriction of the *ius soli* required a referendum.[2] The referendum easily carried. Over 80 per cent of the population voted in favour of the measure with the implicit understanding that the principle of *ius soli* would be weakened. What is important to note however is that the referendum did not result in the amendment of Article 2; this stayed as it was. It was Article 9 that was amended. Prior to the twenty-seventh amendment, Article 9 read thus:

1.1 On the coming into operation of this Constitution any person who was a citizen of Saorstát Éireann immediately before the coming into operation of this Constitution shall become and be a citizen of Ireland.

1.2 The future acquisition and loss of Irish nationality and citizenship shall be determined in accordance with law.

1.3 No person shall be excluded from Irish nationality and citizenship by reason of the sex of such person.

2. Fidelity to the nation and loyalty to the State are fundamental political duties of all citizens.

The amendment involved two new clauses being inserted, thus:

2.1 Notwithstanding any other provision of this Constitution, a person born in the island of Ireland, which includes its islands and seas, who does not have, at the time of the birth of that person, at least one parent who is an Irish citizen or entitled to be an Irish citizen is not entitled to Irish citizenship or nationality, unless provided for by law.

2.2 This section shall not apply to persons born before the date of the enactment of this section.

Therefore, it remains the constitutional birthright of every person born on the island of Ireland and its islands and seas to be a member of the Irish nation, but this is not the same as a constitutionally guaranteed right to Irish citizenship. What the Constitution can be seen to represent is a novel and ingenious distinction between nationals and citizens. To be a national, a member of the nation, is ultimately a subjective matter; one is Irish if one feels oneself to be so. Citizenship is more profound, involving, as it does, rights against the state. The Irish government's information service Oasis implicitly confirms this distinction when it defines citizens as 'formal members of the Irish community, that is, the Irish community living in Ireland and the Irish community living abroad'.[3]

Demarcating citizens

> The highest privilege of citizenship is the possession of political rights... It is [through]... the entitlement to and exercise of these rights that one's status as a 'citizen', as a member of the body politic, will be established. The line that divides members from strangers, citizens from foreigners, the 'we' from the 'they' are drawn most sharply around these privileges. (Benhabib 1999: 724)

Before the late 1980s, the question as to whether Irish citizens who do not live in Ireland ought to have political rights in the Republic's legislature was raised sporadically, most often in the context of debates over electoral legislation, with little response. However, by the end of the 1980s the scale of the new wave of emigration, and the more pro-active approach which the state was beginning to adopt, set the context for an attempt to extend the franchise. In 1991, the Labour Party TD Gerry O'Sullivan lodged an amendment notion to the Electoral Bill. The principal features of the amendment were:

- Those over 18 who had emigrated within the last fifteen years would be entitled to a postal vote, those under 18 would retain voting rights for fifteen years when they reached 18;
- Those elections in which emigrants would be entitled to a postal vote included Dáil elections, European Assembly elections, Presidential elections and all the referenda.

The second-stage reading of the Bill took place during the first two weeks in March 1991. The rhetoric of condemnation over the Irish government's successive record on emigration was much in evidence. In making his pitch Deputy O'Sullivan lacerated past governments:

> It is to the eternal shame of our native Governments that, for nearly 70 years, they have continued the tendency to do nothing to address this shameful haemorrhage of our people... I suggest that, while conditions of transport and communications have improved and have been modernised, the basic rights of Irish people to participate actively and fully in their national affairs

have not changed. Many of our exiles who have been forced to seek work abroad have not reneged on their responsibilities at home. Many a hard earned pound has found its way back home to help educate the young brothers and sisters and to keep the old in relative comfort...We hear much about investment going out of Ireland but we hear very little about the inflow of emigrants' earnings. Money earned on the building sites, in the bars and offices in Boston and Birmingham has filtered back to Ballinrobe, Ballyhaunis and Ballydehob to help those in need, the unemployed, the old and the young. (*Dail Eireann* Official Report, 5 March 1991, Vol. 405, Cols 2389 and 2391)

So the case for the recognition of Irish emigrants by the Irish state is thus: emigrants were forced into leaving, they hoped to return some day, and they continued to contribute to the economic maintenance of people in Ireland. Yet they were disenfranchised once they left the state.

The substance of the government's reply to O'Sullivan can be summarised in a few key points:

- The Irish electoral system is of such sophistication that a few third preferences could decide the outcome in any constituency; therefore the electorate needed to be equally sophisticated and emigrants could never be as fully informed as citizens in Ireland.
- The constitutional time-limit between the calling and the holding of elections would present difficulties in the garnering of votes from citizens outside these islands given the global scale of Irish emigration.
- The fact that, by definition, emigrant voting would take place outside the state meant that a potential for abuse existed.
- The representatives of the Irish abroad, for instance the London based Federation of Irish Societies (FIS) indicated that it was not at all clear that Irish citizens abroad wanted voting rights anyway.
- The 'one man one vote' argument. Irish citizens in Great Britain already have a vote and hence a political voice, though in the British not the Irish legislature.
- The size of the diaspora and the generous definition of citizenship meant that 'the number of non-resident electors could exceed those at home' (*Dail Eireann*, Official Report, 5 March 1991, Vol. 405, Cols 2403-5).

If we examine each of these points in turn, they will be found to be prevarications rather than principled objections. The inference that an understanding of 'the issues' ought to be a prerequisite for entitlement to vote is the kind of elitist conceit that historically has informed the exclusion of groups from the political community. The denial of political rights to women was often justified on the grounds that 'the issues' were too complex. The second and third points are not convincing: there is no reason why voting cannot take place in embassies or consulates, overseen by Irish state officials, to ensure the integrity of the count and of the repatriation of the vote. The next point four is arguably disingenuous; Flynn was referring to a meeting held by the Federation of Irish Societies (FIS)[4] in 1989, when the issue of voting rights for emigrants was discussed. The reservations expressed by FIS concerned the problem whether the voting rights of Irish citizens in elections in Great Britain would be affected by additional voting rights in Ireland. But the phenomenon has not affected the rights of British citizens in Ireland to retain a political voice in the UK and to be treated as de facto Irish citizens. This in turn undermines the fifth point: there are numerous examples of people having political rights to vote in different jurisdictions. Indeed, in the EU, this is the norm; Irish 'citizens' are the exception (Honohan 2001).

The most weighty objection seems to be the last point, namely the potential size of the external electorate. In other words, the government was using the size of the external citizenry as a way of justifying its exclusion from the political community. The then-leader of the Labour Party, Dick Spring, was forthright in his support for allowing the external Irish to participate in Ireland's internal political process. He argued:

> We in the Labour Party see no reason why Irish citizens should be deprived of one of the most basic rights of any citizen simply because they have been forced to live abroad. Ireland is one of the few remaining countries in the European Community which disenfranchises its emigrants. If the Government accept our Bill, this will bring Ireland into line with our EC partners who have provided voting rights for their emigrants in some or all of their elections. Most Deputies are familiar with the principal features of this Bill. The Fianna Fáil Party are missing a glorious opportunity to correct a weakness in our voting system in relation to citizens who have been forced to emigrate. We have

been [1074] alerted to the possibility of a constitutional challenge. I do not believe we should be intimidated. We are legislators with the right to legislate (*Dáil Éireann* Official Report, 13 March 1991, Vol. 406, Cols 1072–4)

Despite Labour's ringing endorsement and principled arguments in support of external participation, the Amendment Bill never reached committee; it was defeated at the second reading (albeit relatively narrowly, by 66 votes to 62).

It was four years before the Dáil revisited the issue. By then Fianna Fáil was gone from government and the Dáil had installed the John Bruton-led 'Rainbow Coalition', with Labour as one of the three parties in the coalition. The specific context was President Mary Robinson's address to both houses of the Oireachtas, titled 'Cherishing the Irish Diaspora' (2 February 1995).[5] According to President Robinson,

> our relationship in this country to those who have left it is a moral relationship ... if cherishing the diaspora is to be more than a sentimental regard for those who leave our shores, we should not only listen to their voice and their viewpoint. We have a responsibility to respond warmly to their expressed desire for appropriate fora [sic] for dialogue and interaction with us by examining in an open and generous way the possible linkages (*Dáil Éireann* Official Report, 2 February 1995, Vol. 448, Cols 1145–58)

The actuality of President Robinson's 'fora for dialogue and interaction' reduced to ensuring access to news from home. Given modern information technology, she suggested that news from home should be even easier to access and should be made so by the government.

The more substantive issue of emigrant participation was dealt with in the Dáil that evening. In response to questions put by Fianna Fáil and Progressive Democrat TDs as to what the government intended to do to facilitate external participation, Brendan Howlin, as Minister for the Environment, responded thus:

> The Government has authorised the drafting of a Constitution Amendment Bill to provide for the election of three Members of the Seanad by Irish emigrants ... It is intended that the

referendum on the Bill will be held at the same time as the proposed referendum on divorce. I am preparing detailed proposals
for legislation to govern such matters as entitlement to vote at
elections of emigrant representatives to the Seanad, registration
of electors and conduct of the elections. These proposals will be
announced well in advance of the proposed referendum. (*Dáil
Éireann*, Official Report, 2 February 1995, Vol. 448, Cols
1232–3)

Howlin went on to argue that:

this proposal is a substantial advance on the rhetoric of the
past. It is the first concrete proposal to give emigrants a voice in
the Houses of the Oireachtas and has been welcomed. I am
aware that there is pressure being brought to bear to grant them
representation in this House...but it is a substantial advance.
(*Dáil Éireann*, Official Report, 2 February 1995, Vol. 448, Cols
1232–1233)

This proposal – to allow three Seanad (Upper House) seats for emigrants – had been floated for some time. In the 1991 debate, Fine
Gael had formulated it as a compromise. It is interesting that in
1995 it was a Labour TD who recommended emigrant representation in the Seanad. As we saw above, in 1991 Labour was fully
behind external participation. In 1995 Fianna Fáil was in
opposition, and it was they and the PDs who were pushing for what
they had rejected four years earlier.

Two years later (1997) Fianna Fáil, in coalition with the PDs,
were back in power. However, notwithstanding their earlier
enthusiasm for external participation, since 1997 the issue has
virtually disappeared from the political arena.[6] On the one hand,
economic conditions changed dramatically in the latter half of the
1990s. The so-called 'Celtic Tiger' has resulted in net migration;
emigration, despite continuing, no longer has a politically sensitive
high public profile. On the other hand, the issue was put on the
back burner by being given over to the All-Party Oireachtas
Committee on the Constitution (APOCC), established in October
1997 to examine and report on the functioning of Ireland's
parliament.[7]

Recognition in lieu of participation

The APOCC published its report in March 2002 – in other words, at the same time as the Task Force on Emigration was conducting its research. Both reports referred to the changed context consequent upon the Good Friday Agreement and, given this, to the way the state ought to relate to the external Irish. The contrast in the conclusions drawn appears striking at first sight; but, on analysis, the reports are complementary.

The tone and the aspirations of *Ireland and the Irish Abroad* are that the state recognises, endorses and materially supports the transterritorial Irish nation. One of the clearest tangible expressions of this newfound sense of obligation has been the funding distributed by the Díon (Irish word for 'shelter') Committee. It was in the context of the re-emergence of substantial emigration that the Irish government in 1984 established the Díon Committee under the auspices of the Republic's then-Minister for Labour, Ruairí Quinn. The committee is an advisory group. Its terms of reference were, and remain:

> To advise and report on emigrant welfare services in Britain. To make recommendations on the provision of financial assistance to organizations to employ professional workers to assist with the welfare problems of Irish emigrants there... consider and make recommendations on specific questions at the request of the Minister for Foreign Affairs. (Díon Strategic Plan 2005)

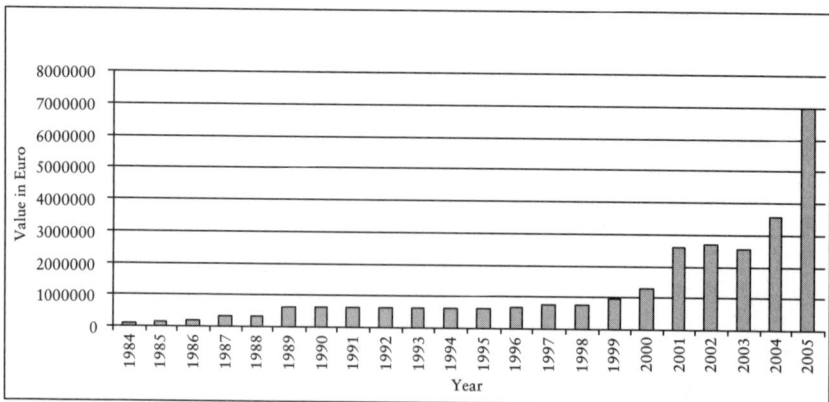

Figure 4.2 Irish exchequer funding for distribution by Díon Committee, 1984–2005 (Díon Strategic Plan 2005)

Its initial funding was not exactly generous; in 1984 Díon was allocated the equivalent of 86,000 euro. The increased awareness of the scale of emigration, following the publication of the results of the Republic's 1986 census and the vocal demands on the part of Irish community activists, led to a rapid increase in funding. As can be seen from Figure 4.2, there has been a substantial increase in the funds made available to Díon since 1984, most especially between 2003 and 2005 when funding increased by 160 per cent from 2.7 million euro to just over 7 million euro.

The largest recipient of this Irish exchequer largesse is the aforementioned Federation of Irish Societies (FIS). Through Irish state patronage the FIS has evolved from what one Irish Ambassador to London described as a collection of drinking clubs to a highly sophisticated ethnic lobby group and the Irish government's approved representatives of the Irish in Britain. In response to this largesse, the FIS has moved away from the issue of external political participation. Leading FIS figures were important members of the Emigration Task Force. *Ireland and the Irish Abroad* steers clear of discussing the issue, taking its cue from the APOCC report published five months previously. The Task Force recommended that the issue be kept under review.

The APOCC report is striking in the way it explicitly demarcates the Irish political community from the Irish ethnic community. It draws a clear line between the citizens of the Republic, resident in the Republic, and the external citizenry. Chapter four of the report, 'Northern Ireland and emigrant participation in national political life', deals explicitly with the arguments for extending the boundaries of the political community to include Irish citizens in Northern Ireland and outside the island of Ireland. The bulk of the chapter deals with the issue of representation of people from Northern Ireland in the Oireachtas in the wake of the Good Friday Agreement. Its conclusion is that the precedent of representation in the Seanad should be continued or even extended. However, the Dáil:

> [is] the primary gathering-place of the representatives of the people of this state, who are bound by the laws enacted by the Oireachtas and who are served by a government drawn primarily from the Dáil and accountable to it. Those citizens resident in Northern Ireland are not affected to anything like the same degree by the actions of the Dáil as are those within the state. (APOCC 2002: 50)

It could be argued that emigrants are a category of Irish citizens that have been most fundamentally affected by the actions of the Dáil:

> The committee unanimously agrees that the history of the state's relationship with emigrants from it leaves ample cause for regret, despite a number of positive initiatives in recent years... This is, however, an argument in favour of a thorough examination of the ways generally in which links between Ireland and the Irish abroad, including emigrants, might be enhanced, and not necessarily an argument in favour of direct emigrant participation in the central institutions of the state (APOCC 2002: 50)

The centrality of political rights to the content of citizenship is the basis of those who argue against the disenfranchisement of emigrants. The committee, however, used precisely the Republic of Ireland's generous citizenship regime as an argument in favour of this disenfranchisement. If citizenship is indivisible, 'it is not clear to us... why in principle someone who left Ireland at the age of two should be entitled to vote whereas the child of an emigrant should not'. The entitlement to political participation is and should remain the entitlement of Irish citizens ordinarily resident in the state. Given that even the 'thinnest' conception of citizenship assumes at least the formal right to engage in the political process, those 'citizens' normally resident outside the state should either be given a voice in the legislature or else designated as something other than citizens.

Conclusion

We have, then, a concentric set of relationships between the state and 'the Irish', which have been radically recycled in the last two decades but which continue to exhibit striking continuities. The discourse of 'diaspora' has become part of the everyday political, media, and popular discourse of modern Ireland. The scale of this diaspora is unclear; estimates are based on a mixture of essentialist ascriptions, dubious statistics and wishful thinking. Consider Tim Pat Coogan's 'green gene' essentialism in the opening pages of *Wherever Green is Worn: The Story of the Irish Diaspora*:

> Some 70 million people in the globe are entitled to call themselves Irish, a remarkable statistic when one considers that there

are only five million people on the island of Ireland itself. (Coogan 2000: ix)

Coogan does not elaborate on what 'entitles' someone to call themselves Irish. In this he is not alone; the figure of seventy million has obscure origins, but it became part of the discursive construction of modern Ireland.[8] The Irish nation has been redefined as a transterritorial, transnational global diaspora. The state, through mechanisms such as the Díon Committee, is distributing record sums of money amongst ethnic Irish organisations precisely at a time when former Irish emigrants constitute by far the largest component of Ireland's inward migration (Hayward and Howard 2007). In other words, as the Irish citizenry abroad is shrinking, the state is supporting the ethnic Irish abroad more extensively than ever before. However, despite these recycled connections, the political community remains co-terminous with the state, in a series of concentric relationships between the Irish state and the putatively wider Irish community. The outer ring is the so-called diaspora, the extraordinarily nebulous 'global family' of the ethnic Irish. Within it are the estimated six million 'second-order' citizens, the Irish nationals located in Northern Ireland, in the rest of the UK, in Europe, USA, Australia and New Zealand, and so on. At the core are the Irish citizens resident in the state.

NOTES

1   The term 'diasporans' comes from Gabriel Sheffer (2003).

2   The details of the referendum can be accessed at the Referendum Commission's website, www.refcom.ie/RefCom/RefComWebSite.nsf/0/E8DACBFC3CD2BB0480256EA5005C 6A50 (accessed 26 May 2006).

3   'Your right to Irish citizenship', available at http://oasis.gov.ie/moving_country/ migration_and_citizenship/your_right_to_irish_citizenship.html (accessed 26 May 2006).

4   FIS is he leading representative organisation of the ethnic Irish in Great Britain and the largest recipient of Irish government funding. See the FIS website at /www. irishsocieties.org/ (accessed 26 May 2006).

5   The full text of this speech is available at http://www.oireachtas.ie/Viewtxt.asp? UserLang=EN&fn=/documents/addresses/2Feb1995.htm (accessed 26 May 2006).

6   poignant symbol of this is the website of the activist group Glór an Deoraí. Its last posting, dated October 1997, 'The story so far', finishes with the promise to 'update you as soon as news is forthcoming'. www.iol.ie/~gad/gadstor.htm (accessed 26 May 2006).

7   A copy of this report is available at http://www.constitution.ie/reports/7th-Report-Parliament.pdf (accessed 26 May 2006).

8   One of the earliest references to this figure of 70 million may be found in Kearney (1988:7).

REFERENCES

Action Group for Irish Youth. 1986. *Chairman's Report*. AGIY: London.

All-Party Oireachtas Committee on the Constitution. 2002. *Seventh Progress Report: Parliament,* Dublin: Stationery Office.

Anderson-Paul, Rachel. 2001. 'Grassroots mobilisation and diaspora politics: Armenian interest groups and the role of collective memory', *Nationalism and Ethnic Politics,* 6 (1), 24–47.

Anthias, F. 2000. 'Evaluating diaspora, beyond ethnicity?', *Sociology,* 32 (3), 557–80.

Benhabib, S. 1999. 'Citizens, residents, and aliens in a changing world: Political membership in the global era', *Social Research,* 66 (3), 709–44.

Brubaker, R. 1996. *Nationalism reframed: Nationhood and the National Question in the New Europe.* Cambridge: Cambridge University Press.

Castles, S. and A. Davidson, 2000. *Citizenship and Migration: Globalisation and the Politics of Belonging.* London: Macmillan.

Citizens Information. 2006. www.citizensinformation.ie (10.03.07).

Coakley, J. and M. Gallagher (eds) 2004 [4th edn]. *Politics in the Republic of Ireland.* London: Routledge in association with PSAI Press.

Commission on Emigration. 1954. *Emigration and Other Population Problems.* Dublin: Stationery Office.

Constitution of Ireland. www.taoiseach.gov.ie/upload/publications/ 297.htm (04/02/2006).

Coogan, T. P. 2000. *Wherever Green is Worn.* London: Hutchinson.

Council of Europe. 1999. *Links Between Europeans Living Abroad and their Countries of Origin.* Stasbourg: CoE.

Courtney, D. 2000. 'A quantification of Irish migration with particular emphasis on the 1980s and 1990s', in A. Beilenberg (ed.), *The Irish Diaspora.* Harlow: Pearson, 287–316.

Delaney, E. 2000. *Demography State and Society.* Liverpool: Liverpool University Press.

Díon Committee. 2005. *Strategic Plan 2006.* Dublin: Department of Foreign Affairs. http://193.178.1.205/information/DionStrategic Plan2006_000.htm (accessed 12/12/06).

Federation of Irish Societies. 2007. www.irishsocieties.org (10/03/2007)

Fitzgerald, P. 1992. 'Like crickets to the crevice of a brew-house: Poor Irish migrants in England, 1560–1640', in Patrick O'Sullivan (ed.) *The Irish Worldwide: History, Heritage, Identity. Volume One: Patterns of Migration.* London: Leicester University Press, 13–35.

Glór on Deoraí. 1997. 'Votes for the Irish Abroad in Irish Elections: The story so far', www.iol.ie/~gad/gadstor.htm (26/05/06)

Greater London Council. 1984. *Ethnic Minorities in London: Policy Report on the Irish Community.* Ethnic Minorities Committee: London.

Hayward, K and K. Howard, (2007) 'Cherry-picking the diaspora', in Bryan Fanning (ed.), *Immigration and Social Change in the Republic of Ireland.* Manchester: Manchester University Press, 47–62.

Honohan, I. 2001. *Civic Republicanism.* London: Routledge.

Howard, K. 2006. 'Constructing the Irish in British: Ethnic recognition and the 2001 UK Censuses', *Ethnic and Racial Studies,* 29, 102–23.

Jackson. J. 1963. *The Irish in Britain.* London: Routledge Kegan Paul.

Jopke, C. 1999. 'Immigration is changing citizenship: a comparative view', *Ethnic and Racial Studies,* 22 (3), 629–52.

Kearney, R. (ed.), 1988. *Across the Frontiers: Ireland in the 1990s.* Dublin: Wolfhound Press.

Keogh, D., O'Shea, F. and Quinlan, C. 2004. *Ireland in the 1950s: the Lost Decade.* Cork: Mercier Press.

Lee, J. 1989. *Ireland 1912–1985: Politics and Society.* Cambridge: Cambridge University Press.

McLaughlin, J. 1997. *Location and dislocation in contemporary Irish society.* Cork: Cork University Press.

National Economic and Social Council, 1991. *The Economic and Social Implications of Emigration.* Dublin: NESC.

Oireachtas Debates http://historical-debates.oireachtas.ie. (11/03/07)

Panayi, P. 2000. *An Ethnic History of Europe since 1945.* Harlow: Longman.

Parekh, B. (2000). *The Future of Multi-Ethnic Britain.* London: Profile.

Referendum Commission www.refcom.ie (14/12/06)

Ryan, L. 1978. *Irish Catholics in England, Report on the Annual Emigrant Congress.* Dún Laoghaire: Glenprint.

Shain, Y. and B. Bristman. 2002. 'Diaspora, kinship and loyalty: The renewal of Jewish national security', *International Affairs,* 78 (1), 69–95.

Sheffer, G. 2003. *Diaspora Politics: At Home Abroad.* Cambridge: Cambridge University Press.

Shirlow, J. 1999. 'Globalisation, western culture and Riverdance', in A. Brah, M. J. Hickman and M. Mac an Ghaill (eds), *Thinking Identities: Ethnicity, Racism and Culture.* Basingstoke: MacMillan, 200–220.

Soysal, Y. 1994. *Boundaries and Identity: Immigrants in Europe.* Florence: European University Institute.

Spencer, I. R. G. 1997. *British Immigration Policy Since 1939: The Making of a Muli-Racial Britain.* London: Routledge.

Task Force on Emigration, 2002. *Ireland and the Irish Abroad.* Dublin: Department of Foreign Affairs.

Turner, B. S. 2001. 'The erosion of citizenship', *The British Journal of Sociology,* 52 (2), 189–211.

Weil, P. 2004. *Nationality and the Child.* Strasbourg: Council of Europe.

5

Boundaries of citizenship: The continued exclusion of Travellers

Una Crowley

In 1922, following the War of Independence, the twenty-six county Irish Free State began its course as an independent nation. The strong social homogeneity of the new state gave Catholic and nationalist leaders a largely uncontested ability to construct and define notions of Irishness.[1] Irish citizenship was conceived in contractual and assimilationist terms, a fact which established a theory of Irish nationality that stressed cultural unification, Catholicism, whiteness and a common Gaelic past – all underpinned by an assumed sedentarism. In a state noted for its narrow-mindedness and stultifying conservatism, those who did not fit the accepted stereotypes were denied full spiritual communion with the Irish nation. This included Protestants, Jews and, as this chapter shows, Travellers (Lyons 1982; Brown 1985; Lee 1993; Longley 2001).

Today the hegemonic 'soft focus' construction of modern Ireland is one of a pluralistic, multicultural, liberal, open society. However, this construction is not opposed to the rhetoric of conservative 'old' Ireland as entirely as it may at first seem, and it occludes as much as it includes. Through a focus on Travellers, Ireland's indigenous nomadic population, this chapter demonstrates how recent moral–legal discourse in relation to Travellers, contrary to its 'progressive' rhetoric, masks a continuum in the exclusionary conception of citizenship which has marked the early decades of the Irish state. This conception is 'one that explicitly understands that excluding people from their rights, not only as citizens, but also as thinking, acting persons is both good and just' (Mitchell 1997: 306). It is also one that is contrary to the rhetoric of European Union models of citizenship, social inclusion and freedom of movement. Through an examination of historical discourse, of policy and legal responses to nomadism, and, in particular, of Section 32 of 1998 Traveller Accommodation Act and of the recent amendment to the Criminal Trespass Legislation, the chapter exposes the limits of the concept of modern citizenship and reveals how this concept can be recycled through structures of regulation and confinement (Bell 1995).[2]

These exclusionary acts are not isolated pieces of legislation/policy coming from a cultural or political vacuum. On the contrary, today Travellers are targeted by restrictive legislation and conceived of by many as 'anti-citizens' – as a community living mainly through crime, deliberately avoiding the duties of taxation, using their mobility to evade justice from the law, and deliberately destroying land and property. This conception is due to a pernicious combination of interlocking discourses originating in both pre- and post-Independence Ireland. Indeed, over the last two hundred years each discourse has been added cumulatively to the ones previously established, thus multiplying the possibilities for anti-nomadic discourse (see Table 5.1). Today, anti-Traveller reactions can be stimulated through any of these factors, alone or in combination (Adams 1997).

Bearing this in mind, I will approach the discussion by briefly examining some historical motives for the prevalence of anti-nomadic discourse and for the stereotypical thinking which is constantly reinforced by the dominant sedentary culture and ideology in Ireland. These powerful discourses, with their inherent claims to 'truth', have led, at least in part, to the present situation – where Travellers have been singled out for special attention by the state in this new legislation and denied the full rights of citizenship. Part Two of the chapter examines the implications of Sections 32 of the 1998 Traveller Act and of Section 24 of the 2002 Housing (Miscellaneous Provisions) Act by questioning not only the discourses surrounding these Acts but also the restrictions accruing to Travellers. The main concern here is with the way space and spatial fixity continue to be 'recycled' as structuring features of citizenship and the way legislation seeks to erode Traveller citizenship by defining the spaces within which the Travellers can act unhindered by political interference (Fyfe 1995).

Discourses of exclusion

Travellers as 'abject'

As detailed in Table 5.1, oppression exerted on nomadism has been documented in writings as early as the sixteenth century, yet it wasn't until the second half of the nineteenth century, as the British government and the Catholic Church took an interest in 'civilising' and 'settling' the Irish peasants, that the Travellers became a target of government.[3] Since then, an accumulation of discourses have been mobilised in order to exercise control over Travellers and each set of discourses builds upon rather than replacing previous discourses.

Discourses were rooted in Enlightenment rhetoric and in the popular debates of the time, related to health, policing, spatial fixity, moral order, citizenship and so on, as modes of governmentality moved into a new episteme (Foucault 1979). These discourses have created and reproduced specific stereotypes that cast Travellers in a negative light, for example by representing them as dirty/diseased, ungodly, unpatriotic, uncivilised, sub-human, economic exploiters and anti-citizens. In combination, these discursive practices have been materially grounded through exclusionary measures such as shunning, imprisonment, evictions, harassment, enforced settlement, segregation and territorial exclusion. In general terms these discourses, stereotypes and material practices can be divided into four time periods: 1830–1922, 1922–57, 1957–90, and 1990 to the present day.

In the first period (1830–1922), discourses on religion, disease/health, wilful poverty and social Darwinism led to the Traveller being constructed as immoral, dirty/diseased, sub-human and a malingerer (see, for example, Borrow 1862; Hackett 1862). Legal discourses pronounced the Travellers as carriers of lice and running sores, deliberately disfiguring themselves or feigning injury in order to be considered objects of sympathy and better receive alms (Kent 1980). The Vagrancy Act, 1847, made begging and homelessness illegal, and the Summary Jurisdiction (Ireland) Act of 1851 imposed penalties on vagrants and nomads for grazing their animals on private property.[4] The 1908 Prevention of Cruelty to Children Act reaffirmed the illegality of childhood begging and imposed penalties on adults whose wandering life prevented their children from receiving an education (cited in the *Report of the Commission on Itinerancy* [COI] 1963: 19, 66, 91). The *Oxford Dictionary* entry of 1896 noted that the term 'tinker' was an abusive term in Ireland. Travellers were oppressed through shunning, exclusion from aid and imprisonment.

	Informal spatial regulation		Formal spatial regulation	
Time period	*1830–1922*	*1922–1957*	*1957–1990*	*1990–present*
Context	Civilising project and enlightenment	Independence/ nation-building	modernisation	Europe and citizenship
Discourses (i.e. accumulation of themes)	Social Darwinism religion disease/health wilful poverty mobility general legislation	Nationalism Social conservatism sedentarisation xenophobia disillusionment	Utilitarianism Paternalism assimilation criminalisation	individualisation active citizenship social inclusion traveller 'specific' legislation
Stereotypes (i.e. oppressed for being)	abject ungodly dirty/diseased malingerers immoral sub-human	unpatriotic uncivilised frauds threatening 'other'	exploiters criminals lawless racially inferior	anti-citizen extortionists irresponsible
Material consequences (i.e. oppressed via)	shunning exclusion from aid imprisonment	evictions harassment transformation of space increased surveillance	enforced settlement segregation economic restriction resistance vigilante attacks	self-regulation inclusion and rewarding of 'socially adjusted' Travellers legislation territorial exclusion

Table 5.1 Discourses, stereotypes and material practices towards Irish Travellers, 1830–present (adapted from Adams 1997: 197).

Travellers as 'unpatriotic'

Throughout the second period (1922–57), discourses mobilised by Independence, nationalism and nation-building increasingly fragmented Irish society through the production, articulation and normalisation of the 'good' and 'bad' citizen; the patriotic citizen and those 'out for themselves'; the moral and immoral person; the disciplined and 'undisciplined' body. Although the Protestant minority initially bore the brunt of these discourses (see Brown 1985; Tanner 2002), the tiny size of the Traveller population did not spare them either.[5] As Allen (1997: 65) notes, 'hatred and dislike of Protestants, Jews and Gypsies became officially quite acceptable [and] Gypsies were regarded as akin to alien beings'. From the 1930s on, politicians in the Dáil increasingly voiced concerns about the Travellers' unhygienic living conditions and 'increasing numbers' (Helleiner 2000).[6] One deputy suggested interning Travellers, in order to prevent the spread of foot and mouth disease (Meaney *Dáil Debates* 1941).

Another deputy, O'Donnell, suggested placing the Travellers in work camps, in order to make 'useful citizens' of them (*Dáil Debates* 1945). Travellers were variously seen as a 'menace to the social order', accused of destroying property, of being cruel to their animals and children, and representing a 'serious danger'.[7] These successional, exclusionary, disciplining discursive and material practices meant that by the late 1950s Travellers were firmly established as a 'threat' and 'pariahs' of the new state. Verbal assaults on Travellers continued to escalate; they were regularly accused of stealing, of criminality and fraudelance, of being anti-citizens, and so on.[8]

Travellers as 'inferior'

The spread of these ideas was given an increased impetus from 1957, as the Irish government embarked on a new strategy of foreign led industrialisation. Travellers were categorised as a sub-group that held back the general welfare and life of the Irish people, and their increasing numbers and visibility became an embarrassment. For many, the settlement and assimilation of Travellers was seen as a necessary part of the larger project of national economic and social development (MacLaughlin 1995; Helleiner 1997, 2000). Efforts by elites to remove Travellers from public space became progressively more pervasive, and there was increased pressure on central and local government to introduce legislation and to 'control and settle itinerants'. Health inspectors voiced concern about the 'insanitary conditions of their dwellings'; they had received complaints from property owners, business people and farmers (Gmelch 1985).

For the Travellers, the material consequences of these discourses were various forms of harassment, eviction, colonisation of traditional halting-sites and mounting surveillance. Nomadism was increasingly becoming a condition of rejection rather than of otherness. The arrival of Travellers in an area constituted a presence that marked the social space as much as the geographical – they were drop-outs, trespassers, alcoholic and criminal. Radical action was thus required to regulate boundaries that contained them and arrest any sign of diffusion. The crucial problem was now rehabilitation: recalling them from their state of abjection and reintegrating them into respectable society (Procacci 1991).

Travellers placed outside the space of citizenship

Official action against nomadism

In 1960, the Irish government set up a commission to investigate and report on the 'problem' of itinerancy. In 1963, after the publication of the *Report of the Commission on Itinerancy* (COI), the government embarked on a national programme for the 'settlement', 'assimilation' and 'rehabilitation' of its nomadic population. The report marked a shift to a new, more systematic means of governing and controlling the Travellers and of extending and consolidating state power. Within the report and the settlement strategies that followed, the diverse lives and lifestyles of Ireland's nomadic population was homogenised, refashioned and reconstructed through elite discourse and the use of statistical inscriptions which permitted the characterisation of Travellers as a 'group', a 'community' in need of reform.

The report, with its inherent claims to 'truth' and expertise, provided the limits within which the discursive objects – Travellers – could act and exist. What was involved, to use Jacques Donzelot's phrase, was a 'systematic grafting of morality on to economics' (Procacci 1991: 157). The ostensible humanitarian discourse of the report disguised and obscured the political and material aims of a modernising Irish nation. Settlement involved the fabrication of a new moral geography, and from the 1960s onwards, the mapping of the Travellers' personal mobility became an intrinsic part of governmental strategy. It was assumed that these proposals would put an end to nomadism, transgression, unauthorised camping and littered scrap. Training centres and social workers would provide supervision and uninterrupted surveillance. Houses and halting-sites would provide disciplined spaces and make the official 'gaze' geographically and socially specific.

Paradoxically, however, as technologies and strategies of government sought to assimilate Travellers and to bring an end to nomadism and its accompanying lifestyle, government agents who were supposed to operate and implement the National Settlement Programme exploited it for their own ends. Many programmes were hampered by both settled and Traveller resistance by territorial rivalries between local authorities and by the impossibility of producing the practical conditions that would make the programme work – for example reliable statistics, individual distinguishability, spatial fixity, efficient communications systems, clear lines of command and political will (Rose and Miller 1992; Helleiner 2000). Local authorities increasingly used the Sanitary Act (1948) to prohibit, evict and discourage Travellers from moving into, or remaining in, a jurisdiction. Travellers were ordered to vacate or face summonses for trespass. Once Travellers were on the move, an unofficial 'boulder policy' was used to ensure that they could not return to a site.[9] The continuing erosion of the social and geographic space within which Travellers traditionally moved meant that most of them were now unable to continue with their customary occupations (for example, scrap collecting), with the result that an overwhelming majority had become dependent on social welfare.

As other minorities, however, Travellers can and do push up against the regulations which constrain the limits of their spaces of citizenship (Bell 1995). Very quickly they became conversant with the law in relation to where they could encamp and how long the process of getting prohibition orders would take. As soon as the order came, they would move on to another area, where the legal process of eviction would begin all over again.

By the 1980s it was clear that the Commission on Itinerancy had merely intensified the problem it sought to tackle: there were more Travellers on urban roadsides than ever and the permanent solution promised by the settlement movement was clearly not materialising (Rottman et al. 1986). Mounting frustration and disillusionment with the lack of progress in settling, rehabilitating and assimilating Travellers increasingly produced forms of knowledge and a political rationality that viewed Travellers as a group 'without value and beyond improvement' (Dean 1999: 146). Liberal forms of government increasingly slipped from implementing 'well-intended' schemes to improve Travellers condition to adopting others, which overtly confined, contained and coerced, if only by prevention, those who continued to travel.

Inflammatory public discourse on Travellers

The press throughout this period largely reproduced and supported elite statements. The Travellers were consistently and increasingly constructed as a negation of health, of discipline and of civilisation. There were calls in the press to '[g]et tough on this tinker terror culture', to enact legislation to 'protect law abiding citizens'. County councillors were quoted in national newspapers making inflammatory statements about Travellers, such as: 'Killarney is literally infested by these people' (*Cork Examiner*, 18 July 1989); 'They are dirty and unclean. Travelling people have no respect for themselves and their children' (*Irish Times* 13 March 1991); 'They are a constant problem, moving from one open area to another and creating problems' (*Cork Examiner* 13 June 1990). A reader's letter in the *Evening Herald* (31 May 1996) stated:

> These people have never paid tax or rent or anything else in their entire lives. They are milking the system dry, and they have to account to no one, not even when they leave miles of rubbish and broken prams and fridges, etc. behind them...the corporation should leave 'decent areas for decent people'.

Among these refrains there were more outrageous statements. One Fianna Fáil county councillor from Waterford stated: 'The sooner the shotguns are at the ready and these travelling people are put out of our country the better. They are not our people, they aren't natives' (*Sunday Independent* 14 April 1996). Travellers were held responsible for a perceived new crime-wave, particularly in rural areas, and were used in the media to exemplify a perceived breakdown in law and order (McVeigh 1998: 155). Sensationalist headlines were commonplace: 'Long history of attacks by small gangs of travellers on old people in rural areas' (*Irish Times* 3 February 1996).

The standard image of the dirty, impoverished, petty criminal gave way to that of a repulsive, threatening creature. The image of the Traveller was recast in racial, cultural and even biological terms and nomadism was viewed as a form of social debasement. The idea of race was increasingly used to define Travellers, to explain their social behaviour, to essentialise their social and cultural practices and to legitimise their relegation to the outer edges of Irish society (MacLaughlin 1999). In a much-quoted article headed 'Time to get tough on tinker terror "culture"', controversial journalist Mary Ellen Synon states that Traveller culture,

> is a life of appetite ungoverned by intellect...it is a life worse than the life of beasts, for beasts at least are guided by wholesome instinct. Traveller life is without the ennobling intellect of man or the steadying instinct of animals. This tinker 'culture' is without achievement, discipline, reason or intellectual ambition. It is a morass. (*Sunday Independent*, 28 January 1996).

Travellers, however, were not, and are not, passive victims in the stereotyping process. Some Travellers were engaged in 'cash to move on' disputes which created further tensions, and there were regular reports of extortion by the Travellers in the papers.[10] Also, many Travellers left large amounts of rubbish behind when they departed from unofficial sites, and some of them desecrated and destroyed lands by dumping vast amounts of industrial waste.

Moral tactics of control: Discourses of citizenship

By the 1990s the obvious failure of the settlement programme, the substantial and rapid growth in the Traveller population and the mounting tensions between the two communities had led to increased pressure on government to find a 'solution'. It was also clear that the government would have to find alternative methods of representing and intervening in the aspects of Traveller life it sought to govern. Under pressure from the inside to enact legislation so as to prevent nomadism, and from the European Community to protect Travellers' rights, the state was faced with a dilemma. How could it single out the Travellers for legislation and prevent nomadism without being seen to infringe on Travellers' democratic rights? The government needed, and ultimately pursued, a functional substitute for confinement in the disciplinary control of Travellers as 'free' citizens: an approach that would enlist the support of Travellers, local authorities and the settled community, a strategy and technique to render the settlement programme operable.

The governmental technique used consisted in invoking the powerful and emotional discourse of citizenship. Citizenship discourse within the European Union is often referred to in the context of belonging, identity, equality, rights and inclusion. However, it is also very much about who does not belong – about exclusion and the denial of identity. There is, as MacKian (1995: 209) has argued, a huge gap between discussing citizenship in terms of who should or should not be a citizen, and the 'actuality of being a citizen'. There is a need to go beyond the formal allocation of rights if we are to enable ourselves to account for the barriers in the way of realising these rights and of actively participating as full citizens (Roche 1997: 155).

'Active citizenship' discourse, the conception of citizenship used in relation to Travellers, has conceptualised the citizen in terms of obligation ('citizenship as practice'). The emphasis on social rights as being central to citizenship is downplayed ('citizenship as status'). The 'genuine' citizen (once given the opportunities) is viewed as someone responsible, involved in the community and making a positive contribution to society. Active citizenship discourse works a double alliance. First, it allies itself to political authorities, translating the political concerns of ill health, poverty, uncontrolled mobility, criminality and pathology into a vocabulary of management – a mechanism for rendering the Travellers 'reality' amenable to certain kinds of action. It then works in alliance with the Travellers, translating the same concerns into a range of techniques for improvement (Rose and Miller 1992).

The moralising rhetoric of the previous decades has been transformed into a language of Travellers helping themselves and having a responsibility towards their environment and locality. Discussions on the expanding and retracting spaces of citizenship repeatedly turn to this notion of locality and towards inclusion (MacKian 1995). Vast amounts of resources and energy have been introduced into area-based partnerships, programmes and services aimed at tackling Traveller exclusion, marginalisation and discrimination, and many local authorities make genuine efforts to work with Traveller groups and families in their localities (see Report of the High Level Group on Traveller Issues, 2006). Indeed, as Powell and Geoghegan's research on community development demonstrates (2004: 169), 'working with Travellers was often a criterion for funding' related to social and economic issues. These inclusion and empowerment policies are combined with a legislation that recognises the

Travellers' right to accommodation (1998 Traveller Accommodation
Act) and to non-discrimination (Prohibition of Incitement to Hatred
Act 1991, Equal Employment 1998, Equal Status 2000). Yet despite
these ostensibly inclusionary strategies and the tiny size of the
Traveller population (representing only 0.6 per cent of the Irish
population), Travellers remain one of the most disadvantaged and
discriminated against groups in Irish society, faring badly on every
indicator of disadvantage (including unemployment, illiteracy,
poverty, health status, access to decision-making and political
representation). In addition, many nomadic Travellers have refused
to engage in the process while others have refused to alter their
social and spatial behaviour – continuing to trespass, and some
continuing to perform anti-social behaviour and to undertake black-
market trade.

Implicit in active citizenship discourse is the idea that 'inclusion is
good, exclusion is bad'. Even if groups reject the dominant economic
and social models of integration, they are nonetheless coerced into
inclusion (Rogers 1995: 52). Also, there is a persistent, implicit
assumption that the locality will represent the means for social
inclusion, the base from which the individual will articulate their
citizenship. Indeed, the entitlements to many social rights (for
example the right to vote, education, social welfare) remain
dependent on spatial fixity. But what if, as MacKian (1995: 213)
asks, there is no locality, no territorial unit to which an individual
relates, no specific material geography?

Far from being automatically inclusive, the active citizenship
promoted by the European Community and Irish government, with
its fixed relation to 'locality', can impose a grid of definition on the
possibilities for 'citizen Traveller' that serves both to exclude and to
highlight those who do not 'play by the rules'. Travellers who refuse
to subordinate a crucial aspect of their identity to citizenship are
portrayed as irresponsible and as anti-citizens (Taylor 1998). Within
the active citizenship framework, the nomadic Travellers are denied a
voice and their non-conforming territoriality is seen as their own
wilful exclusion from the entitlements and responsibilities of
citizenship. Ironically, the more economic success nomadic Travellers
attain, the more vulnerable they are to stereotyping as criminals and
economic exploiters. What is really happening through 'active
citizen' discourse is the construction of nomadic Travellers as an
ensemble of adversaries who confront the social project – to use
Procacci's words, 'the constituting of a different subject from the

productive subject: a subject aware of its duties, a civil and political subject' (1991: 163).

This representation of Travellers serves both to rationalise hostile sedentary community action and to justify restrictive legislation and state policies which deny them the full, inclusive rights of citizenship based on the acknowledgement of diversity. After all it was not aimed at all the Travellers, but just at those who rejected the responsibilities and obligations of citizenship. Travellers who refuse to participate actively in the social, economic and political 'project' according to the set 'ground rules' are made to forfeit the rights of citizenship. The dominant power relations inherent in this discourse are 'obscured by the political fictions of the decontextualised and universal citizen' (Kofman 1995: 124). The debate is polarised in terms of one being 'either for or against the common good' – if one is against the common good (for example, by camping on public grounds) then the public is victimised and the perpetrator must be excluded (Bell 1995: 146).

Legal tactics of control

The Traveller Accommodation Act

The Traveller Accommodation Act (1998) is one part of a larger process of legal reform aimed at protecting minorities and the Irish ratification of international human rights legislation.[11] In effect it constituted the Irish government's undertaking of its duty to Travellers by providing accommodation. The Act was justified as a necessary measure in the drive for successful settlement and enhancement of individual Travellers' quality of life and citizenship status. For the first time in the history of the state, the Act required each local authority, in consultation with Travellers and with the general public, to prepare and adopt a five-year Traveller Accommodation Programme by 31 March 2000. As such, local authorities became obliged to meet the existing and projected accommodation needs (to include transient sites for short-term stays) of (indigenous) Travellers within its administrative area.

The Act works on a quid pro quo basis, wherein the State provided sites, accommodation and rights as long as Travellers comply with the law. In turn, parts of the law were made more restrictive. For example, Section 32 replaced and strengthened the powers of local authorities and of the police to evict Travellers from public land and from the side of the road. It empowered local authorities to act where an unauthorised temporary dwelling is within five miles of a serviced site if the trailer could be accommodated on such a site. As such, Travellers can be forced to move to sites with limited facilities (which are often overcrowded and unsanitary). This may include just one tap between several families. Travellers are not allowed to camp within a one-mile radius of any Traveller accommodation provided for Travellers by local authorities, whether or not other accommodation is available (in the meantime, this has been updated to include any local authority accommodation). Travellers' homes can also be confiscated or removed if they are: considered unfit for human habitation due to a lack of proper services (this could affect almost all the illegally camped caravans); likely to obstruct, or interfere with, the use of public or private amenities; or likely to constitute a significant risk to personal health or public safety. Justifying Section 32, deputy Molloy stated that: '[t]he purpose of these provisions is to protect residents in Traveller accommodation' (Dáil Debates, 31 May 2001). Thus the Act helped to highlight the difference that active citizenship made through its increased powers on the one hand to help Travellers by providing sites and accommodation, on the other to exclude nomadic, non-compliant Travellers from public space (or at least to exclude behaviours which make it possible to live their way of life). The result was that sections of the Act that make living a nomadic life almost impossible were downplayed; after all, they only applied to Travellers who refused their responsibilities to society.

While funding was made available by the Department of the Environment, Heritage and local Government for the provision of Traveller accommodation, many local authorities have openly resisted implementing the Traveller Accommodation Act, and in many cases they intensified disciplinary actions against nomadic Travellers. To date, there has been very little attempt to create a network of transient sites (with the exception of two in Donegal and one in Westmeath), and many official temporary sites remain poorly serviced and maintained in unhealthy and dangerous conditions. The 'indigenous clause' (wherein Travellers have to be registered in a county in order to receive accommodation there) has allowed local authorities to continue to evict Travellers who were not in their jurisdiction at the time their accommodation plans were drafted.

Ironically, local authority surveys were carried out in the summer months when many transient families were away and therefore not included in estimates (Irish Travellers' Movement (ITM) 2001: 2). Others have lost their places on accommodation lists through eviction. Incongruously, the legislation contains no sanctions should accommodation plans not be implemented, and by 2002 only 111 of a recommended 2,200 Traveller-specific accommodation units had been provided (*Irish Times*, 9 March 2002). The Second Report on Ireland of the 'European Commission against Racism and Intolerance' warned that:

> the fact that no sanctions are provided for in the Housing (Traveller Accommodation) Act against authorities who do not take measures to provide accommodation for Travellers may weaken its effectiveness (ITM 2003: 20).

According to the *Annual Count Figures* (2005) of the Department of the Environment, Heritage and Local Government, there are still 589 Traveller families living on unauthorised sites without basic facilities such as water or electricity and a further 280 families are living on temporary halting-sites with very limited facilities, whereas 212 families are sharing accommodation on halting-sites.

Further still, many local authorities have continued, and indeed accelerated, their unofficial 'boulder policy' – the practice of digging trenches or placing large boulders where Travellers traditionally camp. As one 'pro-Traveller' councillor stated:

> It's not an official policy but you tell me what you can do when hundreds descend on a place? They just devastate the whole place, negotiations have to start to try get them to leave and you know they always look for money. The only thing you can do is stop them in their tracks before they arrive. Just close off the places.[12]

This situation, coupled with the lack of short-stay halting-sites and the slow provision of other accommodation, has meant that Travellers who wish to remain nomadic or those waiting for accommodation increasingly camp on vacant industrial land, near housing estates or estates in the process of construction, or on amenity land, and at times arrive in large numbers (this strategy is often used against eviction). There is simply nowhere else to go. For the most part, local authorities refuse to provide sanitation or rubbish facilities to these encampments, which results in the accumulation of rubbish and sewage – although, again, it must be recognised that some Travellers make little effort to tackle waste issues.

Housing (Miscellaneous Provisions) Act (2002)

In the face of growing hostility to 'illegal' Traveller encampments, along with a shunning of the opportunity extended to Travellers by the state, and on the basis that existing criminal sanctions and civil remedies were inadequate to deal with Traveller anti-social behaviour, Deputy Olivia Mitchell (Fine Gael) introduced a new Bill to Dáil Éireann in December 2001. Initially, however, the government was opposed to any changes in the law. Binchy (2002: 5) states that, on the 30 May 2001;

> Mr Bobby Molloy, Minister of State at the Department of the Environment and Local Government with special responsibility for Housing and Urban Renewal, was forthright in his rejection of the argument by Mr Brian Hayes TD that there was a need to change the law in respect to trespass. Mr Hayes argued that the accommodation programme would not be successful because people would 'not accept the continual flouting of the law' as a result of the Minister's actions.

Minister Molloy stated in his address to Dáil Éireann (cited in Binchy 2002: 5):

> I introduced the Traveller accommodation legislation and the local authorities have drawn up and adopted their accommodation plans. The accommodation proposals require the provision of transient sites. If local authorities in Dublin had been active in implementing these proposals and if the transient sites were in place, this type of difficulty would not arise.
>
> Local authorities which have taken action on this issue no longer experience difficulties to the same extent as heretofore... Where facilities are not provided, one cannot simply push people on. There is a responsibility on local authorities to provide transient sites to cater for Travellers and that has not yet been achieved to a desirable extent.

However, as the General Election of 2002 came closer, the government altered its view so as to make it more attuned to the electorate. In an about turn, the government now saw the problem as being the Travellers themselves, rather than the failure of authorities to provide transient sites. This was part of a broader strategy of appearing 'tough on crime', in which Travellers were portrayed as lawless. The outcome was the sudden publication of an amendment to the Housing (Miscellaneous Provisions) Bill, which passed quickly through the Dáil and Seanad on 27 and 28 April 2002. The amendment inserted a new Act – Part 11A – into the Criminal Justice (Public Order) Act (1994) which further strengthens the powers of local authorities and of the Gardai to evict Travellers from public spaces. The provision also amended Section 32 of the Traveller Accommodation Act and made trespass a criminal rather than a civil offence. Nomadic Travellers face fines of 3,000 euro and/or one month's imprisonment if found guilty of criminal trespass (Binchy 2002). Furthermore, a Garda can arrest any person without a warrant and can remove their possessions (including their homes) and store them. Travellers can be forced to move on without any alternative accommodation being provided. As a consequence of the legislation, it is now almost impossible for nomadic Travellers to keep within the confines of the law.[13]

The new legislation is in direct conflict with the provisions of the Traveller Accommodation Act (1998), which specifies that the annual patterns of movement of the Travellers should be taken into account and provided for. It also gives local authorities an 'opt out' clause in the provision of accommodation, in that they can now evict from their jurisdiction Travellers who are camped illegally (even if awaiting accommodation). The views and wishes of Travellers were ignored in the consultation process for the new legislation. Indeed, the amendment to the Criminal Justice Act (1994) was undertaken without any regard for the consultative processes that had been established in recent years. Paradoxically, the Department of Justice, Equality and Law Reform had set up a committee made up of government officials, Garda, Traveller and local authority representatives, in order to investigate the issue of large-scale encampments. This committee had recommended no change in the law, but its views were discounted (ITM 2003).

Enduring moral assumptions behind legal reforms

The 1998 Traveller Act and the amendment to the Criminal Justice Bill of 1994 represent an extension to a number of Acts ratified since the foundation of the state and designed to regulate Traveller lives and to delimit Traveller spatial mobility with respect to housing, trespass, use of roads, ownership and control of animals, destruction to property, anti-social behaviour and trading (see Table 5.2).

Legislation	Year	Function
Local Government (Sanitary Services Act) Section 20	1925	empowers sanitary authorities to confiscate tents or caravans comsidered 'a nuisance or injurious to health'
Local Government (Sanitary Services Act) Section 31	1948	Control of Temporary Dwellings: this Act has the power to move caravans if considered unsanitary or likely to cause a nuisance
The Planning and Development Act	1963	empowers a local authority to remove Travellers who are camped unofficially and to confiscate their dwellings
Road Traffic Acts	1961, 1968, 1993	prohibits temporary dwellings on side of road
Housing (Miscellaneous Provisions Act	1992	Section of this Act empowers local authorities to remove Travellers who are camped unofficially to an official site anywhere within a five-mile radius of where they are
Local Government Act (1994)	1994	strengthens a local authority's power to make bye-laws in relation to the use of temporary dwellings under the Local Government Act (1948)
Casual TradingAct	1995	requires market traders to apply to each local authority for a casual licence for any market in their area; this results in increased costs for engagement in market trading. Previously only one licence was required for the whole country
Control of Horses Act	1997	places restriction on the ownership of horses
Housing (Miscellaneous Provisions) Act	2002	makes trespass a crime rather than a civil matter

Table 5.2 Legislation affecting Irish Travellers' spatial mobility

These Acts legislate for certain moral claims: to the affect that the right to a nomadic way of life is inappropriate and illegitimate. Territorial exclusion is much more subtle and destructive than segregation; it means that nomadic Travellers now have nowhere to camp legally (except for a handful of transient sites), and moving from one camp to another involves nothing more liberating than moving from one criminal trespass charge to another. They are only allowed to exist as long as they are on the move. Travellers simply cannot lead a nomadic lifestyle without breaking laws (Campbell, 1995; Mitchell 1997; Binchy 2002). This intervention in urban aesthetics attempts, in effect, to remove nomadic Travellers from public space, delimit their geography and enforce their invisibility. What perhaps can be seen as the most detrimental effect of territorial exclusion in terms of achieving equal citizenship is the tendency of the marginalised to find localised solutions. Painter and Philo (1995: 116) refer to 'the tendency to avoid public spaces where 'proper' citizens go and instead to seek and carve out safe havens away from the 'terrorism' of such spaces', increasing their invisibility, lack of voice and place in society. All Travellers are victimised for the crimes of a few.

The degree to which these Acts curtail the freedom of Travellers seems to be disregarded by policy makers and legislators. Not only are they presented as rational and reasonable, but they are justified with some conception of right; they see themselves as protectors of 'decent' citizens, the common good and national interests. Theirs is not simply a good or just cause, but a very necessary one. Law exhibits its own 'will to truth', declares the guilt of offenders and exerts a 'pressure', a 'power constraint' on other discourses (Hunt 1994). There is no need to take a hands-off approach to Travellers who do not conform to the norms and values of settled society and act as responsible citizens, they are after all of no economic value to the nation and their nomadism is seen by many as an excuse for unlawful activities.

Conclusions

Since the mid to the late 1990s, the Irish state has actively and substantively engaged Irish Travellers in the policy process, providing new forms of participation and new outlets for representation at local and national level (for example, area-based local partnerships, and the inclusion of Traveller groups like Pavee Point, Irish Traveller Movement, and National Traveller Women's Forum). Active citizenship strategies are represented by government and state agencies as a way of promoting the interests of Travellers and are referred to in the context of belonging, identity and equality. However, as this chapter has demonstrated, within active citizenship programmes and policies there is also an inherent 'drive to exclusion' – operating against 'other ways of living' and 'other ways of being' (Taylor 1998: 147). Although specifically targeted at Travellers, state policies and programmes remain framed by a culturally specific agenda (geared towards sedentary living and sedentary society's acceptance of Travellers' worth), which then defines the proper parameters of political action and the institutional framework appropriate to those limits. Involving Travellers in the policy process has allowed the government to renegotiate, consolidate and recycle its dominant position of influence, and has firmly positioned the state and state actors as the only route to significant social change, (and this even in the face of overwhelming evidence to the contrary – for example the repeated failure of accommodation and health programmes) (Powell and Geoghegan 2004). Government is thus presented as democratic and pluralistic by accepting otherness.

Also, it must be remembered that active citizenship processes are not taking place in a political or social vacuum. There is a long history of failed attempts to bring the Travellers and their organ- isations into alignment with sedentary society (apart from national- scale policies, there were countless confrontations between Travellers, sedentary society and local authorities around the country). As a consequence, the media, the local authorities and the sedentary society in general do not engage with the Traveller subject in the here and now but are in fact responding to, and building upon, discourses and stereotypes mobilised in the past (for example, references to Travellers not paying taxes, to filth and dirt, to anti- citizen behaviour); discourses and stereotypes they seem largely unable to move beyond. Likewise, the Travellers themselves are often sceptical of the state's intentions and of the ability of sedentary society to start to become more inclusive, given its deep-rooted negative attitudes and systematic discrimination, and continue to act in a resistive and confrontational manner.

It is difficult not to conclude that active citizenship strategies in relation to Irish Travellers are, at least to some degree, merely reproducing, consolidating and legitimising the exclusionary, coercive and paternalistic ideologies and practices that emerged in the early decades of the Irish Free State. The underlying ideology persists and space, place and spatial fixity continue to be recycled as structuring features of citizenship with the attempt to add Travellers to existing standards, to convert the Traveller from 'something into something else' – only this time Travellers are doing it for themselves and for the sake of their culture.

Acknowledgements

The author would like to thank Professor Rob Kitchin for his constructive comments on an earlier version of this chapter and for his supervision of the PhD thesis from which this chapter is drawn.

NOTES

1 In the 1926 census, 92.6 per cent of the population classified themselves as Catholic and 61 per cent lived outside towns and villages.

2 An amendment to the Housing Act 2002 (Section 24) inserts a new section – Part 11A – into the Criminal Justice (Public Order) Act 1994, making trespass a criminal rather than civil offence.

3 Sir Henry Sidney executed itinerants in Cork in 1575 and extracted a promise that the native lords would forgo their practice of hiring 'idle men'. His successor continued the executions of 'loose and masterless men' (Canny 1976: 104–6).

4 Vagrancy (Ir) Act (1847), Section 3: 1476–1477, cited in the Report on Vagrancy and Related Offences, (1985), 8–10.

5 A census of 'vagrants camping out' was taken in 1944 and produced a figure of 5,151 Travellers.

6 Deputy Cogan referred to 'the enormous increase in the numbers of hawkers, tinkers and vagrants who are using the public roads as camping places and causing great inconvenience and annoyance to rural dwellers' (Dáil Debates, 2 October 1940, Vol 81, Col. 40). Deputy O'Donnell stated that '[t]hey do not seem to bother much about birth control...they marry young and breed like rabbits...' (Dáil Debates, 19 April 1944, Vol. 93, Col. 1032).

7 For example, Deputy O'Neill asked the Minister for Justice if he was aware of the 'menace to the social order which is caused by the increasing number of tinkers and other vagrants who infest remote areas in every county; that the children of these people do not attend school and grow up illiterate, learning nothing but the elements of crime to which their conditions make them easy addicts' (Dáil Debates, 19 September, Vol. 94, Col. 1528).

8 According to Mr Bourke, Travellers were 'a menace in the city...Every place they go, as the last speaker and other speakers have said, they cause a lot of trouble' (Dáil Debates, 13 July 1955, Vol. 152, Cols 737–8); Mr Lynch argued that Travellers destroyed property. 'They cut the wire fence, roll it up, take it away to other areas and sell it. They remove gates, they go in and graze the new grass, and in the harvest time they go in and steal from the fields'(Dáil Debates, 11 July 1956, Vol. 159, Col. 665).

9 This consisted in the 'unofficial' placing of large boulders on, or the digging of ditches

around, Travellers camping sites once they moved on. The practice has been in existence since the 1960s.

10 It was alleged in the High Court that Travellers on another site near Kilruddery had demanded £2,000 for every man, woman and child from a development company, in return for moving (*Irish Times*, 29 August 1994).

11 For example, the Irish government introduced laws such as the Prohibition of Incitement to Hatred Act (1991), the Equal Employment Act (1998), and the Equal Status Act (2000) in order to protect minorities, including Travellers, from discrimination.

12 Interview with the author, 15 July 2002, Co. Meath.

13 Notably, the legislation was justified in the media as helping to free up resources to *deserving* and compliant Travellers: 'Most Travellers could benefit from the new legislation if it helps local authorities prioritise their accommodation rather than having to police the excesses of "trader Travellers" who have accommodation elsewhere' (*Irish Times*, 29 March 2002).

REFERENCES

Adams, M. (ed.). 1997. *Teaching for Diversity and Social Justice*. London: Routledge.

Allen, K.1997. *Fianna Fáil and Irish Labour: 1926 to the Present*. London: Pluto Press.

Bell, D. 1995. 'Pleasure and danger: the paradoxical spaces of sexual citizenship', *Political Geography*, 14 (2), 139–53.

Binchy, W. 2002. 'The criminal trespass legislation: What does it do and is it constitutional?', Paper presented at the conference on Criminal Trespass Legislation: Implications for Human Rights Protection in Ireland, July 2002, Trinity College Dublin.

Borrow, G. 1862. *Wild Wales*. London: John Murray.

Bourke, P. J. Dáil Debates, 13 July 1955, Vol. 152, Cols. 737–8

Brown, T. 1985. *Ireland: A Social and Cultural History 1922–1985*. London: Fontana Press.

Campbell, S. 1995. 'Gypsies: The Criminalisation of a way of life?', *Criminal Law Review*, 28, 28–37.

Canny, N. 1976. *The Elizabethan Conquest of Ireland: A Pattern Established, 1565–76*. Brighton: Harvester Press.

Cogan, Dáil Debates, 2 October, 1940, Vol. 81, Col. 40.

Commission On Itinerancy (COI). 1963. *Report of the Commission on Itinerancy*. Dublin: The Stationery Office.

Daiken, L. 1947. 'Parasites without power', in J. Lindsay (ed.), *Anvil: Life and the Arts*. London: Meridian Books.

Dean, M. (1999). *Governmentality: Power and Rule in Modern Society*. London: Sage.

Department of the Environment, Heritage and local Government. (2005). *Annual Count Figures*. www.environ.ie.

Foucault, M. 1979. *Discipline and Punish: The Birth of the Prison*. London: Allen Lane.

Fyfe, R. N. 1995. 'Law and order policy and the spaces of citizenship in contemporary Britain', *Political Geography*, 14 (2), 177–89.

Gmelch, G. 1985. *The Irish Tinkers: The Urbanisation of an Itinerant People* [2nd edition]. Wavelength Press: Prospect Heights.

Gordon, C. (ed.). 1991. *Knowledge/Power: Selected Interviews and Other Writings 1972–1977*. New York: Pantheon Books.

Hackett, W. 1862. 'The Irish Bacach or professional beggar, viewed archaeologically', *Ulster Journal of Archaeology*, 9, 256–71.

Helleiner, J. 1993. 'Traveller settlement in Galway City: Politics, class and culture', in C. Curtin (ed.), *Irish Urban Cultures*. Belfast: Institute of Irish Studies, QUB, 181–201.

Helleiner, J. 1997. 'Discourses of exclusion: The Irish Press and the Travelling People', in S.

Riggins (ed.). *The language and Politics of Exclusion: Others in Discourse.* London: Sage, 109–30.

Helleiner, J. 2000. *Irish Travellers: Racism and the Politics of Culture.* London: University of Toronto Press.

Hunt, A. 1994. *Foucault and the Law: Towards a Sociology of Law and Governance.* London: Pluto Press.

Irish Folklore Commission Survey. 1952. *Tinker Questionnaire.* Vols. 1255–6. Unpublished material in the archives of the Department of Folklore, University College Dublin.

Irish Traveller Movement (ITM), 2001. *A Lost Opportunity? A Critique of Local Authority Traveller Accommodation Programmes.* Irish Traveller Movement: Dublin.

Irish Traveller Movement. 2003. *Charting a Future Strategy for the Delivery of Traveller Accommodation.* Irish Traveller Movement: Dublin.

Keane, J. B. 1987. *The Field.* Cork: Mercier Press.

Kent, L. 1980. '*In the House of Strangers': The Impact of Government Policy on Irish Travellers.* Unpublished PhD thesis, University of Oregon.

Kettner, J. H. 1978. *The Development of American Citizenship, 1608–1870.* Chapel Hill, NC: University of North Carolina Press.

Kiberd, D. 1995. *Inventing Ireland.* London: Jonathan Cape.

Kofman, E. 1995. 'Citizenship for some but not for others: Spaces of citizenship in contemporary Europe', *Political Geography,* 14 (2), 119–35.

Latour, B. 1987. *Science in Action.* Cambridge, MA: Harvard University Press.

Lee, J. J. 1993. *Ireland 1912–1985.* Cambridge: Cambridge University Press.

Lynch, T. Dáil Debates, 11 July 1956, Vol. 159. Col. 665.

Lyons, F. S. L. 1982. *Culture and Anarchy in Ireland: 1890–1939.* Oxford: Oxford University Press.

Longley, E. 2001. 'Multi-culturalism and Northern Ireland: Making differences fruitful.' In E. Longley and D. Kiberd (eds), *Multi-culturalism: The View from the Two Irelands.* Cork: Cork University Press, 1–44.

MacKian, S. 1995. 'That great dust-heap called history', *Political Geography,* 14 (2), 209–16.

MacLaughlin, J. 1995. *Travellers and Ireland: Whose Country, Whose History?* Cork: Cork University Press.

MacLaughlin, J. 1999. 'European gypsies and the historical geography of loathing', *Review,* XXII (1), 31–59.

Marston, S. A. 1990. 'Who are 'the People'? Gender, citizenship and the making of the American nation', *Environment and Planning: Society and Space,* 8, 449–58.

Marston, S. A. 1995. 'The private goes public: Citizenship and the new spaces of civil society', *Political Geography,* 14 (2), 194–8.

McVeigh, R. 1998. 'Irish Travellers and the logic of genocide', in M. Peillon and E. Slater (eds), *Encounters with Modern Ireland: A Sociological Chronicle 1995–1996.* Dublin: IPA, 155–64.

Meaney, C. Dáil Debates, 4 June 1941, Vol. 83, Col. 1445.

Mitchell, D. 1997. 'The annihilation of space by law: The roots and implications of anti-homeless laws in the United States', *Antipode,* 29 (3), 303–35.

Molloy, R. Dáil Debates, 31 May 2001, Vol. 537, Col. 996.

Ni Shuinear, S. 1997. 'Why do Gaujos hate gypsies so much, anyway? A case study', in T. Acton (ed.), *Gypsy Politics and Traveller Identity.* Hertfordshire: University of Hertfordshire Press, 26–53.

O'Donnell, W. Dáil Debates, 19 April 1944, Vol. 93, Col. 1032.

O'Donnell, W. Dáil Debates, 12 April 1945, Vol. 96, Cols 2022–3.

O'Neill, E. Dáil Debates, 19 September 1944, Vol. 94, Col. 1528.

Painter, J. and C. Philo, 1995. 'Spaces of citizenship: an introduction', *Political Geography,* 14 (2), 107–20.

Pile, S. 1995. '"What we are asking for is decent human life": SPLASH, neighbourhood demands and citizenship in London's docklands', *Political Geography,* 14 (2), 199–208.

Powell, F. and M. Geoghegan. 2004. *The Politics of Community Development.* A&A Farmer: Dublin.

Procacci, G. 1991. 'Social economy and the government of poverty', in G. Burchell, C. Gordon and P. Miller (eds), *The Foucault Effect: Studies in Governmentality.* Chicago: University of Chicago Press, 151–68.

Prunty, J. 1999. *Dublin Slums: A Study in Urban Geography.* Dublin: Irish Academic Press.

Report of the High Level Group on Traveller Issues, 2006. Dublin: Stationery Office.

Report on Vagrancy and Related Offences, 1985. Dublin: Stationery Office.

Roche, M. 1997. 'Citizenship and exclusion: Reconstructing the European Union', in Maurice Roche and Rik van Berkel (eds) *European Citizenship and Social Exclusion.* London: Ashgate, 3–22.

Rodgers, G., Gore, C. and Figueiredo, J. (eds) 1995. *Social Exclusion: Rhetoric, Reality, Responses.* Geneva: International Institute for Labour Studies.

Rose, N. and P. Miller, 1992. 'Political power beyond the state: Problematics of government', *British Journal of Sociology,* 43 (2), 172–205.

Rottman, D., A. Tussing and M. Wiley. 1986. *The Population Structure and Living Conditions of Irish Travellers: Results from the 1981 Census of Traveller Families.* Dublin: The Economic and Social Research Institute.

Sahlin, I. 1995. 'Strategies for exclusion from social housing', *Housing Studies,* 10 (3), 381–401.

Sampson, J. 1890. 'Tinkers and their talk', *Journal of the Gypsy Lore Society,* 1 (2), 204–20.

Scott, J. 1998. *Seeing Like a State: How Certain Schemes to Improve the Human Condition Have Failed.* London: Yale University Press.

Tanner, M. 2002. *Ireland's Holy Wars: The Struggle for a Nation's Soul 1500–2000.* Yale University Press.

Taylor, C. 1998. 'The dynamics of democratic exclusion, *Journal of Democracy,* 9 (4), 143–56.

6

Developmental welfare once again: Growth and human capital

Bryan Fanning and Tina MacVeigh

This chapter examines changes and continuities within Irish social policy, concentrating on shifting understandings of, and commitments to, developmental welfare – from the 1960s to the present. The specific focus is on how ideological conceptions of nation-state developmentalism dating from the 1960s have become recycled so as to articulate a project of 'welfare state' restructuring, in response to globalisation. The development project of the 1960s emphasised an expansion of human capital to be driven by education. More recent reforms have depicted other welfare goods and services as having a developmental function. What has become recycled here is a perceived compact between the state and the citizen as welfare subject. Specifically, a post-World War II limited Keynesian welfare settlement, which prioritised economic growth above welfare security for Irish citizens, has become recycled as a social policy adopted in response to globalisation. In this new context, social protection is primarily understood in terms of individual participation in the labour market.

The OECD/Irish Government 1965 report *Investment in Education* has been credited with jolting the focus of Irish education, from character development and religious formation to one on economic development and the human capital needed for industrial growth (O'Sullivan 1992: 447). In the debate surrounding this report there was a degree of populist emphasis, by politicians, on the principle of equal educational opportunity. *Investment in Education* and contemporaneous policy documents introduced a two-fold emphasis on developmental welfare. They were making the case for educational reform to support the economic development objectives, and at the same time suggesting that improved and extended educational facilities should 'help to equalise opportunities by enabling an increasing proportion of the community to develop their potentialities and raise their personal standards of living'. For example, in the *Second Programme for Economic Expansion*, expenditure on education was described as 'an investment in the fuller use of the country's primary resource – its people – which can be expected to yield increasing returns in terms of economic progress' (Ireland 1964: 193). Some four decades, later in 2005, the National Social and Economic Council (NESC) published a report entitled *The Developmental Welfare State (DWS)* (NESC: 2005). This document was proposing ways for the various challenges facing twenty-first century Irish social policy to be met by the state and by other actors in the Irish welfare economy. To some extent it recast the now long-standing approach to developmentalism outlined in the *Investment in Education*. At the same time it offered a broader conception of developmental welfare, which focused on services and social protection as well as on education.

The most significant change precipitated by *Investment in Education* was the introduction of universal 'free' secondary education. While this expansion in education (and subsequently the expansion of third-level provision) has been credited in the meanwhile for later economic prosperity, the initial case advanced by political leaders was one which also promised greater equality of opportunity in the future. However, the Irish educational landscape remains a profoundly unequal one forty years after *Investment in Education*. To invoke a cliché, the rising tide of developmental education did not lift all boats. The persistence of profound educational inequality in Ireland suggests the need for a cautious assessment of the expanded developmental claims of the 2005 NESC Report. If, as NESC suggests, an expansion of developmental welfare is to come as a partial trade-off for some existing forms of social protection – for, unlike in the 1960s, no overall expansion of entitlements is implied – then the legitimate expectation is that there will be, again, losers as well as winners. Developmental education benefited the economy but the human capital stratifications it produced meant that the benefits of growth were experienced differentially.

As a text, the *Developmental Welfare State* did not engage much with past ideological Irish conceptions of welfare. Instead, it located an agenda of change within a well-rehearsed and internationally successful neo-liberal critique of the welfare state, borrowing somewhat from the 'Third Way' between left and right which had been promoted by Tony Blair and Anthony Giddens. But theirs was a very different political context to the Irish one. Giddens discussed the breakdown of a British 'social democratic' consensus around welfare while outlining a programme for its renewal (Giddens 1998: 16). Almost a decade later *DWS* engaged in a similar task, but from the very different vantage point of a competitive corporatist consensus. *DWS* emerged in a context where the state was a far smaller actor in welfare economy than it was in Britain. Despite the *DWS* title reference to a 'welfare state' the Republic of Ireland has had no such thing. It had a mixed economy of welfare with long-established voluntary, market and state sectors, which *DWS* sought to reconstitute as a developmental welfare economy. Its ideological pedigree combined nineteenth and early twentieth-century liberalism, which defined a limited role for the post-Independence Irish state in the area of social security and Catholic doctrine, which defined welfare activities in areas such as education and health (Fanning 2004a: 13). Arguably, the real value of this borrowed critique of social policy was its perceived capacity to address the individualisation of Irish society. With no welfare state to dismantle or rebuild, the proposed developmental 'welfare state' was characterised by consistencies (the architecture of the welfare economy in terms of who does what) as well as changes (conceptions of welfare/well-being which affect who gets what).

Change and continuity in the Irish welfare economy

Basic architecture of the Irish welfare economy

In Ireland as elsewhere, social policy goals have frequently been shaped by economic ones. Both in turn can be influenced by ideological, cultural or nation-building imperatives. Through the publication of *Investment in Education*, a post-Independence, economic and culturally isolationist, nation-building project had given way to one centred on economic modernisation and openness. Much of the Republic's social infrastructure had predated Independence. Social protection systems emerged as a functional consequence of nineteenth century industrialisation and urbanisation, just as denominational mass education fostered the mass identities, religious and cultural, which had been institutionalised within the state after Independence. Under British rule, a minimalist social protection system emanating from the state had developed, for instance, through the Poor Law (1838) and the two-tiered social and retirement insurance system, introduced between 1908 and 1911. Here the imperatives were those of industrial Britain. With industrialisation and urbanisation, economy and social infrastructure became increasingly interlocked. The nuclear family was the product of an industrial workplace. The separation of home and social care from paid employment and the risks of cyclical unemployment were managed through a state system of social protection for the male breadwinner. The case for social insurance was initially justified in terms of the economy – it was a means of managing the economic cycle of upturns and downturns by offering workers a safety net against the risk of unemployment. Welfare goods and services (education, health and social hygiene) have often been conceptualised as serving nation and economy – in essence, a developmental role – by producing workers fit for economic activity. Social security, too, had a developmental role, insofar as it supported the workforce through economic downturns and compensated for market failure (Creedy and Disney 1985: 17). Different ideological approaches to welfare emerged which reflected differing ideological conceptions of the good society. For example, Esping-Anderson identifies three prevalent worlds of welfare capitalism in the West often seen to overlap in the politics of specific countries. These are the conservative or *ancien régime* tradition of welfare associated with Catholic countries, which has persisted within post-World War II Christian democracy; a liberal individualist tradition, born out of contestations of the *ancien régime*; and a socialist tradition galvanised by the social inequalities associated with liberal individualism (Esping-Anderson 1990). Within the actual welfare systems characterised by these ideological archetypes, functionalist relationships between economy and social policy can be seen to persist.

For much of this history of the state, the basic architecture of the Irish welfare economy has remained unchanged, notwithstanding significant gradual changes in levels of provision and in entitlements to welfare goods and services. Much of it emerged prior to Independence, with the development of state provisions in the areas of social protection. Non-contributory benefits date from the 1838 Poor Law onwards. Unemployment and retirement age benefits date from the 'new-liberal' legislation introduced in 1908 and 1911.[1] Here the measures introduced in Ireland had much to do with the social protection and developmental needs of industrial Britain. The resultant system provided stratified but residual levels of social protection. A limited gradual expansion of employment-related social protection contrasted with the 'big bang' post-World War II expansion of the same system in the United Kingdom. This phenomenon was influenced like others by the – then prevalent – Keynesian economic orthodoxies (Rottman and O'Connell 2003: 82–3). As noted in *DWS*, Ireland used a 'moderate to low' proportion of national resources to provide services and a small proportion to provide cash transfers by EU15 standards (NESC 2005: 104). It was concluded that: 'cash transfers as a percentage of GNP are low compared to other countries principally because of the lower bill for pensions but also because of the Irish welfare state's high reliance on means-testing. Ireland is exceptional within the EU for the high proportion of its social spending which is means-tested' (NESC 2005: 104). In essence, levels of state provision and the basis for who got what owed much to what the British left behind rather than to what the 'welfare state' introduced after the World War II.

The 1958 *Programme for Economic Expansion* marked a turning point in Irish economic policy, from an emphasis on protectionism to one on economic development. It emphasised that any welfare expansion must be dependant upon economic growth (Kaim-Caudle 1967: 103). A belated Keynesian settlement emphasised growth rather than security. The pursuit of economic growth was prioritised over welfare and infrastructure growth, notwithstanding the interrelationships between all these. Irish Keynesianism never included the 'growth and security' commitment to full employment and social protection, characteristic of its British version (Hughes 1998: 27). The Irish 'growth and security' compact applied only to some relatively privileged sectors, notably unionist workers and public servants (Fanning 2004a: 12). In this context, the state's transfer payment system proved inadequate as social protection, the proof being in high emigration. In a context where there was little emphasis on human capital – a fact evident in the prevailing elite view that emigration was a good thing (Lee 1989: 374) – and not much of an industrial economy, social insurance was not envisaged as having a developmental role. Ideological conflicts, insofar as they emerged, were prompted by Catholic anxiety about state encroachment upon the second significant domain of Irish welfare economy, the religious voluntary sector, which included education and health and was controlled by the Church. In this context the rare political ruptures that opened up between Church and state – notably around the 'Mother and Child Scheme', in 1951 – were demarcation disputes between two functional and ideologically different domains of social policy (Fanning 2006).

The enduring role of the Church in the welfare economy

From Catholic Emancipation onwards, the Catholic Church dominated education and health provision. The former was crucial to the inter-generational reproduction of Catholicism. It contributed hugely to Irish nation-building before and after Independence. Catholic values became constitutionally enshrined. The key encyclicals of social doctrine which set out a Catholic welfare ethos, *Rerum Novarum* (1891) and *Quadragesimo Anno* (1931) emerged in response to liberal and state socialist conceptions of social policy. This Catholic 'Third Way' resisted unnecessary encroachment upon the family and upon the voluntary sector by higher institutions such as the state. This principle of 'subsidiarity' held that the state should not usurp the relationship between Catholic institutions such as schools and the family. Both encyclicals offered fairly sophisticated engagements with liberalism and socialism, which allowed for elastic thinking about how the state and other actors should address changing social conditions. Theory aside, neo-Thomism became politically associated with a static, anti-modernist and anti-developmental *Gemeinschaft* conception of the good society.[2] Irish education in the decades after Independence was shaped by theological rather than economic goals. Post-Independence 'Irish-Ireland' nation-building combined Catholic conservatism with post-colonial economic isolationism.

A school system developed under state administrative control from the nineteenth century on. However, the ethos of denominational schools was constitutionally protected up until the Education Act (1998).[3] The expansion of provisions which followed *Investment in Education* did not supplant Church control over schools. The settlement that emerged allowed for vocational education eventually to co-exist alongside traditional secondary provision. The Church had opposed the development of vocational education outside of its control (Garvin 2004). It achieved a controlling 'patron' status over vocational provisions. The crucial changes which occurred in the wake of *Investment in Education* were cultural ones. The expansion of education from the 1960s on arguably fostered secularism among those in the first generation to benefit from free secondary education (Garvin 1982: 31). In the longer term, this prompted a rise in individualism – one more open to neo-liberal than Catholic conceptions of welfare.

After Vatican II, the Catholic-dominated voluntary sector acquired something of a developmental focus, witnessed by urban community development programmes and social justice anti-poverty activism (Irish Commission for Justice and Peace 1998). This sector had been a long-standing leader of efforts to redress rural decline, even if the communitarian goals being pursued (the preservation of 'traditional' Catholic communities) were conservative ones. A gradual shift in focus from such conservatism mirrored the mainstream political shift from isolationalism, epitomised by the different leaderships of de Valera and Lemass. This amounted to a conviction that there could be no bucolic, static, Catholic communities (with or without the comely maidens dancing at the crossroads, invoked in de Valera's 1941 'dream speech') without some element of economic modernisation. Opposition to developmentalism was by no means limited to Catholicism. The big theme of Joe Lee's magisterial *Ireland 1914–1985* was the prevalence of psychological determinism in Irish society, together with a fatalism which blocked development (Lee 1989: 646). Post-famine experiences of underdevelopment accepted emigration as inevitable. The prevailing mindset, as depicted by Lee, placed little emphasis on human capital.

Post-Vatican II Catholic approaches to social policy emphasised communitarian and social-justice goals over economic ones. From the 1980s on, Church activism sought at times to increase the role of the state in social policy (Irish Commission for Justice and Peace 1998). Here it could be seen to take a role associated elsewhere with the left: that of promoting decommodification.[4] The last major policy document influenced by social Catholicism, *Strengthening Families for Life* in 1998, advocated basic income measures aimed at rewarding the unpaid work of women in the home.[5] By then, tax individualisation policies which aimed at encouraging the economic participation of women in the labour market were strongly advocated by the government. So, too, were initiatives to dismantle the community development 'social economy' of paid voluntarism, which owed much to the 'welfare-to-work'/'work-as-welfare' initiatives championed by New Labour (Deloitte and Touche 1998). Catholic conceptions of a right, for mothers and volunteers, not to undertake paid employment, and the remedies (proposed by the Church, such as the basic income advocated by the Catholic Non-Governmental Organisations, conflicted with a 'Celtic Tiger' emphasis on maximising human commodification.

For some theorists, past underdevelopment has itself been the key factor in explaining the underdevelopment of the role played by the state in the provision of welfare goods and services (Peillon 1995:184). In the absence of real possibilities for rapid welfare expansion in the post-war era, questions about the role of the state in social policy did not become politicised to the same extent as in Britain. In the Irish context there was little impetus to restructure the basic architecture of the mixed economy of welfare; welfare innovation tended to occur in the voluntary sector both in terms of acknowledging 'new' social needs, such as those for people with disabilities, and in terms of the development of subsequent provision. The state took an increased role in funding voluntary welfare without acquiring control. That being said, from the 1960s on the voluntary sector was characterised by secular expansion, for instance in the area of urban and rural community development (Rush 1999: 167)

Education and development

Promoting human capital

The 'can do' mentality evident in *Economic Development* signaled a cultural break with the fatalism described by Lee (1989: 420). Developmentalism, as articulated there, in subsequent policy documents, and by political parties (notably Fianna Fáil), emphasised a human capital role for the state in developing public-sector enterprises. Human capital itself came to be understood as a key requirement for economic growth (Breen et al. 1990: 126).

In this context, according to Denis O'Sullivan, *Investment in Education* amounted to a paradigm shift whereby a combined mercantile and human capital paradigm broke with an earlier dominant theocentric one (2005: 105). A 1954 Council for Education report described the former in the following terms:

The school exists to assist and supplement the work of parents in the rearing of children. Their first duty is to train their children to love and fear God. That duty becomes the first purpose of the primary school. It is fulfilled by the school through the religious and moral training of the child, through the teaching of good habits, through his instruction in the duties of citizenship and in his obligations to his parents and community – in short, through all that tends to the formation of a person of character, strong in his desire to fulfil the end of his creation. (cited in O'Sullivan 2005: 109)

O'Sullivan explains subsequent paradigm shifts in terms of the sort of expertise that informed educational goals. Religious expertise, epitomised by papal encyclicals and episcopal pronouncements, was displaced, from the 1960s onwards, by World Bank policy, OECD Reports, EU funding protocols and whatever was deemed from time to time to constitute 'best practice' (O'Sullivan 2005: 115). *Investment in Education* did not aim to secularise education, but it advanced strategic goals which were at odds with the traditional Catholic ethos. In effect it replaced the theocratic expertise that dominated education policy with what O'Sullivan calls mercantile expertise. This emphasised a utilitarian approach to education and the use of managerial indicators to measure and classify its outcomes. *Investment in Education* steered education policy on a new 'mercantile' cultural trajectory which continues to be followed. (O'Sullivan 2005: 129). As the report itself outlined,

[a] country must seek in designing its education system to satisfy, amongst other things, the manpower it needs for the future. If the range and levels of skills required to convert economic potential into economic achievements are not available, a country is unlikely to have the resources needed to provide education of the quality and variety that is being increasingly demanded. As education is at once a cause and a consequence of economic growth, economic planning is incomplete without educational planning. Education, as well as having its own intrinsic values, is a necessary element in economic activity. (Ireland 1965: 350)

Investment in Education and subsequent reports also emphasized a human capital education paradigm. This differed from the mercantile paradigm in its focus on the benefits to the individual rather than to the economy. In the simplest of terms investment in education led to economic growth; education was seen to deliver, at an individual level, higher incomes and status. By expanding the provision for education, the state could create more opportunity and maximise human capital. As put in the *Second Programme for Economic Expansion*: 'Since our wealth lies ultimately in our people, the aim of educational policy must be to enable all individuals to realise their full potential as human persons' (Ireland 1964: 17). Such human capital perspectives imply a functional emphasis on equality of opportunity, one that is meritocratic and allows for social mobility without being preoccupied by class, gender, or demographic factors that might affect educational outcomes (Drudy and Lynch 1993: 35). *Investment in Education* promoted meritocracy through addressing the wastes and inefficiencies of the existing system. In the words of Joe Lee (1989: 361):

> [t]he report collected important statistical data for the first time, intended to indicate the resources available, and the efficiency with which they were used. It provided striking evidence of the lack of opportunity for poorer children to proceed to secondary and higher education. After its exposure of the waste of talent fostered by an educational system based on low intellectual and relatively high financial entry requirements to advanced levels it was no longer possible to sustain fond illusions.

In this context, a 1969 OECD report described the introduction of free secondary education as 'a move in the direction of equality of opportunity'. That same year, the then Minister of Education, Brian Lenihan, described equality of educational opportunity as 'our most urgent social and national objective' (cited in Greaney and Kelleghan 1984: 27). What precisely this meant had been set out by an earlier Minister, Dr Patrick Hillery, who stated that it would be an uplift to the morale of the country, 'if it were generally understood that the child of even the poorer, if he is of sufficient ability, would have the opportunity of . . . climbing right to the top of the educational ladder' (ibid.). The human capital rationale for such equality of opportunity was also acknowledged by the National Industrial Economic Council, the predecessor of NESC which represented tripartite employer, trades union and state interests:

Of all kinds of inequality, inequality of opportunity is by far the most damaging to the ethos, efficiency and material welfare of a society. If those with the innate ability to benefit from it are denied access to further education, their reasonable ambitions are thwarted, their potential contributions towards achieving the society's objectives are reduced and social cohesion is endangered (NESC 1966 cited in O'Sullivan 2005: 271).

The impact of 'Investment in Education'

Reforms in the wake of *Investment in Education* included the removal of secondary level fees, the standardisation of the curriculum, the implementation of nationwide standardised examinations at the intermediate and leaving certificate, the rationalisation of small schools in most rural areas and the introduction of free school transport. The rise in secondary participation was dramatic. In 1964, one quarter of 17-year-olds remained in full-time education and 5.9 per cent were estimated to be in third level. Participation in second level education had grown by one half in 1979. A two-thirds growth in participation rates occurred at third level over the same period, with some 20 per cent of young people entering a third level institution by 1979 (Rottman and O'Connell 2003:45).

Developmental welfare in the wake of *Investment in Education* overwhelmingly accrued to relatively advantaged socio-economic groups within Irish society. Writing in 1982, in a special issue of the journal *Administration* aptly entitled *Unequal Achievement*, Rottman and O'Connell concluded that this had produced a virtual upper middle-class monopoly of advantages from education:

> The importance of education institutions within the society was greatly enhanced. The population was better or at least more extensively educated, and the content of that education was greatly altered. But the expansion of education, and particularly the opening of opportunities through 'free education' in the 1960s and 1970s, did more to consolidate the advantages of propertied and professional middle class families than to facilitate social mobility: the strong encouragement to educational accomplishment was disproportionately taken up by children from middle-class backgrounds. The qualifications so obtained were used to secure for those families the bulk of opportunities becoming available in white collar and skilled

industrial employment and self-employment. Participation in second and third level education was and remained severely restricted along social class lines, with children from substantial proprietorial and upper middle-class professional families forming a share of the student population at higher levels which vastly exceeded their share of the student-aged population. Middle-class dominance is strongly evident at the Leaving certificate standard and in the late 1970s nearly three quarters of the children of members of the major professions entered a third level institution, in contrast to less than four per cent of the children of unskilled workers. (Rottman and O'Connell 2003: 46)

Educational disadvantage, and disadvantage in general, is associated with a number of factors, including unemployment and limited social mobility (MacVeigh 2006). While advances have been made in the participation at third level education of individuals from lower socio-economic groups, their representation at third level remains significantly lower than in other income groups (Clancy 2003: 13; O'Connell, Clancy and McCoy 2006: 9). A succession of social-partnership accords from the 1990s onwards emphasised the policy goals of addressing social exclusion and persistent educational disadvantage, though with limited success in the case of the latter.

The Developmental Welfare State

Recasting the Irish social debate

The 2005 *Developmental Welfare State (DWS)* NESC report outlined a broad conception of developmental welfare, which included social protection benefits, transfer payments, and a range of services in addition to education. It offered a broad blueprint for 'recasting the Irish social debate', which, it maintained expressed 'a significant convergence of views on the Council on what the core social challenges in Ireland now are and the lines along which Ireland's welfare state needs reform' (NESC 2005: 6) *DWS* located this competitive corporatist consensus in social and ideological shifts. It portrayed a new, individualist Ireland, which had broken with traditional understandings and practices of social solidarity. There was, *DWS* argued, 'a stronger appreciation of the individual and of her/his life as something to be personally shaped' (NESC 2005: 6). Significant erosion has taken place in the legitimacy of traditional 'religious, political, business and professional' sources of authority. This, it was argued, created new demands for accountability, witnessed by 'a stronger social awareness and a growing unease at the extent of social disparities', increased exposure to other countries' standards and practices, and greater access to information (NESC 2005: 2). All this suggested opposition to any strong role for the state as a provider of welfare goods and services – an opposition rooted in antipathy to the authoritarianism that had previously characterised Irish institutions as well as political ideology. The stated political context for reform – that of a welfare-state legitimacy crisis, the failure of past welfare efforts to address inequalities of opportunity and the need to recalibrate in the face of globalisation-drew to some extent on the style and substance of the 1990s 'Third Way' proposals to reform the British welfare state and the more recent one concerning the future of social Europe. Conceptually the *DWS* can be seen to acknowledge a shift from nation-state to market–state (Bobbitt 2003). Politically, it did so from a specific post-Keynesian neo-corporatist perspective characterised by an emphasis on open economy, innovation and competitiveness, as well as on the subordination of social policy to economic policy (Jessop 2000: 178).

In particular, the *DWS* echoed the conception of an 'individualised risk society' developed by Giddens from Ulrich Beck's account of 'reflexive modernity'. This conception emphasised the need for individual and societal reflectivity to manage individually and collectively experienced risks (Beck 1992). As applied by Beck to the British case, it identified an institutionalised individualism in opposition to neo-liberal market individualism. Beck argued that most rights and entitlements associated with the British welfare state were designed for individuals engaged in paid employment: 'In many cases they presuppose employment. Employment in turn implies education and both of these presuppose mobility. By all these requirements people are invited to constitute themselves as individuals: to plan, understand, design themselves as individuals' (Beck, cited in Giddens 1998: 36). Under the 'Third Way', as defined by Giddens, the developmental role of the welfare state – redefined as a social investment state – was to support individual reflexivity in managing risks and hazards across the human lifecycle (pp. 99–118). As outlined in *DWS*: 'A fundamental standpoint from which to judge the adequacy and effectiveness of overall social protection is to access the risks and hazards which the individual person in Irish society faces and the supports available to them at different stages of the lifecycle' (NESC 2005: xxiv).

In making the case for a radical welfare reform both mercantile and human capital concepts of developmentalism were invoked. *DWS* linked economic competitiveness with the development of a knowledge-based economy. All welfare goods and services, not just education, were deemed to have a developmental function. *DWS* primarily focused on forms of developmental welfare which removed barriers to economic participation – notably social and market child care and elder care services, destined to support the rise in female participation in paid employment without a corresponding decline in birth rate, which would bring about 'the type of demographic crisis currently confronting the systems of social protection in other member states' (NESC 2005: 37). Here, the developmental emphasis was upon choice, individual autonomy, enhanced individual opportunities, social conditions that would nurture and sustain individual adaptability, flexibility and risk-taking; a 'sustainable balance between dynamism and security' as articulated by Giddens (1998) and Beck (1997). In short, a radical rethinking was needed, which addressed the following questions:

- '[w]hether the number of people turning to privately provide social services (health, education, child care) and with a negative perception of the quality of publicly provided services is now so large that no government in the foreseeable future can expect an electoral mandate to fund more and better public services by raising tax';
- '[w]hether increased income transfers are at the heart of alleviating poverty or can only produce better outcomes if they are linked to improved support services and clear conditionality to reduce people's duration on welfare-only incomes';
- '[w]hether the state should remain the key provider of essential social services or whether more public money should be channelled (under new arrangements for accountability) to private and not-for-profit bodies' (NESC 2005: 5).

Ireland, *DWS* argued, 'needs to participate actively in the search going on within the EU and throughout the industrialised world for the forms of social protection which better equip people and their societies to meet the demographic, social and economic challenges of the 21st century' (p. 4). Social protection paid for by the state did not have to be provided by the state; welfare expansion through private and non-profit organisations was likely to achieve the best balance between accountability, innovation and efficiency (p. 160).

DWS advocated a radical expansion of services aimed at facilitating higher levels of labour market participation. Labour market participation was defined in turn as the only really viable form of social protection. Within this 'work-as-welfare' equation, 'the radical development of services' was identified as the single most important route to improving social protection (p. xix). This recast the view of welfare expansion as a form of social redistribution and benefit of growth: 'Formally advances in social protection were largely thought of as a societal dividend which democratic political processes extracted *after* the event from successful economic performance' (p. 9). A key *DWS* argument is that strong economic performance now allowed for a services dividend and that future growth depended on the expansion of services. However, while 1960s developmentalism hinged on the expansion of 'free education', the *DWS* emphasised the purchase of caring services. Whereas the organisational principle the 1960s project emphasised was universalist, the *DWS* emphasises the development of targeted provision by public bodies (NESC, 2005: 23).

DWS also advocated radical shifts in social protection, aimed at requiring jobless people to participate in the open labour market. Here, the emphasis – as in earlier reports (Kelleghan 2002: 21) – was upon groups experiencing social exclusion and educational disadvantage:

> Significant minorities in Ireland's population are currently experiencing multiple forms of social disadvantage, and present strategies and policies are not proving adequate in helping them. This is evidenced by the scale of educational disadvantage, the long duration of dependence on means-tested social welfare of a large number of people, and the extent to which people are found in similar predicaments in the same areas from one generation to the next. (NESC 2005: 2)

DWS advocated using welfare payment arrangements to encourage 'as many people's eventual participation as possible in employment or other social activities' (p. 157). Developmental welfare included a human capital emphasis on 'stemming educational disadvantage' so as to 'increase people's employability and productivity and strengthen their attachment to the world of work' (p. 33). The *DWS* case for addressing inequality of opportunity was a developmental one: 'Children receive priority because of the greater awareness of the later problems that result from a poor start in life'. But a societal consensus that such inequalities of opportunity should be addressed was also presumed: 'It is accepted that parental circumstances should not be the cause of any child being denied access to key developmental opportunities; while all children are supported, some are supported more than others (progressive universalism)' (p. 157).

The limits of developmental welfare

However, in keeping with *Investment in Education*, much of the developmental emphasis fell upon relatively advantaged groups. Emphasis on raising skill levels tended to focus on the already employed and on those with higher levels of educational attainment (NESC 2005: 23). These were seen to play a key role in securing the 'workforce quality that underpins a competitive, knowledge-based economy' (p. 139). At the same time, the *DWS* acknowledged that low-skilled jobs had not gone away; 'jobs in occupations typically held by people with less than upper secondary schooling dropped from 43 per cent of all jobs in 1991 to 32 per cent in 2001 but they still grew by 26,000 in absolute terms', with expectations that such jobs would in 2010 constitute 30 per cent of overall employment (pp. 25–29). In this context, the emphasis was to be on removing welfare-dependency disincentives to work, lower taxes, retention of secondary benefits and higher entry level wages, in order to make such employment attractive (p. 28). As such, it was implied that developmental welfare meant different things for different groups, ranging from life-long learning for reflective individualists to benefit carrots and sticks for those dependent on low-skilled employment or on benefits.

The *DWS* appeared at a time when potential immigrant job displacement and replacement of low-skilled Irish workers had yet to be politicised. It noted that low-skilled immigration has been needed to fill 'large proportions of vacancies in hotels, catering, factory production, child care and other areas' (p. 198) It suggested that many immigrants did not face the same constraints as Ireland's jobless; for example, that more of them are single or without dependants. Indigenous jobless were therefore likely to be less flexible than immigrants, less likely to accept low-skilled, low-paid jobs. The *DWS* acknowledged that immigrant competition for such jobs would benefit consumers (users of services provided by immigrants) but not long-standing Irish losers in the human capital sweepstakes (p. 198). Such acknowledgements tacitly accepted the limits of a purely developmental welfare approach. The overall argument was that pushing the employment rate higher implied a focus on 'hitherto relatively neglected groups in the working-age population, the obstacles they face and the supports they need' (p. 77). However, it was admitted that, from a utilitarian perspective, the impetus to address the developmental needs of this residual rump was undermined by access to immigrant labour.

A new welfare paradigm?

The *DWS* proposed no radical structural change to the existing Irish welfare economy. It acknowledged continuities in proclaiming that, '[s]ince the beginning of the State in 1921, public authorities in Ireland have been able to build public services around the multiple contributions of private-non-profit organisations' (NESC 2005: 37). It identified and endorsed the ongoing and long-standing development of market provision:

> Significant commercial providers of health services, medical insurance, child care, elder care, schooling and other forms of social protection now exist in Ireland. Employers also provide significant levels of social protection, particularly in the form of occupational pensions and by supporting the health, life/work balance and skill levels of their employees as well. For example, 20 percent of the value of all health insurance premiums is estimated to be paid by employers as employee benefits. (Department of Health and Children, cited in NESC 2005: 37)

The *DWS* noted a long-standing role of the voluntary sector in service provision and innovation and characterised such initiatives as being 'akin to the R&D [Research and Development] sphere of the Developmental Welfare State' (NESC 2005: 186). Such organisations were seen to respond to social needs not met yet – initially in a particular and one-off manner but with implications for mainstream service provision that are systematically identified. To a considerable extent, the *DWS* would build on the well-established principle of state regulation of the voluntary sector (NESC 1990: 213-4). All this suggests much institutional continuity, notwithstanding a gradual expansion of various sectors of the welfare economy over time and a bias towards the market and not-for-profit sector within this expansion. However, the *DWS* has superimposed a new welfare/well-being paradigm upon such broad institutional continuities. This has reconceptualised the purpose of welfare goods and services. It has mobilised understandings of welfare/well-being that drew upon theories of individualisation, 'reflective modernity' and 'risk society'. In this context, human capital and mercantile developmentalism became extended beyond education to welfare goods and services (see Box 6.1).

Conclusion

The *DWS* developmental welfare/well-being paradigm proposed a balance between mercantile and human capital goals that saw individual human capital as shaped by a number of factors which could be positively addressed through welfare goods and services. This might be termed as a 'growth and opportunity' compact, as distinct from an archetypical Keynesian 'growth and security' one. The *DWS* can be located within the half century-old developmental nation-building project that replaced previous post-colonial isolationism. Effectively, it attributes to welfare goods and services a nation-building role which was previously the province of education. During the late 1990s, a conflict played out between Catholic communitarian conceptions of welfare prevalent in the past, exemplified *Strengthening Families for Life*, and those hegemonic now, articulated in the *DWS*. The emphasis given in this chapter to the former serves to demonstrate the extent of the welfare/well-being paradigm shift claimed by the *DWS*. Responses of the *DWS* to social change, for instance the growing participation of women in paid employment, emphasise a commodification of care (Rush 2006). The *DWS* offered a monocultural account of the Irish welfare economy which makes scant reference to immigration except in terms of its effect on the developmental welfare needs of indigenous groups. Immigrants, no less than other members of Irish society, have welfare needs resulting from their participation in paid employment, as they are parents and carers just like the others. This neglect is unsurprising for two reasons. The *DWS* emerged from established corporatist groups. Secondly, immigration policy, no less than the

Box 6.1 Welfare changes and continuities, 1966–2005.

Investment in Education within Irish limited nation-state Keynesianism	*The Developmental Welfare State* within market state/open economy
• developmental education as nation-building	• proposed developmental welfare to meet requirements of globalisation
• highly targeted (means tested) benefits	• proposed highly targeted (tailored universalism) services
• growth seen as a prerequisite for welfare expansion	• the case for a 'service dividend' from growth and as prerequisite for future growth
• emphasis on developmental (free secondary) education	• advocacy of developmental welfare (services provided by the market, voluntary sector or state) and developmental education
• emergence of the mercantile developmental paradigm	• persistence of the mercantile developmental paradigm
• emergence of the human capital paradigm, to be fostered through education and meritocratic competition	• persistence of human capital paradigm, to be fostered through developmental welfare that requires individual reflexivity and responsibility
• meritocratic/equality-of-opportunity expectations	• critique of persistent inequalities of condition as system failure; emphasis on accountabilities and targeting to redress inequality of opportunity within provision.
• voluntary/privatised care within households	• market and social care services to support individual autonomy within labour market
• prevalence of Catholic communitarian and liberal approaches to social policy	• secular communitarianism/social capital approaches vie with neo-liberal approaches to social policy
• mixed economy characterised by Catholic anti-welfare statism, state activism to promote economic development and strong reliance on religious voluntary sector	• mixed economy characterised by neo-liberal anti-welfare statism, competitive corporatist activism to promote economic development and strong reliance on 'not-for-profit' sector and the market

DWS, still tends to be expressed in terms of economic development goals (Office for Social Inclusion 2004: 77). The availability of low-skilled immigration labour was identified as the Achilles Heel of developmental welfare. Immigration was strongly supported insofar as it contributed to overall economic development. Yet it removed any imperative to invest in the human capital of marginal groups (see Crowley, this volume). In this context, exclusions from human capital that were encountered by marginal groups in an era of high emigration are potentially replayed in an era of high immigration. In this respect a tension between mercantile and human capital goals can be seen to persist. This points to the incapacity of the developmental welfare paradigm to address all the needs and, as ever in social policy debates, to solve a problem of reconciling ideology with practice.

Within these debates, it is not so much the state that has become recycled as various understandings of the relationship between the citizen and the state. Historically, the capacity of the state to provide universal safety-nets was inevitably stunted by its limited role within the Irish welfare economy. Economic prosperity arguably makes possible a new expansion of universal welfare goods and services. What the *DWS* offers is a services dividend rather than an expansion of state provision. The sort of compact articulated within the (misnamed) *Developmental Welfare State* is one between the state as regulator of the welfare economy (distinct from the state as provider) and the citizen as user. The role of the state presented here is one recycled from the 1960s when, after all, the expansion of education took place mostly through provision owned by the religious voluntary sector.

NOTES

1   The Old Age Pension Act 1908 and the National Insurance Act 1911.

2   The philosophical influence here was the Aristotelian concept of 'natural law', introduced into Catholicism by Thomas Aquinas. An anti-modernist neo-Thomism became influential in seminaries at the end of the nineteenth century. The ideological emphasis in Catholic social thought was upon pre-modern forms of community – what Emile Durkheim refered to as 'mechanistic solidarity' and Ferdinand Toiennes called *Gemeinschaft* – and of social relationships, characterised by shared values and goals (Fanning 2004b: 43).

3   The Education Act (1998) represented a new settlement within Irish education, which took account of the declining numbers of clerical teachers and the demands for greater lay-teacher and parental involvement in the management of schools, while protecting the latter's religious ethos.

4   The term 'decommodification' is used in the field of comparative social policy to measure

the extent to which entitlements to state provision allow people to withdraw from the labour market. Simply put, it measures the extent of coverage offered by social security. It is an index of levels and durations of benefits and of conditions of eligibility and access (Esping-Anderson 1990).
5   Conference of the Religious in Ireland's influence was evident in this 1998 Report of the Commission on the Family.

REFERENCES

Beck, U. 1992. *The Risk Society; Towards a New Modernity.* London: Sage.

Beck, Ulrich, 1998. 'The Cosmopolitan Manifesto' *New Statesman* (20 March 1998)

Bobbitt, P.C. 2003. *Marketing the Future of the State.* London: New Statesman.

Breen, R. (et al.) 1990. 'Education: The promise of reform and the growth of credentialism', in *Understanding Contemporary Ireland.* Dublin: Gill & Macmillan.

Clancy, P. 2003. *Supporting Equity in Higher Education: A Report to the Minister for Education and Science.* Department of Education and Science, Dublin, May 2003.

Commission on the Family 1998. *Strengthening Families for Life.* Dublin: Stationery Office.

Creedy, J. and R. Disney. 1985. *Social Insurance in Transition: An Economic Analysis.* Oxford: Clarendon.

Deloitte and Touche 1998. *Review of the Community Development Programme.* Dublin: Stationery Office.

Drudy, S. and K. Lynch. 1993. *Schools and Society in Ireland.* Dublin: Gill & Macmillan.

Esping-Anderson, G. 1990. *The Three Worlds of Welfare Capitalism.* Cambridge: Polity.

Fanning, B. 2003. 'The construction of Irish social policy (1953–2003)', in B. Fanning and T. McNamara. *Ireland Develops: Administration and Social Policy 1953–2003.* Dublin: Institute of Public Administration, 3–20.

Fanning, B. 2004a. 'Locating Irish social policy', in Fanning, B., Kiely, G., Kennedy, P. and Quin, S. (eds), *Theorising Irish Social Policy.* Dublin: University College Dublin Press 6–22.

Fanning, B. 2004b. 'Communitarianism, social capital and subsidiarity', in B. Fanning et al. (eds), *Theorising Irish Social Policy.* Dublin: University College Dublin Press, 42–60.

Fanning, B. 2006. 'The new welfare economy', in B. Fanning and M. Rush (eds), *Care and Social Change in Irelands Welfare Economy.* Dublin: UCD Press, 9–25.

Garvin, T. 1982. 'Change and the political system', in Litton, F. (ed.), *Unequal Achievement: The Irish Experience 1957–1982.* Dublin: Institute of Public Administration, 21–41.

Garvin, T. 2004. *Preventing the Future: Why Ireland Remained So Poor for So Long.* Dublin: Gill and Macmillian.

Giddens, A. 1998. *The Third Way: The Renewal of Social Democracy.* Cambridge: Polity.

Greaney, V. and Kelleghan, T. 1984. *Equality of Opportunity in Irish Schools: A Longitudinal Study of 500 Students.* Dublin: Educational Research Centre.

Hughes, G. 1998. 'Picking Over the Remains: The Welfare State Settlements of the Post-Second World War UK', in G. Hughes and G. Lewis (eds), *Unsettling Welfare: The Reconstruction of Social Policy.* London: Routledge, 3–38.

Ireland. 1964. *Second Programme for Economic Expansion.* Part II. Laid by the Government before each House of the Oireachtas, July 1964. Dublin: Stationery Office.

Ireland. 1965. *Investment in Education.* Dublin: Stationery Office.

Irish Commission for Justice and Peace. 1998. *Re-Righting the Constitution: The Case for New Social and Economic Rights: Housing, Health, Nutrition, Adequate Standard of Living.* Dublin: Irish Commission for Justice and Peace.

Jessop, B. 2000. 'WNS to the SWPR' in G. Lewis, S. Gerwitz and J. Clarke, *Rethinking Social Policy.* London: Sage, 171–84.

Kaim-Caudle, P. 1967. *Social Policy in the Irish Republic.* London: Routledge.

Kelleghan, T. 2002. *Approaches to Problems of Educational Disadvantage.* Paper presented to National Forum on Primary Education and Ending Disadvantage, St Patrick's College, Dublin, 1–5 July 2002.

Lee, J. J. 1989. *Ireland 1912–1985: Politics and Society.* Cambridge: Cambridge University Press.

Leo XIII. 1891. Rerum Novarum: On Capital and Labour. http://www.vatican.va (accessed 15/03/07)

MacVeigh, T. 2006. 'Education, life chances and disadvantage' in B. Fanning and M. Rush (eds), *Care and Social Change in Ireland's Welfare Economy.* Dublin: UCD Press.

National Social and Economic Council. 1990. *A Strategy for the Nineties.* Dublin: Stationery Office.

National Social and Economic Council. 1993. *A Strategy for Competitiveness, Growth and Employment.* Dublin: Stationery Office.

National Social and Economic Council. 2005. *The Developmental Welfare State*: Report No. 113. Dublin: Stationery Office.

O'Connell, P., D. Clancy and S. McCoy, 2006. *Who Went to College in 2004? A National Survey of New Entrants to Higher Education.* Dublin: Higher Education Authority.

O'Sullivan, D. 1992. 'Cultural strangers and educational change: The OECD Report *Investment in Education* and Irish Educational Policy', *Journal of Education Policy,* 7 (5), 445–469.

O'Sullivan, D. 2005. *Cultural Politics and Irish Education since the 1950s: Policy Paradigms and Power.* Dublin: Institute of Public Administration.

Office for Social Inclusion. 2004. *Reconciling Mobility and Social Inclusion: The Role of Employment and Social Policy.* Dublin: Stationery Office.

Peillon, M. 1995. 'Interest groups and the state', in P. Clancy, S. Drudy, K. Lynch, K. and L. O'Dowd, (eds), *Irish Society: Sociological Perspectives.* Dublin: Institute of Public Administration, 358–78.

Pius XI. 1931. Quadragesimo Anno: On the Reconstruction of the Social Order, http://www.vatican.va (accessed 15/03/07)

Rottman, D. and P. O'Connell. 2003. 'The Changing Social Structure', in B. Fanning and T. MacNamara (eds), *Ireland Develops: Administration and Social Policy 1953–2003.* Dublin: Institute of Public Administration, 36–59.

Rush, M. 1999. 'Social partnership in Ireland', in G. Keily, A. O'Donnell, P. Kennedy and S. Quin, (eds), *Irish Social Policy in Context.* Dublin: University College Dublin Press, 155–177.

Rush, M. 2006. 'The politics of care' in B. Fanning and M. Rush (eds), *Care and Social Change in Ireland's Welfare Economy.* Dublin: UCD Press, 46–65.

Whitaker, T. K. 1958. *Economic Development.* Dublin: Stationery Office.

7

Continuity and adaptation in local government
Mark Callanan

The story of Irish local government is a mixture of continuity and adaptation, as well as proposed reforms which lie in the 'waiting room' – some of which may never see the light of day and others which could perhaps be resuscitated at some future point. This chapter will discuss a number of themes in local government related to the three areas of statehood: definition, representation and participation. For example, the themes of continuity and adaptation, as outlined in Chapter 1, relate closely to issues of identity and community at local level, local representative democracy and political structures, and creating avenues for participation in local decision-making.

The fundamental features of the traditional system remain largely intact, and, while reforms have been introduced, the fundamentals have been recycled through this process of change. Therefore the chapter argues that, while a number of profound changes have taken place in recent years within Irish local government, including managerial reforms and the establishment of new participative structures, far-reaching reforms have also been proposed which have not been implemented. These include provisions to introduce directly elected mayors, while revisions of local government boundaries which directly challenge deeply-rooted territorial identities have never been seriously considered. The general powers and finance-raising abilities of local government, as well as the relationship between central and local government, have also been characterised by a remarkable continuity, albeit one punctuated by occasional and largely ad hoc adaptation.

The rationale for any system of local government is the premise that local communities should, through democratic structures, have the right to make decisions based upon their own priorities and needs. Local government is therefore the 'government of difference', acknowledging the largely uncontested fact that, for example, the needs and therefore the priorities of highly urbanised areas, like Dublin city, are likely to be different from those of a sparsely populated rural county. To a large extent, the existence of local government structures allows for (at least some) decisions and services to be adapted to the particular local circumstances that exist in different areas through directly elected fora. However, the way in which this is done in Ireland, and some of the institutional norms and limitations on the ability of local authorities to fulfil this mandate, have been remarkably persistent since the foundation of the state.

The first section of this chapter examines the question of territory and local government boundaries, as well as the issue of internal structures within local authorities. Developments in traditional representative structures, local electoral turnout and more contemporary participative experiments are explored in the second section. The third and fourth sections look at the related issues of the powers of local government and the ability of elected local authorities to raise finances to pay for local services and activities. Lastly, the critical relationship between central and local government is discussed. Each of these issues is assessed from an historical perspective which enables the illustration of particular areas of continuity, adaptation and recycling.

Rigid boundaries, altered internal structures

Over a century of local territorial affinity and stability

Local government in Ireland predates the existence of the central state. In fact the counties, as administrative units, originally emerged over an extended period during the middle ages (Haslam 2003: 14; Daly 2001: 2–3). The establishment of the present structure of elected councils is based on the Local Government (Ireland) Act 1898. This legislation, adopted by the Westminster Parliament before independence, provided for the establishment of county councils and maintenance of the city and town system, which had undergone reforms earlier under the Municipal Reform Act of 1840.

The present-day system of local government in Ireland consists of a number of different structures. These include county, city, town and borough councils.[1] There are five city councils and twenty-nine county councils in Ireland. Both have a similar range of functions. The county councils and city councils are designated in law as the primary units of local government in Ireland, and together they cover the entire territory of the state. Then there are seventy-five town councils and five borough councils. Some of the town councils and all the borough councils have similar functions to those of the county and city councils but increasingly, given their size, are tending to devolve their main functions up to the county councils.

These territorial structures have proved remarkably resilient to change. The only system-wide restructuring that has occurred was the decision, by the newly independent state in 1925, to abolish rural district councils – a sub-county structure originally established through the 1898 Act. The only significant change to the *county* borders came through the Local Government (Dublin) Act (1993), whereby the old Dublin County Council was replaced by three new administrative counties, namely Dún Laoghaire-Rathdown, Fingal and South Dublin. The iron rigidity of Irish county and city structures is unusual in comparative terms, given that the territorial boundaries of local government have in most countries been subject to a system-wide revision or overhaul at least once in contemporary times. In Scotland, for example, local government boundaries have been revised on no less than four different occasions since the late nineteenth century, in 1889, 1929, 1975 and 1996 (Wilson and Game 2002: 52–9, 70–3). The 1971 White Paper on Local Government Reorganisation typifies the reluctance of successive Irish governments to revise local government structures. It rejected the concept of breaking up the counties into European-style municipalities based on town and hinterland, arguing that, despite its imperfections, the county structure was 'powerfully supported by local sentiment and tradition', and that it should remain 'the basic unit of local government' (Government of Ireland 1971: 24–5). Similarly, while the 1991 Barrington Report proposed new sub-national structures at both regional and sub-county levels, it equally argued that, in deference to territorial loyalties, the county was central to the basic local government framework and should remain responsible for key local government services, as well as for a number of services that could be devolved to local government (Barrington Report 1991: 29).

As the 1971 White Paper intimates, the most common reason

given for leaving local government structures untouched is the general affiliation most Irish citizens have with county structures and symbols (such as the county colours), not least due to the popularity of Gaelic games. This factor, which relates to the concept of the definition of political communities presented in Chapter 1, must in part account for the strong loyalty to the county structure, which local government units in other countries cannot rival. This situation is also reflected in the difficulties encountered in getting agreement on individual requests for boundary changes that challenge county allegiances – even when in practice towns and cities have expanded beyond their nominal boundary. Much as these proposals may have a rationale in terms of reflecting the reality of modern-day growth in urban areas, local opposition tends to emerge quickly in response to proposals for boundary extensions. Examples include unsuccessful proposals for Limerick city to expand into County Clare, Waterford city into County Kilkenny, and Carlow town into County Laois. In addition to the strength and popularity of Gaelic games, Daly (2001) argues that the fact that an increasing number of political and social groups and associations (and indeed some paramilitary movements) in Ireland during the nineteenth and early twentieth century began to organise along county lines helped to embed the county as the primary sub-national unit.

In comparative terms, however, the county and city structures are rather large units of local government, covering relatively large populations. Local authorities in virtually all European countries and in the United States have a much lower population base than is the case in Ireland. In fact, with the exception of Britain, Ireland has the fewest local authorities per capita in Europe (John 2001: 35). The size of the Irish county and city councils, and the large areas and populations they have to cover, have sparked a process of adaptation through 'internal devolution' in a number of areas, where citizens can avail themselves of services on a more localised basis, rather than having to travel sometimes long distances to the main county town (Callanan 2003: 488). Amongst those spearheading this approach have been Donegal and Meath County Councils, as well as Dublin City Council. Part of the motivation behind this action has been to make services more accessible to citizens, but the move itself is also a tacit recognition of the large size of the traditional county structure.

Adaptation of internal structures

However, there is a contrast between the reluctance in Ireland to tamper with the territorial boundaries and structures of local authorities, and a willingness to make changes to the internal operating structure of local government. A particularly notable development in this area was the establishment of the system of county/city management within Irish local government. This essentially involved the grafting of an American approach towards local executive management, albeit adapted to Irish circumstances, onto what had been until then an overwhelmingly British-influenced model of local government.

Appointments to the position of county/city manager are based on a contract for seven years, with recruitment carried out on a non-political basis through a central independent agency. The manager is an employee of the local authority, acts as head of its administration and advises elected members on policy matters. There is a formal separation of powers within Irish local government law between what is the responsibility of the elected council to determine and what decisions are the responsibility of the manager. National legislation clearly defines the functions of elected members, known as *reserved functions* – these must be decided through a decision of the majority within the elected council. Any other responsibility of a local authority is automatically deemed to be an *executive function* – that is, the responsibility of the county/city manager (or indeed his/her nominees within the local authority's staff).

Essentially, the intention was to delineate clearly the responsibilities of elected members in determining the 'policy framework' for the local authority. The county/city manager must operate within this policy framework set down by the elected representatives, through taking decisions on executive functions. Informally, and in addition to the formal executive powers referred to above, the Irish county/city manager is widely regarded as the main source of policy initiation in local government (Chubb 1992: 278; Collins and Quinlivan 2005: 390–1). The manager is also responsible for providing advice to the council, and the manager as such has a right to attend all meetings (although not also to vote). Thus there has been considerable blurring in the legal distinction between executive and reserved functions, and, in most aspects of a local authority's work, conflict over policy issues tends to be minimal.

This management system has also remained largely intact since it was established across the country in 1940. While some changes have been introduced (such as supervisory powers for elected members and fixed-term contracts for managers) at different intervals, the basic features of the system are now largely accepted.

The means and methods of local-service delivery have also evolved and adapted to new situations, particularly in recent years. One element of this change has involved local authorities stepping back from direct service provision in certain areas. This has happened in a number of ways: either through licensing private companies to provide services previously run by local authorities; or through contracting out service provision to private contractors for a specific task or time period more frequently than in the past; or in some cases through local authorities increasingly working alongside both private and voluntary sector providers to deliver services.

Along with other parts of the public service, in those areas where local government retains responsibility for direct service provision it has borrowed many techniques and mechanisms from the private sector, with a view to ensuring greater efficiencies and effectiveness. Thus a greater emphasis is placed within local government on service users (increasingly termed 'customers'), better quality and more accessible services, innovative use of information technology, modernised human resource practices, improved financial management systems and more emphasis on value-for-money, as well as strategic planning and the use of quantitative indicators to monitor performance. Many of these reforms were heralded in the 1996 White Paper, *Better Local Government* and implemented in the following years. Early assessments of these changes have largely been positive, and seen them as worthwhile (Boyle et al. 2003: 144) and the new approaches to service delivery echo many similar 'New Public Management' (NPM) initiatives introduced by local authorities in many other countries.

Representation and participative structures at local level

Local elections and local representative structures

Elections are held to county, city, borough and town councils every five years. Voter turnout for local elections has been marked by a relatively consistent decline until 2004 (see Table 7.1). While the increase in turnout in 2004 was a positive development, the unusual circumstances of this vote – namely the fact that the local elections occurred on the same day as elections to the European Parliament and a constitutional referendum – suggest that it would be unwise to speculate on whether this marks a reversal of the underlying trend.

Year	Voter turnout
1967	69.0%
1974	61.1%
1979	63.6%
1985	58.2%
1991	55.1%
1999	50.3%
2004	58.6%*

Table 7.1 Turnout in elections to county and city councils, 1967–2004.

Source: Coakley and Gallagher (2005: 469)
*2004 figure from the Department of the Environment, Heritage and Local Government.

Political power at local level is exercised on a collegiate basis through the elected council, through decisions on reserved functions (see above) and through the representational role of elected members. Political parties at local level play a minor role in local government policy-making, and parties in local councils do not tend to organise themselves into alternative policy groups in the context of day-to-day decisions to be taken by elected members. Rather, political control of councils is primarily used for determining issues such as the election of the mayor, or nominations of members onto committees and other bodies (Kenny 2003: 105–16; Collins 1987: 82, 108). One former local politician admits that 'party political differences presented themselves much less often than the public might think' (Gallagher 2001: 90).

The fact that county/city managers are full-time professionals gives them some advantages over part-time politicians, who spend much of their time doing 'constituency work'. Elected members find it difficult to devote sufficient time to policy matters, partly because the PR-STV electoral system encourages competition between

individual politicians (often within the same party) and partly due to
a clientelist political culture, which regards it as the responsibility of
the elected representatives to mediate between the public and public
authorities in order to access public services.[2] This is a facet of Irish
local government already recognised by central government
(Department of the Environment [DoE] 1996: 8, 18), which has
sought to encourage elected members into playing a greater role in
the development of local government policy. Yet recent research,
based on a survey of elected members in Ireland, has concluded that
despite recent reforms, the view of elected members as largely
passive actors in policy-making remains an accurate one (O'Keeffe
2004: 89–90).

Strengthening local political leadership?

The mayor/chairperson of the local council plays a largely
ceremonial role, having none of the executive responsibilities that
may be found in other European systems of local government. In
addition, the fact that the mayor is elected annually by local
authority members has traditionally meant that the position is
rotated amongst different parties and an individual is rarely in office
for more than twelve months. Thus far, the trend of establishing
stronger political executive structures in other countries (either
through strong mayoral positions or through 'cabinet-style'
structures) has not had a major impact in Ireland, although the idea
of directly elected mayors was toyed with in the Local Government
Act (2001).[3]

One possible route towards strengthening political power within
local government, aside from directly elected mayors, lies in a new
structure established in each county and city council during 1998–99
called the Corporate Policy Group (CPG). Each CPG consists of the
mayor of the council, plus the chair of each policy committee of the
council. It certainly could be argued that this represents a move
towards a 'cabinet-style' formation within local government
structures, something that has emerged in some countries as an
alternative to directly-elected mayors as a means of strengthening
local political leadership and executive powers (see John 2001).
While it could not be said that the CPG is currently playing this role
in the Irish context, the structure may possibly evolve into a stronger
political executive in the future.

New participative structures

Local governments in various countries have been experimenting with different ways of listening to what local communities want and allowing local people to participate in local affairs beyond the ballot box. For example, there has been an increased emphasis on the importance of local authorities consulting local people on local issues more regularly – through conducting surveys, setting up focus groups and holding public meetings (Local Government Customer Service Group 2005: 8–10). A new trend, influential in recent years, has been the desire to create new and more innovative channels for local groups to influence, as well as participate in, decision-making at local government level.[4] New structures such as strategic policy committees, community and voluntary fora, and county/city development boards have emerged to create new opportunities for local groups and citizens to make their voices heard.

During the years 1998–99, the committee arrangements of county and city councils were restructured, and a new structure of 'strategic policy committees' (SPCs) was put in place. This new arrangement involved the preparation of policy decisions by these new committees, which contain both elected council members and representatives of local interest groups (Callanan 2005a). The committees make policy recommendations to the full council, which still has the final say on policy matters. Two thirds of the membership of each of these policy committees are comprised of elected members, with the remaining one-third consisting of 'sectoral interests' – a grouping made up of representatives of social partners, community and voluntary groups and other relevant interests at local level, for instance business, agriculture and environmental interests. The SPC structure was partly designed to replicate, at local level, the social partnership process that had been in existence at national level since 1987, through the establishment of structures designed to involve specified interests in local policy-making.

Another participative structure recently established at local level in Ireland has been that of the county and city development boards (CDBs). The CDBs are, to a large extent, a reaction to the fragmentation of service delivery at local level, and an attempt to ensure better coordination in addressing local problems by different state and non-state actors, through ensuring that there were agreed priorities for the locality, coordinated service delivery, and clarity on roles and responsibilities. Local government is given a key facilitation role in the process. Representation on the boards is given to local government, local development bodies, state and national public bodies operating locally (such as the police force, health agencies, bodies responsible for economic development) and the social partners and community and voluntary sector (see Keyes 2003).

One of the key differences between the SPCs and the CDBs (apart from their differing composition) is that the former are focused on the functions and responsibilities of the local authority. Their mandate is to make recommendations on policy to the elected council with regard to local government functions. By contrast, the CDB has a much broader mandate: it must provide a ten-year strategy as a template for *all* public bodies operating within a county or city area, including the local authority. The local authority must approve the strategy, but the strategy will also affect the operation of health services, tourism, education, policing, vocational training, industrial development and local development in the area. Each strategy sets a goal for where a particular county or city wants to be in ten years time, and identifies the contribution of each public-service provider towards achieving that goal. However, the recycling theme again emerges, as the CDB structure does not challenge directly the continued operation of a multitude of public bodies operating at local level. These are left intact, and, instead, the CDB arrangements seek to provide a forum for coordination of service delivery at local level.

Needless to say, these structures also provide opportunities for stakeholders to influence local decision-making: they constitute a further example of attempts to institutionalise structures which are participative in local decision-making. While problems and diffi-culties with some of these different participative structures remain (see Callanan 2005a), there is a general view that the latter 'have led to a better understanding and trust between local government and other stakeholders in the local community' (IPA 2004: 42).

Functional continuity and adaptation

Local government in Ireland is responsible for the delivery of a number of essential services and functions. Notwithstanding the importance of these services, in comparative terms Irish local government is generally considered to possess a narrow range of functions (see for example Collins and Quinlivan 2005: 389). Local authorities in most other EU countries provide at least some services which in Ireland are supplied either by central government departments or by state agencies operating within state determined policy parameters. This is most notable in the areas of social service provision, education and healthcare (Callanan 2004: 67). Irish local government has traditionally been focused on what might be described as 'engineering functions', which contribute to the development of society in an important but limited range of areas such as social housing, transportation, and environmental services. In contrast, local authorities in other countries tend to have a much broader socio-economic remit.

A succession of different reports has made the case for a wider range of local government functions. The Barrington Report (1991) proposed that local authorities be given an expanded and substantive role in health, policing, education, social welfare, tourism, heritage, and local development. On foot of these recommendations, a Devolution Commission was established by Government in 1995 to examine which functions could be devolved to local authorities. The Commission argued that there was a number of areas that were candidates for a stronger local government remit, including tourism, economic development, social welfare and employment, education, heritage, consumer protection, health, agriculture and policing (Devolution Commission 1996: 27–8).[5]

These proposals have been largely ignored. Instead, there has been a steady dilution in local government responsibilities through a series of different decisions taken at different intervals, whereby more and more responsibilities were assigned to agencies at national, regional or local level. For example, local authorities had been responsible for healthcare until the establishment of regional health boards in 1970. Many areas that were the responsibility of local government have been given to national agencies such as the Environmental Protection Agency and National Roads Authority, whereas services that could have been assigned to local government were instead given to newly established local development agencies independent of local government, such as Leader groups, local area partnerships, and county/ city enterprise boards.

Until 1991, local authorities were constrained by the principle of *ultra vires*: this dictated that local authorities could only carry out activities that related to specific responsibilities, conferred on them by law. If an activity did not relate to one of these statutory responsibilities, local authorities would be acting 'beyond their powers'.

This effectively put a constraint on the ability of local government to respond to local wishes and needs in areas outside of their formal legal powers. In 1991, however, local authorities were given a 'general competence'. According to the current legislation on the general competence of local government, local authorities may undertake any activity they consider necessary 'to promote the interests of the local community', which may include either directly or indirectly 'social inclusion or the social, economic, environmental, recreational, cultural, community or general development of the administrative area (or any part of it) of the local authority concerned or of the local community' (Local Government Act 2001, Section 66).

One can of course argue that the freedom and discretion implied by the general competence is purely hypothetical if local authorities lack the staff or financial resources necessary to respond to local demands or to strike out in new directions – thus to a large extent the general competence could be seen as having primarily symbolic rather than practical value (see Blair 1991: 51). On the other hand, regardless of some of these restrictions, several local authorities in Ireland have demonstrated their willingness to move beyond their statutory remit, and have quietly taken on an enhanced role in new areas such as social inclusion, heritage and conservation, childcare, environmental awareness, and the provision of broadband infrastructure in rural areas (Larkin 2004: 15; Callanan 2005b: 589).

That said however, it must be acknowledged that, despite the suggestions made in many reports, there has of yet been no structured programme of devolution from central to local government in Ireland – in fact devolution of functions to local authorities has been a notable omission from the local government reform programme launched in the late 1990s.

Financial powers: Many proposals, few changes

The current sources of local government financing derive from: the Local Government Fund (a general-purpose fund from central government); central government grants earmarked for specific purposes (in particular the delivery of state services through local government – for instance national roads, higher education grants); charges levied by local authorities for services; and rates levied on commercial properties.

A decisive moment in local government history was the decision by central government in 1978 to abolish rates on domestic properties. Rates on agricultural land were subsequently removed by a judicial decision in 1982. Despite the popularity of the move to abolish domestic rates, the loss of this source of revenue for local authorities was to have major and long-lasting consequences for local government. The income that would have arisen from domestic rates was to be fully compensated by central government' grant, but successive governments failed to carry through this commitment – particularly during cutbacks in government expenditure during the 1980s.

The abolition of rates on domestic property and agricultural land, coupled with the tendency to cap increases in commercial rates, and the decision in 1997 to abolish domestic water charges, have all served to limit local authority discretion in raising revenue and have increased the local government's dependence on central government for finances. The combined effect of these decisions, added to new obligations on local authorities, has produced the result that local government in Ireland has little in the way of discretionary revenue by comparison with local authorities elsewhere in the European Union.

Over more than forty years, a steady stream of reports has been published highlighting the need for reform in the system of local government financing. These reports have effectively recycled long-standing arguments and proposals for widening the revenue base of local authorities (see Dollard 2003 for details). Most of these studies have argued that the introduction of some form of local property tax in Ireland would be one possible method of financing local authorities, while others have recommended the idea of a local income tax used in some countries. The response from central government to these reform proposals has also been relatively consistent: despite the plethora of analyses, little in the way of meaningful reform has been forthcoming. This was reflected on in the latest of these reports, published in 2006 (Indecon 2005: 133, 193–4). This report projected a major shortfall in the estimated revenue available to local authorities in future years – revenue which would be needed if existing levels of service provision are to be maintained and if emerging expenditure requirements demanded by future national and EU legislation are to be met. The same analysis concluded that 'there is an understandable and widespread frustration among local authorities in relation to the absence of reforms in funding local government systems, despite the unanimous call for reforms in all major previous reviews' (p. 210).

There is a view in political circles that, despite the fact that some form of tax on property exists in virtually every other country in Europe and in the United States, and that this has been proposed by nearly all the recent studies on Irish local government finance, there is a deep-seated public antipathy in Ireland towards any notion of property tax or of a return to rates on domestic properties. The experience of governments introducing and then abolishing both residential property tax and the short-lived farm tax seems to have made politicians reluctant even to contemplate modest proposals on this issue (Callanan 2003: 483). Even the compromise solution proposed by the most recent report[6] was immediately rejected by government in 2006. De Buitléir (2001: 149–50) argues that the political problems associated with reintroducing rates or a local property tax are insurmountable, no matter how good the arguments look on paper.

Central supervision and limits on local discretion

Central and local government share the status of being directly elected by the electorate at large. In fact, aside from the *Dáil* and the Presidency, local authorities are the only other entities in the state that can claim this direct electoral legitimacy. Yet this has not traditionally involved any sense of equality in the relationship between these two elected levels of government – far from it. Of course, local authorities in other countries are also clearly subject to national legislation and, in that sense, subordinate to central government. Nevertheless, the extent of the power imbalance in the central–local relationship is more pronounced in Ireland than elsewhere.

The foundation of the state was a critical juncture for Irish local government, and the approach adopted then was to set the tone for central–local relations thereafter. Due to a combination of historical factors prevalent at the time, semi-ideological factors, and concerns over professionalism and equity, from the beginning of the independent state, central government concerned itself with detailed supervision and control over local government activities (see Garvin 2001; Collins and Quinlivan 2005). Reforms imposed by the centre following independence were designed in part to address identifiable and particular problems in what was admittedly a turbulent period, and in part to ensure central control and compliance by subservient local authorities – the most graphic illustration of the latter was the power of central government introduced in 1923 to effectively overturn the results of local elections and to remove councils from office. The elected members of a number of local authorities were simply removed from office by central government during the 1923–4 period and replaced by an appointed commissioner. Such centripetal traditions remain alive and well to this day. The power of central government to remove elected councillors remains in law, and, although it has not been called into effect since 1985 this power is threatened on individual recalcitrant local authorities on a regular basis, and is seen as an effective method of ensuring compliance (Callanan 2002: 247–9).

The range of central government controls over local authorities is by now well established as part of Ireland's administrative tradition. These controls were succinctly described in 1992 by a then backbench TD, and later to become the Minister responsible for local government (Roche 1992: 22–5), as including:

- the many statutory instruments, regulations or orders drawn up by central government to detail the precise intention of the law, which 'are so tightly drawn that, with their explanatory memorandum, they severely limit any chance of local inventiveness arising at the implementation stage';
- subtle forms of control such as 'the notes, comments and explanations of legislation and regulation which flow continuously from central government to local government';
- the need to secure sanctions and prior approvals from central government for many activities (for example before preparing tenders, going to tender and accepting tenders);
- technical inspectors;
- enquiries which can be set up by Ministers;
- financial controls and audit;
- cash limits, budgetary restrictions and the ability of central government to 'cap' increases in rates.

The conclusion of this summary was that 'local government is in effect controlled to a virtual standstill' (Roche 1992: 25).

Detailed regulation and supervision of local government activities is commonplace.[7] Thus Acts of the Oireachtas are often supplemented by more detailed statutory instruments, ministerial regulations, circular letters, 'guidelines' and other material. Usually these will extend to setting out the details of implementation in a prescriptive manner (Callanan 2003: 480–1). As Barrington notes (1991: 147–8) administrative supervision of local authorities takes the form of detailed regulation, rather than framework legislation. The problem of excessive central control has been recognised by central government, including in the most recent White Paper on local government reform (DoE 1996: 7; see also Government of Ireland 1971: 53) but little has been done to tackle the issue in any comprehensive way. In many areas local authorities are presented with detailed instructions regarding implementation, which results in the lack of a 'policy space' to adapt national legislation and policy to suit local circumstances: (IPA 2004: 24–5).

Thus central–local relations range from the paternalistic to the authoritarian. The verdict of one former county manager is that there is an absence of any real philosophy or recognition regarding central–local relations in Ireland, which results in a pragmatic approach towards communication and interaction. The relationship between local authorities and central government 'has evolved as one of principal and agent rather than partnership' (Haslam 2001: 103). This contrasts with traditions in many other European countries, where there is an increasing realisation that, as society becomes more and more complex and diverse, central government becomes poorly equipped to meet many of today's contemporary challenges. These often do not fit neatly into sectoral boundaries but rather consist in area-based or cross-cutting issues and therefore require a concerted effort to tackle multiple problems (Hesse and Sharpe 1991: 611–12; Stewart 1995: 250–1; Jones and Stewart 1997: 23).

Inter-governmental relations in Ireland continue to exist within a centralised paternalistic environment, despite the obvious interdependencies between central and local government. Even from a pragmatic viewpoint, given local government's responsibility for implementation of legislation in a range of areas from social housing to waste management, it is surprising that central government does not regularly tap into this source of expertise and information before new legislation and initiatives are embarked upon. Clearly the top-down tradition where local authorities are regarded as subservient agencies is outmoded and out of line with principles of good govern-ance, which attach value to the expertise of those implementing legislation in the process of policy review and formulation. Forde (2004: 63) states that 'there is no consistent or regular system of consultation between the central and local levels of government in Ireland', while commenting that 'the low degree of consultation appears paradoxical, given that local government is charged with implementing national and EU legislation'. Where consultation between central and local levels does take place, it tends to be ad hoc and informal, for example through written letters or the setting up of temporary working groups.

Political adaptation in local government

As a system of elected government older than the Irish state itself, local government provides particularly intriguing insights into the concept of 'path dependency' and into debates over the question of whether institutional arrangements act to constrain the behaviour and decisions of political and societal actors. Without doubt, there have been important reforms in local government and in the local state in Ireland, but this has occurred within certain non-negotiable frameworks. For example, there has been virtually no change to the boundaries of local authorities, in deference to the traditionally strong feeling of togetherness at county level. Central–local relations have been, and continue to be, underpinned by a widespread culture of mutual distrust, which results in central controls and supervision and in limited discretion at local level. Changes to functional or financial responsibilities have been ad hoc, and limited to relatively minor areas, which do not fundamentally challenge institutional assumptions such as central government control of key public services, or the perceived undesirability of local taxation. Underpinning all of this is the remarkable resilience of beliefs, norms, traditions, conventions and formal and informal procedures within the Irish polity on local government issues.

In many respects, the adaptations and changes that have been introduced in Irish local government mirror those introduced in many other countries, both in Europe and further afield, pointing to international as well as domestic influences (see John 2001 and Denters and Rose 2005). However, while some of the influences have been transnational phenomena, the precise approach used is often mediated through a domestic lens. For example, one challenge faced by representative democracies is to close the gap between the representatives and the represented (see Chapter 1). A key mechanism (though not the only one) to give effect to this objective at local level in Ireland are the SPCs, which were heavily influenced by the domestic approach towards social partnership at national level.

Steyvers et al. (2005:26) observe that New Public Management-style managerial reforms with a strong emphasis on producing greater efficiencies, complemented by the establishment of partici-patory mechanisms, have been introduced in many continental European, Nordic and Anglo-Saxon countries. However, they also believe that countries with a traditional separation between political and administrative responsibilities at local level (such as Ireland) are more open to managerial reforms and less open towards strength-ening local political leadership through initiatives such as directly elected mayors. This illustrates that, despite the importance of international trends, national foundations and traditions within different local government systems continue to shape the precise form and extent of change (see also Pilet et al. 2005: 635–6).

Some fundamental reforms have been introduced to Irish local government, reflecting the changed environment in which local government operates. These include new participative structures that complement traditional representative democracy. Major changes have also been introduced to the internal operation of local authorities, including new management structures and procedures – those introduced in recent years have taken on a distinctly 'New Public Management' flavour. Despite the importance of these reforms, however, the basic elements of the 'local state' have been recycled, or in some cases have been left untouched entirely. There has been no major restructuring of local government boundaries, no significant progress in devolving functions to local authorities, and little in the way of substantive reform of local fund-raising powers. It looks as though future change is likely to develop within the confines of these basic features of the 'local state'.

NOTES

1   Changes of title introduced in 2002 (for example county boroughs became city councils) were nominal only – they did not imply any change in boundaries or in responsibilities. For the sake of consistency, this chapter uses the contemporary local-authority titles.

2   As one councillor has put it, 'if somebody comes to me with a medical card and they're under the limit, I send it down to the Health Board and they send it back to me and I hand it into their hand...we spend too much time you know doing work for people that they're entitled to anyway, glorified messenger boys' (quoted in Carey 1986: 309).

3   MacCarthaigh and Callanan (forthcoming) note that, while the initiative concerning directly-elected mayors was abandoned in 2003, the idea remains popular with a number of political parties, and one cannot discount the possibility that the plan will see some sort of revival. By the same token, it is clear that even within those political parties

formally supporting the idea, significant opposition remains, and resistance amongst the ranks of national and local politicians may be difficult to overcome.

4   The importance of fostering the involvement of local voluntary associations and economic and social interests in local government can been traced back to earlier proposals (Government of Ireland 1971: 44–6).

5   More recent reports have also remarked on the high degree of centralisation in Ireland, and called for devolution of powers to local government (Harris 2005: 98–104).

6   Namely a local tax on second (or indeed third) houses but leaving principal private residences exempt from tax (Indecon, 2005, pp. 185–6 and 200–1).

7   Of course it should be noted that a host of other accountability mechanisms that apply to state bodies generally, from the Ombudsman's office and independent audit and financial control to provisions on freedom of information and ethics in public office, also apply to local government.

REFERENCES

Barrington, T. J. 1991. 'The crisis of Irish local government', in J. J. Hesse (ed.) *Local Government and Urban Affairs in International Perspective*. Baden Baden: Nomos Verlagsgesellschaft, 141–66.

Barrington Report. 1991. *Local Government Reorganisation and Reform – Report of the Advisory Expert Committee*. Dublin: Stationery Office.

Blair, P. 1991. 'Trends in local autonomy and democracy: reflections from a European perspective', in R. Batley and G. Stoker (eds), *Local Government in Europe: Trends and Developments*. Basingstoke: Macmillan, 41–57.

Boyle, R., P. Humphreys, C, O'Donnell, O. O'Riordan, J. and V. Timonen, 2003. *Changing Local Government: A Review of the Local Government Modernisation Programme*. CPMR Research Report No. 5. Dublin: Institute of Public Administration.

Callanan, M. 2002. *Local Government Act 2001*. Dublin: Thompson Round Hall Press.

Callanan, M. 2003. 'Where stands local government?', in M. Callanan and J. F. Keogan (eds), 475–501.

Callanan, M. 2004. 'Local and regional government in transition', in N. Collins and T. Cradden (eds), *Political Issues in Ireland Today*. Manchester: Manchester University Press, 3rd edn, 56–78.

Callanan, M. 2005a. 'Institutionalizing participation and governance? New participative structures in local government in Ireland'. *Public Administration* 83 (4), 909–29.

Callanan, M. 2005b. 'Motives for measuring local government services: Own initiative or top down?', in H. Reynaert, K. Steyvers, P. Delwit, and J.-B. Pilet (eds), *Revolution or Renovation? Reforming Local Politics in Europe*. Brugge: Vanden Broele Publishers, 585–614.

Callanan, M. and J. F. Keogan (eds). 3003. *Local Government in Ireland: Inside Out*. Dublin: Institute of Public Administration.

Carey, S. 1986.'Role perceptions among county councillors' in *Administration* 34 (3), 302–16.

Chubb, Basil. 1992. *The Government and Politics of Ireland*, London: Longman.

Coakley, J. and M. Gallagher (eds). 2005. *Politics in the Republic of Ireland*. London: Routledge.

Collins, N. 1987. *Local Government Managers At Work: The City and County Manager System of Local Government in the Republic of Ireland*. Dublin: Institute of Public Administration.

Collins, N. and A. Quinlivan 2005. 'Multi-level governance', in J. Coakley and M. Gallagher (eds) *Politics in the Republic of Ireland*. London: Routledge, 384–403.

Daly, M. E. 2001. 'The county in Irish history', in M. E. Daly (ed.). *County & Town: One*

Hundred Years of Local Government in Ireland, (RTÉ Thomas Davis Lecture Series: Winter 1999). Dublin: Institute of Public Administration, 1–11.

de Buitléir, D. 2001. 'Local government finance in Ireland' in M. E. Daly (ed.), 141–51.

Denters, B. and L. E. Rose. 2005. 'Towards local governance?', in B. Denters and L .E. Rose (eds). *Comparing Local Governance: Trends and Developments*. Basingstoke: Palgrave Macmillan, 246–62.

Department of the Environment (DoE) 1996. *Better Local Government – A Programme for Change*. Dublin: Stationery Office.

Devolution Commission. 1996. *Interim Report*. Dublin: Stationery Office.

Dollard, G. 2003. 'Local government finance: The policy context', in M. Callanan and J. F. Keogan (eds). 325–40.

Forde, C. 2004. 'Local government reform in Ireland 1996–2004: A critical analysis', *Administration* 52 (3), 57–72.

Gallagher, P. 2001. 'The experience of being a councillor', in M. E. Daly (ed.), 88–97.

Garvin, T. 2001. 'The Dáil Government and Irish local democracy 1919–23' in M. E. Daly (ed.), 24–34.

Government of Ireland. 1971. *Local Government Reorganisation – White Paper*. Dublin: Stationery Office.

Harris, C. (ed.) 2005. *The Report of the Democracy Commission – Engaging Citizens: The Case for Democratic Renewal in Ireland*. Dublin: New Island Press.

Haslam, R. 2001. 'The county manager', in M. E. Daly (ed.), 98–108.

Haslam, R. 2003. 'The origins of Irish local government'. in M. Callanan and J. F. Keogan (eds), 14–40.

Hesse, J. J. and L. J. Sharpe. 1991. 'Local government in international perspective: Some comparative observations', in J. J. Hesse (ed.), *Local Government and Urban Affairs*, Baden Baden: Nomos verlagsgesellschaft, 603–21.

Indecon International Economic Consultants in association with the Institute of Local Government Studies at University of Birmingham (2005) *Review of Local Government Financing*. Dublin: Department of the Environment, Heritage and Local Government.

Institute of Public Administration (IPA). 2004. *Review of the Operation of Strategic Policy Committees*. Dublin: Institute of Public Administration.

John, P. 2001. *Local Governance in Western Europe*. London: Sage Publications.

Jones, George and Stewart, John (1997) 'What we are against and What We Are For', in G. Jones (ed.) *The New Local Government Agenda*. Hertfordshire: ICSA Publishing, 1–27.

Kenny, L. 2003. 'Local government and politics', in M. Callanan and J. F. Keogan (eds). *Local Government in Ireland*, 103–22.

Keyes, J. 2003. 'Community and enterprise', in M. Callanan and J. F. Keogan (eds), 285–98.

Larkin, T. 2004. 'Coping with complexity: Implications of the transition from local government to local governance for management styles', *Administration*, Vol. 52, No. 1, 3–18.

Local Government Act. 2001. Dublin: Stationery Office.

Local Government Customer Service Group. 2005. *Customer Consultation: Guidelines for Local Authorities*. Dublin: Department of the Environment, Heritage and Local Government.

MacCarthaigh, M. and M. Callanan (forthcoming). 'The mayoralty in the Republic of Ireland', in J. Garrard (ed.), *Heads of the Local State, Past and Present*. Aldershot: Ashgate, Chapter 5.

O'Keeffe, A. 2004. *Elected Members in Ireland in 2003: A Review of Their Roles* [Unpublished Dissertation Submitted for MSc in Strategic Management and Public Services, Cardiff University].

Pilet, J.-B., K. Steyvers, P. Delwit and H. Reynaert. 2005. 'Conclusion. Assessing local government reforms: Revolution or renovation?', in H. Reynaert, K. Steyvers, P. Delwit, and J.-B. Pilet (eds). *Revolution or Renovation? Reforming Local Politics in Europe*.

Brugge: Vanden Broele Publishers, 615–39.

Roche, D. 1992. 'Irish local government: Controlled to a virtual standstill', in K. Rafter and N. Whelan (eds). *From Malin Head to Mizen Head: The Definitive Guide to Local Government in Ireland*. Dublin: Blackwater Press, 21–5.

Stewart, John (1995) 'A future for Local Authorities as Community Government', in J. Stewart and G. Stoker (eds). *Local Government in the 1990s*. London: Macmillan, 249–267.

Steyvers, K., J.-B. Pilet, H. Reynaert and P. Delwit. 2005. 'Introduction. Local Government in transformation: Momentum for revolution or incremental renovation?', in H. Reynaert et al. (eds), 11–28.

Wilson, D. and C. Game. 2002. *Local Government in the United Kingdom*. Basingstoke: Palgrave Macmillan.

8

Turnout, political support and representation in Ireland

Adrian P. Kavanagh

The introductory section to this book highlights definition, representation and participation as the three dimensions of political adaptation, or of 'recycling' the Irish state, and this chapter will specifically focus on the latter two of these. Its key focus will be on the relationship that exists between political parties and candidates and voter turnout levels in Ireland. The present study takes a unique perspective on this in its use of highly detail marked register turnout data to uncover the manner in which such relationships are framed within specific local contexts.

Low and declining turnouts increasingly became a characteristic of Irish electoral contests from the early 1980s onwards. This has been a particular cause for concern given that high electoral participation rates are important for the proper functioning of Irish democracy (Marsh et al. 2001). At the turn of the millennium, this appeared to have created a situation in which the representative system seemed to be in decline and in which citizen participation is, instead, becoming largely focused on community activity and voluntary organisations, especially in low turnout urban constituencies (Community Workers Co-operative [CWC] 2000). However, the resurgence of participation levels in many atypical low turnout urban areas in the 2004 local, European and Citizenship Referendum elections may point towards the renewed relevance of the representative system in these areas. This has been sparked, in part, by a refocusing of political mobilisation efforts on such low turnout areas, and also by the efforts of non-partisan voluntary organisations such as the Vincentian Partnership for Justice. The situation reflects the arguments of Cassel (1999), Fuchs et al. (2000) and Putnam (2000), who claim that voluntary associations have a role in terms of improving electoral participation levels in providing participants with skills and contexts which encourage them to become habitual voters.

Whether the increased levels of participation evident in the 2004 contests are symptomatic of a reversal in the trend of declining participation level in Irish elections remains to be seen; turnout levels at present are still very much lower than those of the 1960s and 1970s, and there are consequences associated with this state of things as this chapter will argue. As well as appearing to engender a decline in the efficacy of the representative system, low and declining turnouts may lead to distortions in political representation, especially when socio-economic biases exist (Lijphart 1997). In turn, political factors will also influence turnout levels. Changing patterns of political mobilisation, for instance, may help to account for the declining participation rates of the past two decades to some degree, while differential levels of mobilisation across constituencies will shape spatial variations in turnout levels at the sub-constituency level. Therefore this paper will focus on two different, yet related, issues. First, the degree to which partisanship influences, or has influenced turnout variation and turnout decline in Ireland. Secondly, the manner in which socio-economic biases, related to turnout variation, may result in distortions in political representation in Ireland, with subsequent impacts for policy-making. We begin by studying the extent of turnout decline since 1980 and the spatial variations within it.

Turnout in Irish elections: temporal and spatial trends

Electoral turnout in Ireland and in a number of other Western democracies has been in consistent decline over the past two decades. Turnout levels for general elections in the Republic of Ireland reached a post-War peak of 76.9 per cent in 1969, and remained consistently at this level during the 1970s. Turnout, however, declined by 2.4 per cent between the June 1981 and February 1982 elections and the general trend in subsequent decades has been one of declining turnout (Figure 8.1), with turnout in 2002 13.5 per lower than in 1981.

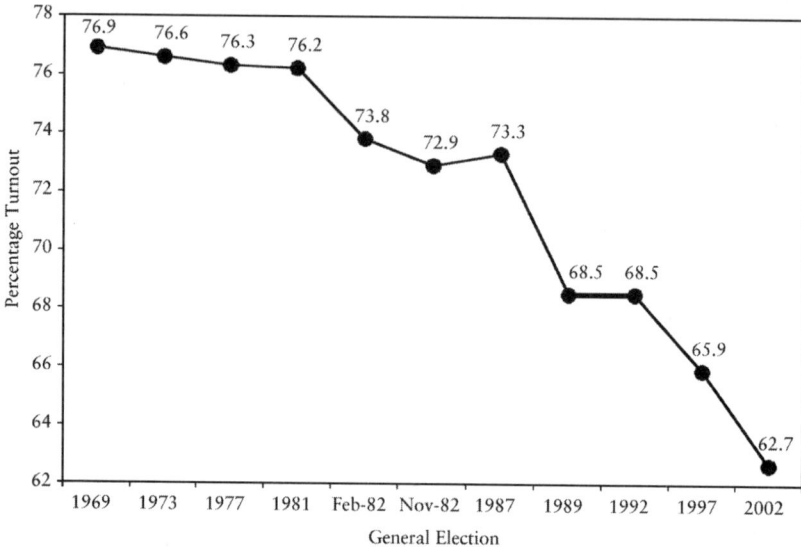

Figure 8.1 Turnout in general elections in Ireland, 1969–2002.

General election turnout declined by 3.2 per cent between 1997 and 2002. The rate of decline was greater within the Greater Dublin region, but turnouts actually increased in Donegal South West, Sligo-Leitrim, Galway West and Kerry North, while other constituencies only experienced a marginal decline (Figure 8.2). With the exceptions of Dublin South West and Dublin Central (largely a result of boundary changes), these constituencies tended to be located mainly in the more rural parts of Ireland. The same constituencies also tended to have the highest actual turnout levels in 2002, whereas the lowest levels were largely associated with constituencies that had experienced the greatest decline between 1997 and 2002; thus the overall trend was to reinforce the strong rural-urban turnout differentials which characterise the geography of turnout in Irish general elections (Kavanagh, Mills and Sinnott 2004).

There have also been significant declines in turnout in European, Presidential and Referendum elections in recent decades (Marsh et al. 2001). In terms of European Community related referenda, the turnout of 34.8 per cent for the Nice Treaty Referendum in 2001 marked a significant decline on previous referenda, contrasting unfavourably with those on accession to the European Economic

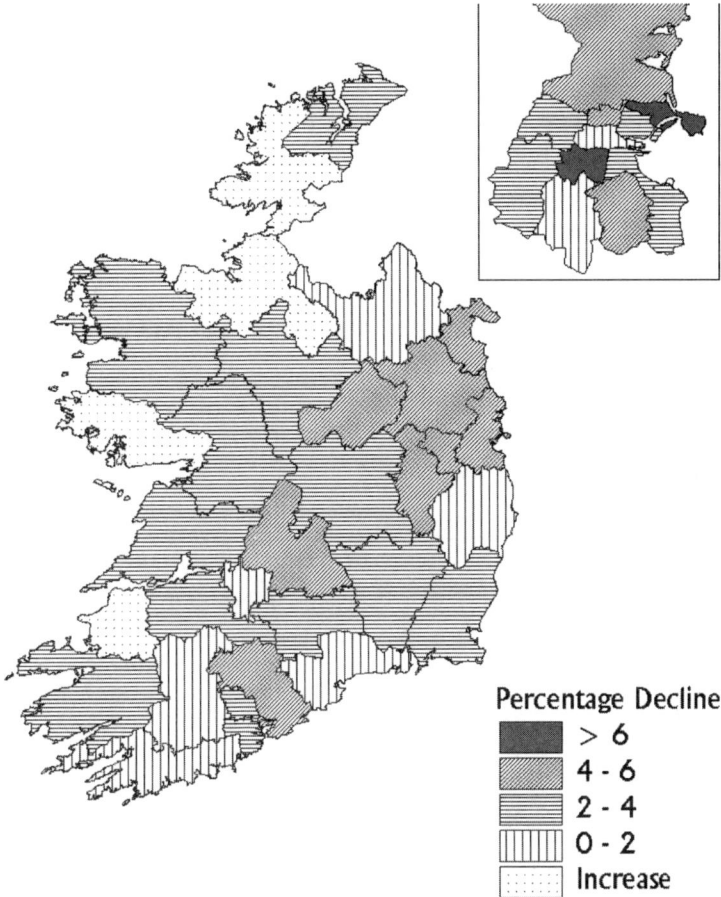

Figure 8.2 *Change in turnout rates by general election constituency, 1997–2002.*

Community in 1972 (70.9 per cent), the Maastricht Treaty in 1992 (57.3 per cent) and the Amsterdam Treaty in 1998 (56.2 per cent). By contrast, there was a significant increase of 14.7 per cent in the turnout rate for the 2002 Nice Treaty Referendum, relative to the 2001 levels, and subsequently there was a strong participation rate in the Citizenship Referendum in 2004, although this high turnout was due in part to the holding of local and European elections on the same day.

An interesting point to note is that the spatial patterns of turnout in referenda contrast starkly with those for general and local elections. Turnouts are usually higher in rural areas for local and general elections, whereas higher than average referendum turnouts are generally associated with urban areas, and particularly middle class urban areas. The correlations in Table 8.1 illustrate a high degree of association between the turnouts for different referenda held between 1995 and 2002, but also a series of weak or statistically inverse associations between turnouts in referenda and general elections. Striking contrasts between spatial patterns of turnout variation and decline for general (and local) elections and those for referenda suggest that different factors may be at play in demobilising electors for different electoral contests. Thus, attempts to arrest Irish turnout decline must have a comprehensive constituency or place-based focus, as concerns about low and declining turnouts may be unique in character in different parts of the country and may be particularly related to specific electoral contests.

	GE 97	RF 02	RF 01	RF 98	RF 96	RF 95
General Election 2002	.92**	−.43**	−.30	−.15	−.23	−.17
General Election 1997		−.31**	−.20	−.01	−.06	−.00
Abortion Referendum 2002			.93**	.747**	.83**	.86**
Nice Referendum 2001				.803**	.86**	.82**
British-Irish Agreement Referendum 1998					.59**	.62*
Bail Referendum 1996						.92**
Divorce Referendum 1995						−

Table 8.1 *Correlations between turnouts in general elections and referenda, 1995–2002.*
*(Note **: p<0.05, *: p<0.01)*

Turnouts in local elections had also experienced a similar decline in the last three decades of the twentieth Century. The 50.2 per cent average turnout rate for the 1999 local elections marked a decline of 5.4 per cent on the 1991 level, and of 19 per cent on that for the 1967 local elections. Particularly high levels of turnout decline between 1991 and 1999 were found in Dublin and the other large urban centres, with especially high levels of decline in Mulhuddart (18.0 per cent), Lucan (16.9 per cent), Ballyfermot (15.6 per cent) and North Inner City (13.9 per cent). There was, however, a significant increase in turnout levels in the 2004 local elections, as noted earlier, with an average rate of 58.6 per cent. Turnouts in urban areas increased significantly with a doubling, or even trebling, in the number of voters turning out in a number of disadvantaged areas in Dublin. There is a number of different reasons put forward for these increased turnout levels, as discussed in Kavanagh (2004); the holding of the contentious Citizenship Referendum on the same day was undoubtedly one of the more significant of these factors, particularly in the more urban areas, where interest levels in referendum elections tend to be highest. Whether the improved participation levels in 2004 represent a reversal in the trend of declining turnouts over the past few decades remains to be seen. The unusually high level of interest in the Citizenship Referendum may have accounted for temporary reversal of this trend. Alternatively, the higher local election turnouts could signify an increased degree of engagement with the Irish representative system, with reinvigorated levels of voter participation rooted in political mobilisation practices that are both old and new and cognisant of local contexts and their issues. This will be addressed in the next section.

Partisan influences on turnout rates

The electoral literature strongly emphasises the extent to which partisan efforts to 'get the vote out' can influence turnout rates. Caldeira et al. (1990) highlight the degree to which electoral participation levels in areas may be heightened by political party organisational efforts, while Taylor and Johnson (1979) and Rallings and Thrasher (1990) register a trend for higher turnouts in areas of high partisan competition. Caldeira et al. (1990:192), however, observe that in some cases parties may prefer to see low turnout in certain areas:

> Aware of their mobilizing potential, party leaders may eschew getting out the vote because they know the electoral realities are such that low turnout will advantage their candidates. Parties can conduct campaigns of obfuscation and confusion, intended to demobilize electorates.

Many political scientists associate declining turnout levels with changes in the nature of political mobilisation, particularly stressing the replacement of door-to-door canvassing by more professional, but detached, campaigning methods, such as TV advertising and leafleting. Rosenstone and Hansen (1993) suggest that a considerable portion of US turnout decline has resulted from a reduction in such face-to-face forms of voter mobilisation, as also noted by Green and Gerber (2001); the latter link this trend to declining levels of party membership. Membership of Irish political parties has declined in recent decades – for instance, Fine Gael membership fell from 33,972 to 23,315 over the 1982–2001 period (Gallagher and Marsh 2002: 57). This has, in turn, led to a decline in levels of party activism and in the number of people available for canvassing duty at election time, leaving parties increasingly reliant on mass advertising campaigns and mail shots to mobilise support. Traditional door-to-door canvassing still remains an important aspect of election campaigns, but limited personnel and resources mean that individual candidates and small parties are unable to reach all electors in their constituencies, especially in condensed campaigning periods; they are forced to focus their canvassing efforts on specific areas and groups and overlook others. Highton and Wolfinger (2001) find strong evidence that non-voters are the least likely to be canvassed during election periods, while low turnout areas tend to be the least canvassed in Irish elections, as will be discussed later (and see also Kavanagh 2002b). Some campaigns may, however, focus more on low turnout areas on the basis either of ideology or localism or, in the case of larger parties, on the basis of a strategic division of the constituency between its different candidates.

Partisan influences on voting are clearest in terms of an analysis of localised influences, as is envisaged in the concept of the 'friends and neighbours' effect, according to which a candidate is seen to poll most strongly in the areas surrounding their home base (or bailiwick). A number of studies, such as (1982) Parker's research on the Galway West constituency, have clearly shown that the 'friends and neighbours' effect strongly influences Irish voting behaviour. In turn, one can envisage a 'friends and neighbours' influence on turnout, as higher turnouts will be expected in areas where a local candidate is running. Figure 8.3 illustrates a strong association between higher turnouts and candidates' homes in County Laois in the 1999 local elections, with the exception of the urban areas of Portlaoise, Griaguecullen and Portarlington. As partisan competition in rural areas, such as Laois, is often characterised by the presence both of a local Fianna Fáil and of a Fine Gael candidate, two or more 'friends and neighbours effects' may often be at play, which results in exceptionally high turnout levels in some rural areas.

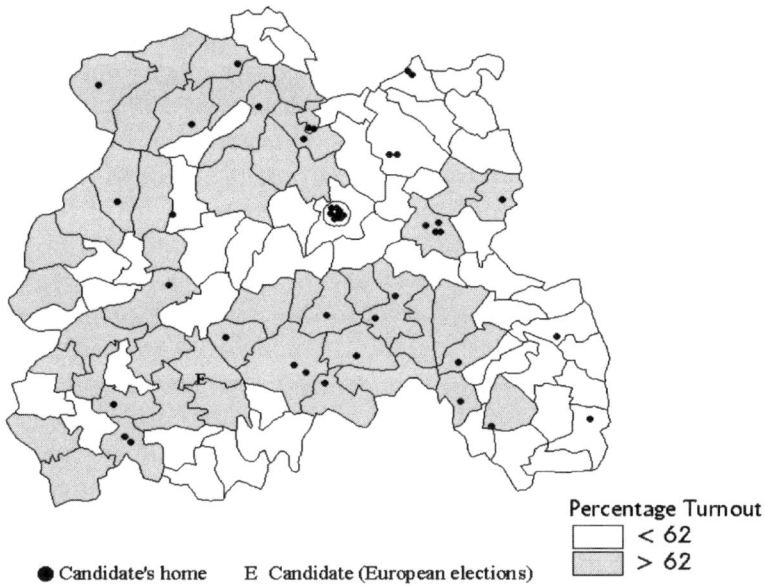

Figure 8.3 *Voter turnout in Co. Laois in 1999 local elections, as related to candidates' homes.*

This 'friends and neighbours' effect on turnout also impacts upon urban constituencies, as in the case of the Clondalkin constituency in the 1999 local elections – even though this constituency had the lowest turnout in these elections (27.9 per cent) at national level. In the home bases of the successful candidates, turnouts were signicantly higher than the constituency average, as illustrated by Table 8.2.

Candidate	Home Area	Turnout %
Therese Ridge	St. Patrick's Avenue	41.7
John Curran	Knockmeenagh Road	44.1
Colm Tyndall	Floraville Avenue	53.3
Colm McGrath	Moyle Park	68.6
Robert Dowds	Castle Park	49.2

Table 8.2 *Turnouts for 1999 local elections in the Clondalkin constituency in home areas of successful candidates.*

The North Clondalkin area within this constituency had one of the lowest turnout levels in the state in 1999, along with Cherry Orchard and Dublin Inner City. As well as the high levels of social deprivation in the area, the very low turnout in 1999 (and in the subsequent 2002 General Election) reflected the low levels of political mobilisation and the lack of strong locally based candidates – a tendency also noted for the South West Inner City of Dublin in 2002. In the 2004 local elections, however, turnout levels in North Clondalkin increased dramatically, largely due to a stronger mobilisation effort in the area and to the contesting of the election by a number of candidates from it. These included Shane O'Connor of Sinn Féin, who succeeded in winning a seat, and Gino Kenny of the Socialist Workers Party. Turnouts increased in a number of estates on account of the stronger mobilisation efforts and local candidate effects. By comparison with the 1999 levels, the numbers turning out to the polls increased by 153 per cent in St Ronan's estate (Kenny's home base), and 110 per cent in Cherrywood Park (O'Connor's home base). In all, while just 3,490 people from North Clondalkin turned out to vote in 1999 (in an average turnout of 23.6 per cent), this number increased to 7,880 in 2004 (average turnout of 45.8 per cent), representing a 125 per cent increase in the numbers turning out to vote. Indeed 1,030 more people in North Clondalkin voted in 2004 than in the 2002 General Election (which had an average turnout of 41.2 per cent).

Similar evidence exists of 'friends and neighbours' influences on participation levels in the low turnout inner city areas of Dublin, with the canvassing efforts of locally-based Sinn Féin candidates pushing up turnout levels in a number of Dublin City Council flat complexes in the 1999 and 2004 local elections. The 1999 local elections in the South West Inner City electoral area were contested by locally based 'official' and 'unoffical' Sinn Féin candidates, which resulted in higher than the (Dublin City) average turnout levels in the latter's home bases – Michael Mallin House (47.9 per cent) and St Teresa's Gardens (40.3 per cent) (Kavanagh 2002a). In 2002, no strong South West Inner City-based candidate contested the general election, and the percentage turnout rate fell by 12.6 per cent in Michael Mallin House and by 13.5 per cent in St Teresa's Gardens. Nevertheless the contesting of the 2004 local elections by a locally-based Sinn Féin candidate, Andrew O'Connell, saw turnout levels more or less rebounding back to their 1999 levels in Michael Mallin House (46.8 per cent) and St. Teresa's Gardens (40.2 per cent).

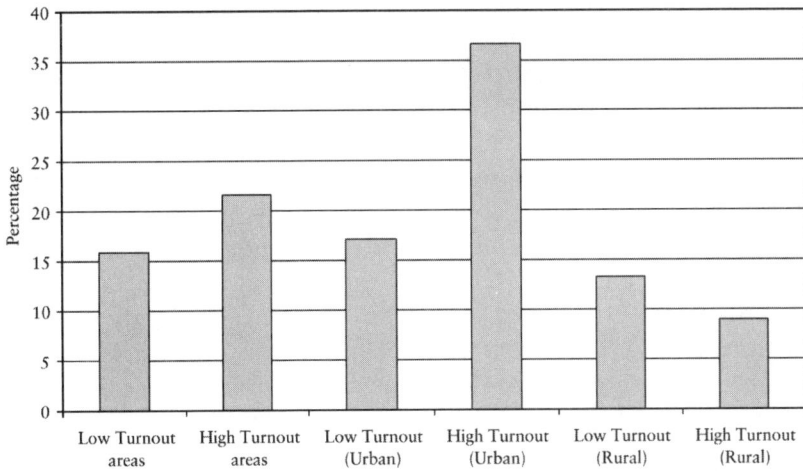

Figure 8.4 Turnout characteristics of areas specifically focused on
in canvassing efforts by politician respondents (N = 96)
Source: Kavanagh 2002b.

Once the evidence of the impact that political mobilisation and
local candidate effects has on turnout levels, both in high turnout
rural and in low turnout urban areas, has been investigated, the final
part of this section will explore the degree to which politicians may
shape their canvassing efforts for elections – efforts arising from an
identification of turnout variations within their constituencies. This
part is based on a survey of politicians' opinions on the issue of
turnout carried out around the 2002 General Elections. Many
respondents saw their strongest support levels being drawn from
groups that they identified as 'high turnout groups', namely the
elderly, the professional classes and the owner occupiers (Kavanagh
2002b). Relatively few claimed that they received strong levels of
support from younger voters, new residents, migrants, and the
unemployed – groups generally identified as having low turnout
characteristics.

The politician respondents were also asked whether their
canvassing strategies took turnout considerations into account. As
illustrated by Figure 8.4, over one third (37.5 per cent) of
respondents claimed they specifically focused on either high turnout
(21.6 per cent) or low turnout (15.9 per cent) areas. (A significant

proportion of the respondents (59.1 per cent) claimed that they did most of their constituency work in low turnout areas.) Urban respondents (53.7 per cent) were significantly more likely to claim that turnout considerations shaped their canvassing strategies than rural respondents were (22.2 per cent). 36.6 per cent of the urban respondents claimed they focused their canvassing efforts on high turnout areas within their constituencies, while 17.1 per cent placed the emphasis on low turnout areas. Rural respondents were slightly more likely to place greater stress on low turnout parts of their constituencies (13.3 per cent). Politicians in high turnout constituencies (5.9 per cent) were considerably less likely to take account of turnout considerations, when planning canvassing strategies, than those representing low turnout constituencies (52.8 per cent) were. Respondents from left-of-centre parties were generally the more likely to focus canvassing efforts on low turnout areas, namely Labour Party (33.3 per cent) and Sinn Féin respondents (50.0 per cent), while Progressive Democrat (71.4 per cent) and Green Party respondents (80.0 per cent) were more likely to target high turnout areas. Fianna Fáil (71.9 per cent) and Fine Gael respondents (72.7 per cent) were the more likely to say that turnout considerations had no influence on what areas they canvassed at election times.

To conclude this section, it must be argued that – given the concerns that declining partisanship levels may result in the further demobilisation of low turnout, often working-class, areas – greater attention should be focused on 'vicious cycles of turnout decline'. With these, low turnouts amongst certain groups and areas may, mindful of the need for parties and candidates to maximise support in the face of declining partisanship, lead to such areas being further ignored by the political machines. With less effort put into canvassing such areas, even lower turnouts will be expected, which will lead in turn to greater socio-economic biases in turnout, greater distortions in levels of support and representation and the further marginalisation of these areas and their specific issues in terms of policy-making and outcomes. However, the significant turnout increases in low turnout working-class areas in 2004 show that this cycle can be broken if these areas are politicised (either through specific efforts of certain political parties or through the engagement of local people in political issues or disputes, as in the case of the bin charges conflicts that took place in a number of working-class areas in Dublin in the lead up to the 2004 elections). With higher electoral participation levels, these areas' concerns will be given greater prominence in political decision-making processes, which may in turn encourage other long-term non-voters to participate if they see the political process impacting 'on the ground' to address the needs of their area.

Turnout, political support and class influences

Just as participation levels are shaped in part by political factors as highlighted in the previous section, the impact that turnout variation may have on the political system also needs to be addressed. One particularly significant issue relates to the likely outcome of socio-economic, demographic or other biases in relation to turnout propensity, wherein distortions in political representation are likely if the composition of the voting population differs significantly from that of the non-voting population. Accelerated turnout decline in a certain area or amongst a specific social group may further marginalise that area or group in terms of future political decision-making, as discussed above. In this scenario, issues specific to these low turnout groups and areas may be increasingly ignored or devalued in policy-making and outcomes, as such issues are seen to be of little, or declining, benefit in electoral terms for politicians (International Institute for Democracy and Electoral Assistance [IDEA] 1999). This mirrors the warnings of Key (1949) and Burnham (1987) that politicians are under no compulsion to address the issues of low turnout classes and groups, as they will see no electoral advantage in doing so.

Lijphart (1997) also expresses concern about class biases in turnout rates, noting that these tend to be strongest in low turnout countries such as the USA and Switzerland. Lijphart argues that such biases will influence levels of electoral success or failure and the subsequent content of public policies. Highton and Wolfinger (2001) query the extent of such class biases on turnout in US electoral contests; they point to the significant proportion of younger and residentially mobile people amongst the non-voting population, neither group being particularly marked by politically distinctive characteristics. Lijphart (1997) and Piven and Cloward (1988), however, argue that such surveys fail to allow for the non-voters' underdeveloped political attitudes and suggest that the views of this group would change if they were mobilised to vote; 'politicians would be prodded to identify and articulate the grievances and aspirations of lower-income voters in order to win their support, thus helping to give form and voice to a distinctive class politics' (Piven and Cloward 1988: 21).

Lawless and Fox (2001) observe an association between higher levels of welfare spending and greater political participation amongst the poor and argue that increasing turnouts amongst the less well-off sections of society is essential to ensure fair representation within the political system. Martinez (1997) largely agrees with this contention and further argues that the size and socio-economic composition of the voting population will largely determine whether tax policies will be regressive or progressive in nature.

Much US-based research focuses on the outcomes that universal turnout scenarios would have. Highton and Wolfinger (2001: 189) found that a universal turnout scenario would have envisaged increases of 4 per cent in the lead Clinton had over Bush in the 1992 presidential election, and 5 per cent in the lead he had over Dole in 1996. Grofman, Owen and Collet (1999) offer a useful typology for addressing the potential effects of turnout variation, involving a partisan bias effect, which would favour left-of-centre parties and candidates, a bandwagon effect, which would benefit the winning party in an election, and a competition effect, which generally acts to the disadvantage of incumbent candidates. Pacek and Radcliff (1995) contend that increases in turnout will generally entail higher shares of the vote for left of centre parties. This association tends to be weakest in countries where class-based politics is the least pronounced, while the bandwagon effect tends to be weaker in countries where class cleavages are strongest. Their analysis, based on national elections in nineteen industrial democracies for the 1950–90 period, finds that the left share of the vote increases by almost one third of a percentage point, on average, for every percentage increase in turnout. This leads Lijphart to argue (1997: 5):

> In short, the overall weight of the evidence strongly supports the view that who votes and how people vote matter a great deal. Indeed, any other conclusion would be extremely damaging for the very concept of representative democracy.

In the Republic of Ireland the proportional representation by single transferable vote (PR–STV) electoral system, with its use of multi-member constituencies, means that Irish general elections do not amount to one single contest, but rather forty-three separate elections, each with its own peculiar circumstances and influenced by national factors to varying degrees (Sinnott 1995). This results in high degrees of localism in Irish electoral contests, as well as in a strong element of marginality, thus rendering Grofman, Owen and Collet's concept of a 'competition' effect redundant and leaving just their partisan and bandwagon effects to be considered. Much of the discussion in this section will centre on the partisan effects of turnout variation. As for the bandwagon effect, there seems to be some evidence of it in relation to turnout variation between the 1992 and 1997 general elections. This was positively, and significantly, associated with gains in Fianna Fáil (r = 0.50) and Fine Gael (r = 0.48) support, the two parties that gained most seats in the 1997 General Election. By contrast, Labour losses in 1997 tended to be greatest in areas with the greatest declines in turnout rates, with a significant negative association between turnout change and Labour gains (r = -0.64), thus further reinforcing the evidence of such a bandwagon effect in the 1997 contest. Just as areas with increased turnout levels tended to be areas with the greatest increases in support for the two most successful parties in 1997, the areas experiencing the greatest declines in turnout were the ones in which the least successful party in this election, the Labour Party, experienced the greatest loss in support.

Correlation analysis in Table 8.3 illustrates the nature of the associations between party support and turnout for the most recent general and local elections, based on constituency-level data. Fianna Fáil and Fine Gael support is positively associated with turnout, with the Fine Gael correlation statistically significant both for the 2002 and 2004 contests. The Labour Party, the Progressive Democrats, Sinn Féin and the Green Party support, by contrast, is inversely associated with turnout. Rather than discounting a class basis to the relationship between political support and turnout, however, the negative association for the Progressive Democrats (and the other parties) is very much a function of the significant rural–urban turnout differentials associated with local and general elections. Support levels for these more urban-based parties will tend to be, generally, inversely correlated with turnout. However the small number of cases involved (forty-three or fewer) does not allow for particularly robust associations between party support and general election turnout, although these associations are largely mirrored for the local elections, which involves a somewhat larger number of cases/constituencies (up to 180).

Party	General Election 2002	Local Elections 2004
Fianna Fáil	0.25	0.42**
Fine Gael	0.66**	0.53**
Labour Party	−0.35	−0.37**
Progressive Democrats	−0.43	−0.10
Sinn Féin	−0.14	−0.20*
Green Party	−0.39	−0.40**

Table 8.3 Correlations between turnout and party support, by constituency, in the 2002 General Election and in the 2004 local elections. (Note **: p<0.05, *: p<0.01)

It could also be argued that the significance of the local elections associations arises from the increased significance of the high turnout rural component of Fianna Fáil support in 2004, and also the low turnout urban component of Sinn Féin, Labour and Green Party support.

Analyses based on constituency-level data, however, offer little information regarding the potential implications of turnout variation for political support, and hence representation. Biases that exist at this level would tend to favour parties who attain the bulk of their support, and representation levels, in low turnout constituencies, since fewer votes will be needed to win seats in these constituencies as quotas will tend to be smaller. In the 2002 General Election, for instance, the quota in the Mayo constituency (with a higher than average turnout rate) was 3,244 votes larger than in the low turnout Dublin South Central constituency. Fianna Fáil won the same number (two) of seats in both these five-seat constituencies, winning them with 15,106 first preference votes in Dublin South Central and 25,380 first preference votes in Mayo.

It is more instructive to look at associations between turnout and political support at the sub-constituency level. Table 8.4 shows associations between turnout and party support for the 2002 General Election and 2004 local elections, based on party support ('tally') figures drawn from the sub-constituency level (polling districts and electoral divisions) and drawn from both urban and rural counties.

Party	2002 General Election	2004 Local Elections
Fianna Fáil	0.30**	0.45**
Fine Gael	0.45**	0.49**
Labour Party	−0.09*	−0.28**
Progressive Democrats	0.19**	0.17**
Independents	−0.17*	−0.12**
Green Party	−0.11**	−0.15**
Sinn Féin	−0.52**	−0.40**

Table 8.4 Correlations between support and turnout in the 2002
General Election and 2004 Local Elections
(Note **: p<0.05, *: p<0.01)

This analysis uncovers significant positive correlations between general (and local) election turnout and support for the centrist, or right of centre, parties; Fianna Fáil, Fine Gael and the Progressive Democrats. Significant negative associations with turnout emerged for the parties of the left, namely Labour, Green Party and Sinn Féin, and the Independents. This suggests that class-based factors may play a role in shaping relationships between turnout and party support in Ireland, which may have an impact, in turn, on how successful these parties are in winning political representation at the parliamentary or local authority levels.

The degree to which class cleavages impact on the Irish electoral system has been debated, with commentators such as Whyte (1974) arguing that Ireland has a political system that is largely without social bases. Other analysts, such as Laver (1986), argue that much clearer links exist between socio-economic factors and party support. Sinnott (1995) accounts for discrepancies that emerge in different research findings by noting how different spatial units are used as the bases for these ecological analyses. Furthermore, the tendency to use constituency-level in geographical studies of turnout and party support figures means that analyses are less likely to detect variations within the data, given that the significant differences often occur within constituencies and not between them. Data illustrating variations at a sub-constituency level prove to be of greater salience to an ecological analysis, as socio-economic and demographic variations are more likely to exist within constituencies, rather than between constituencies.

There is strong evidence of a class basis to Dublin turnout rates, as presented by the associations in Table 8.5; these reflect previous research findings (Kavanagh 2001). Associations between party support and various socio-economic variables, based on observations at the sub-constituency level, suggest a class basis to party support at least in the Dublin region. Table 8.5 shows a significant association between Sinn Féin support and a range of exclusion-related variables (as also for the Socialist Workers Party, Socialist Party and Workers Party). Support for right-of-centre parties, Fine Gael and the Progressive Democrats, is negatively associated with these exclusion-related variables; the associations for the Green Party mirror these associations to a large degree – marking it out as a 'party of protest' for the Dublin middle classes. The associations between these class-related factors and Fianna Fáil/Labour Party support were less defined, however. Associations with Labour support proved to be largely insignificant, while positive associations existed between Fianna Fáil support and some, but not all, of the factors, trends that one would expect for 'catch-all' parties. In 2002 Fianna Fáil's share of the vote in affluent areas within Dublin was roughly similar to their share in deprived parts of the city, while Labour also won roughly similar shares of support, on average, in different social areas.

	Turnout	FF	FG	Lab	PD	GP	SF
Early school leavers	−0.37**	0.39**	−0.58**	0.03	−0.62**	−0.56**	0.66**
Rented council housing	−0.65**	−0.06	−0.48**	0.03	−0.44**	−0.30**	0.67**
Social Classes 5 and 6	−0.42**	0.35**	−0.64**	0.06	−0.63**	−0.48**	0.70**
Lone parent households	−0.44**	0.19**	−0.51**	0.00	−0.48**	−0.51**	0.67**
Blue Collar employees	−0.19**	0.56**	−0.57**	−0.06	−0.51**	−0.47**	0.52**
Unemployment Rate	−0.69**	0.05	−0.55**	0.02	−0.56**	−0.42**	0.71**

Table 8.5 Simple correlations between socio-economic variables and turnout/party support in Dublin for the 2002 General Election.
*(Note **: p<0.05, *: p<0.01)*

Just as Table 8.5 suggests a significant class basis to party support levels in Dublin in the 2002 General Election, Fine Gael, the Progressive Democrats and the Green Party again are shown to achieve higher levels of success in the more affluent parts of the city and Sinn Féin support is considerably higher in the more deprived areas. In 2004, however, Fianna Fáil support levels in the more deprived areas (ranked 4 or 5) were significantly lower than in the more affluent parts of the city (ranked 1 or 2). The Labour Party emerges, as a result, as the classic catch-all party in Dublin in the

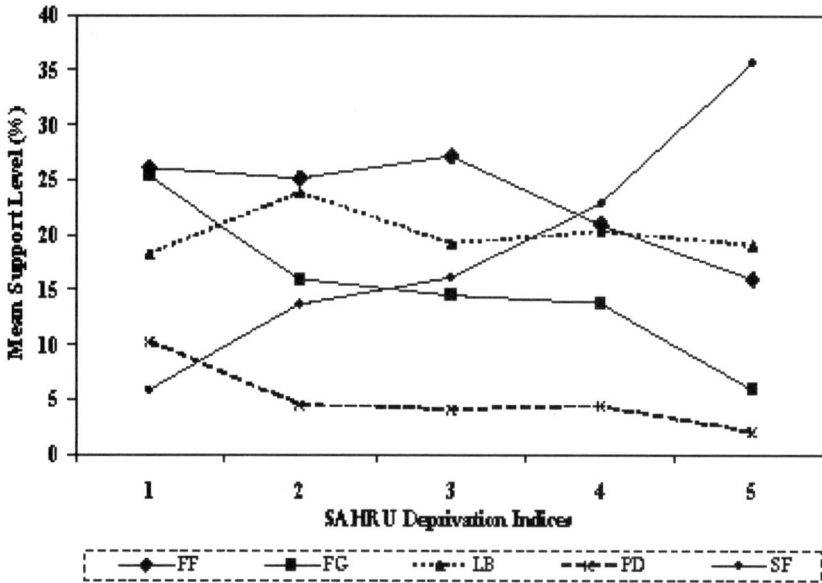

Figure 8.5 *Mean party support in 2004 local elections related to relative affluence of areas in Dublin.*[1]

2004 local elections – the party that wins fairly similar shares of the vote in all types of social areas.

Thus, by and large, there is significant evidence to suggest that, at least in the Dublin context, the parties associated with low turnout areas are those that tend to win markedly higher support levels in working-class and underprivileged areas, which indicates that a socio-economic bias effect is at work. In consequence, parties such as the Socialist Party, Socialist Workers Party and Sinn Féin, which rely on support from low turnout, underprivileged areas in the city, may be unable to mobilise their support to the same extent as other parties, whose main support bases are in high turnout, middle class areas.

An 'equal turnout' simulation model is employed to determine whether an equal turnout scenario, similar to the universal turnout scenarios referred to above, would have resulted in changes in political support and representation levels for the 2002 General Election in Limerick West, Dublin South Central and Dublin Central. Some of these constituencies were of special interest, given that very small margins determined which candidate won the final seat (Limerick West and Dublin Central).

To simulate such an equal turnout scenario, each of the polling stations were allocated the exact number of voters that they would have had if all stations had a similar turnout rate to the constituency average. These votes were then distributed between the different candidates for that polling station in the same proportion as the original vote shares for that station. The methodology for this model is outlined as follows:

Box 8.1. *Methodology for an 'equal turnout' simulation model.*

Let X_{ij} be the votes won by candidate i in polling station j. Let X_i be the total votes won by candidate i. Let T_c be the percentage turnout for the constituency. Let T_j be the turnout for polling station j. To create an equal turnout scenario, the total number of votes in station j is multiplied by T_c/T_j, thus ensuring that $T_c = T_j$ for all polling stations. In turn, the number of votes won by candidate i in polling station j, X_{ij}, is multiplied by T_c/T_j. These simulated votes for each of the candidates in the different polling stations were then added together to produce a new, simulated, total vote for each of the candidates involved, termed X_i^*.

$$X_i^* = \sum_{j=1}^{n} X_{ij} \bullet \frac{T_c}{T_j}$$

Using these new simulated votes for the different candidates and the Electoral Database[2] programme,[3] the election was then rerun on a count-by-count basis, involving the same transfer patterns as in the original election, until the final seat was filled.

In general, left-of-centre candidates gained votes in the different simulations, which usually amounted to gains of roughly 100–300 votes per candidate, while centrist and right-of-centre candidates tended to lose votes. Fianna Fáil support, on average, was not significantly affected in these simulations (with the exception of Dublin Central), as the party strategy of dividing up constituencies between candidates meant that some candidates would hail from high turnout areas and others from low turnout areas. A change in representation would have resulted in Dublin Central had an equal turnout situation existed; Nicky Kehoe of Sinn Féin would have won the final seat there, ahead of Dermot Fitzpatrick of Fianna Fáil.[4] The model suggests that, within constituencies, left-wing candidates are losing votes to centrist and right-of-centre candidates on account of to turnout variations.

The 'equal turnout' simulation employed here has many limitations, mainly due to underlying assumptions in assigning political preferences to non-voters on the basis of the political characteristics of voters in their local areas. Increases in turnout in low turnout stations may prove to be of even greater advantage for left-of-centre candidates than the simulation envisages. This means that the predictions of the model as to the likely impact of an equal turnout scenario are probably under-estimating the likely increase in support for left-wing candidates. It could also be argued that these small socialist parties have already attained as many votes as they can, and that any turnout boost would be in the form of a bandwagon effect, benefiting the winning party nationally. The findings of an Irish Marketing Survey held after the 2002 General Election tend to support the first contention. This survey has found that non-voters in 2002 were proportionally more likely to have supported Sinn Féin, the smaller political parties and Independent candidates, had they decided to vote, and less likely to have supported Fianna Fáil, Fine Gael and the Progressive Democrats (Lyons and Sinnott 2003: 155). The model also assumes that the transfer patterns will be similar to those of the actual election, which is unlikely to be replicated in a real life situation. However, the model as such does succeed in pinpointing the manner in which spatial variations in turnout rates within constituencies may act so as to favour certain parties or candidates, which could determine the destination of final seats in constituencies given the high degree of marginality associated with Irish electoral contests.

More concrete evidence of the impact that turnout has on political support was seen in the significant turnout increases in the 2004 local, European and Citizenship Referendum elections, particularly in the more urban and eastern parts of the state. Large turnout increases were found in a number of working-class urban areas, in part due to the role that parties such as Sinn Féin and the Socialist Party played in mobilising large numbers of people who had previously been long-term non-voters, making them turn out for these elections, in many cases for the first time ever. These increased working-class turnouts, in turn, impacted on the local election results, leading to higher voters for left-wing parties and candidates in a number of constituencies. The higher turnout in the Clondalkin electoral area (turnout increased by 19.4 per cent), the constituency with the lowest turnout in 1999, resulted in an extra 1,916 votes for the Labour Party, 1,799 votes for Sinn Fein and 1,014 votes for the Socialist Workers Party. (Despite the much higher number of voters and running an extra candidate, Fianna Fáil just gained an extra 623 votes, while Fine Gael gained 313 more votes.) In all, left-wing parties won almost half the votes cast in Clondalkin (49.8 per cent); this was a significant increase on the 24.1 per cent share of the vote that these parties won in the low turnout 1999 election.

Similarly, the number of voters increased by 2,453 (turnout increase of 12.5 per cent) in the low turnout South West Inner City electoral area between 1999 and 2004, and the number of votes won by left-wing parties and candidates increased by 2,576, amounting to an increase of 17.0 per cent in their share of the vote relative to 1999. (By contrast, the number of votes won by Fianna Fail fell by 279, as their share of the vote declined from 26.4 per cent to 15.8 per cent.) The trends noted for Clondalkin and South West Inner City, of increased turnout levels (particularly in working-class parts of the constituency) resulting in significant gains for left-wing parties

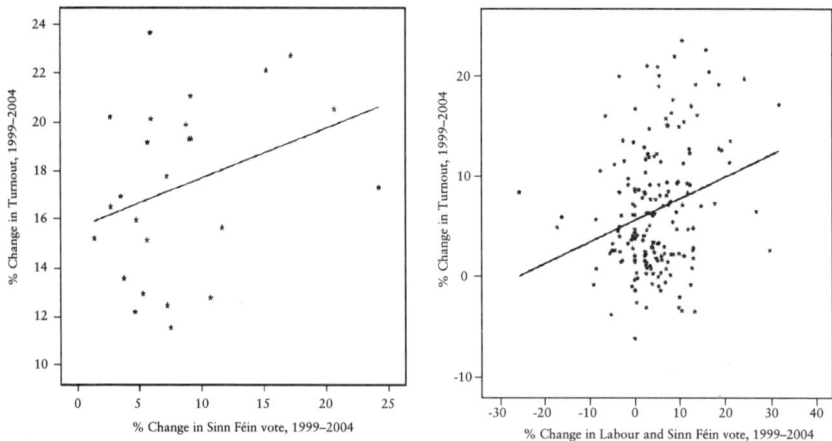

Figures 8.6a and 8.6b. *Scatterplots relating change in turnout levels at the electoral area, between 1999 and 2004 to (a) changing support levels for the Labour Party and Sinn Féin at the national level and (b) changing support levels for Sinn Féin in the Dublin region.*

and candidates, were replicated in other constituencies (such as Ballyfermot, Ballymun-Whitehall and Mulhuddart). This trend is also reflected in the scatterplots in Figure 8.6, wherein positive relationships are uncovered between changes in the turnout rate and changes in support levels for the Labour Party and Sinn Féin at the national level (Figure 8.6a), and for Sinn Féin within the Dublin region (Figure 8.6b).

Conclusions

The Irish public has traditionally been portrayed as highly interested in, and engaged by, political and electoral concerns, but this has ignored Ireland's relatively low voter turnout levels, as compared to other European states, and the significant decline in electoral participation levels since the late 1970s has further put this contention to the test. Given this decline and its likely impact in terms of political representation and policy style, this chapter has focused on the associations that exist between turnout levels and party politics, both in terms of the impact that party mobilisation has on electoral participation levels and in terms of the impact that spatial variations, and declines, in turnout levels have on support levels for election candidates and political parties. In relation to the first theme, the significance of changes in the nature of political mobilisation has been noted, and the reduced use of traditional face-to-face canvassing techniques (resulting from declining levels of party membership and political activism) have been associated, in part, with falling turnout levels in Ireland and other western democracies and with the inflation of turnout variations within constituencies, as the canvassing activities of parties and candidates become more focussed on higher turnout areas. Thus, lower levels of political engagement, associated with significant differences between higher turnout rural and urban middle-class areas on the one hand, and lower turnout urban working-class (as well as commuter-belt) areas on the other, are a significant characteristic of modern Irish politics.

In the late 1990s and early 2000s, as participation levels in deprived urban areas continued to fall, the socio-economic bias to Irish turnout rates was, in turn, influencing political support levels and parties, which were largely reliant on low turnout support bases and were losing votes and possibly also seats as a result of sub-constituency level turnout variations. By the general election in May

2002, which was characterised by the lowest turnout levels in the history of the state and especially low turnout levels in many working class areas, it could have been argued that the recycling of the State was very much associated with an increasingly disengaged Irish electorate, particularly in the poorer urban areas. These lower urban working class participations levels, in turn, were acting to maintain the political status quo as spatial differentials in turnout levels acted to maintain the hegemony of the more conservative political parties. As suggested in an earlier draft of this report, the representative system appeared largely meaningless to disadvantaged urban communities, who were looking to the community and voluntary sectors as a means of promoting the greater political inclusion of their areas.

However, as the 2000s progressed, the limitations placed on community groups by the political system became increasingly obvious, as evidenced for instance in the barriers that these groups experienced in their involvements in various urban regeneration projects during the period. Increasingly, community groups, including those involved in the many locally-based environmental protests of the period, turned anew towards the electoral system in order to promote their political aims. This process, in addition to the growing influence of parties such as Sinn Féin, the Socialist Party and the Socialist Workers Party, reinvigorated mobilisation efforts in low turnout urban areas, especially in cases where this was linked to a local candidate (or 'friends and neighbours') effect; this resulted in significant increases in participation levels in the 2004 elections, as discussed in this chapter.

Linkages between turnout, partisanship and patterns of support and representation are strong. Declining partisanship levels engender declining turnout, and such declines in turnout may further intensify spatial variations and socio-economic biases in turnouts and hence influence patterns of political support and, possibly, of representation, while acting to dismiss the particular policy concerns of low turnout areas and groups. In turn, renewed, locally-focused mobilisation efforts, involving many elements that are traditional in approach, can significantly arrest this trend of turnout decline. If the ongoing recycling of the Irish state is to involve a renewed engagement of its population with the representative system, a sustained and community-based mobilisation of the electorate will be a necessity. Place matters in accounting for political behaviour, as Agnew (1996) and Johnston and Pattie (2004) argue, and thus the renewed engagements of the 'recycled' Irish representative system with its electorate must be mindful of the specific concerns of the different local contexts that these people are located.

Acknowledgements

This chapter initially arose as part of a PhD research project involving a spatial perspective as to the associations between voter turnout and social deprivation in Ireland, which was funded by the Irish Research Council for the Humanities and Social Sciences. The author wishes to thank Dr. Dennis Pringle and Dr. Rowan Fealy, Department of Geography, NUI Maynooth, for helpful comments and assistance during the earlier drafting stage. I would also like to thank the following people for the provision of the various forms of data used in the analyses referred to in this paper: Mr. James Barry of the Dublin City Sheriff's Office, Mr. Sean Fleming TD and Laois Fianna Fáil, Mr. Maurice McQuillan and Dublin Fine Gael, Mr. Charlie McCreevy TD, Mr. Brian Lenihan TD, Mr. Richard Bruton TD, Mr. Sean Haughey TD, Mr. Sean Ardagh TD, Mr. Jim Mitchell TD, Mr. Ruairi Quinn TD, Cllr. Eamonn Walsh, Mr. Conor Lenihan TD, Mr. Brian Hayes TD, Mr Gay Mitchell TD and Ms. Eithne Fitzgerald.

NOTES

1 This analysis uses the Small Area Health Research Unit (Trinity College) Deprivation Index. The higher the index/rank, the greater the degree of deprivation – a rank of 1 relates to the 20% most affluent Electoral Divisions in the State, a rank of 5 relates to the 20% most deprived Electoral Divisions in the State.

2 Copyright Ciaran Quinn, Dublin, accessed from http://election.polarbears.com (01/09/02)

3 For a detailed analysis of the findings arising from the various simulations see Kavanagh 2002b.

4 Fitzpatrick won the fourth seat in Dublin Central on the final count by just 74 votes. The model suggests that Kehoe would have had 6,422 votes and Fitzpatrick 6,178 votes on the final count in an equal turnout situation.

REFERENCES

Agnew, J.A. 1996. 'Mapping politics: How context counts in electoral geography', *Political Geography* 15 (2), 129–46.

Burnham, W. D. 1987. 'The turnout problem', in J. Reichley (ed.), *Elections American Style.*

Washington DC: Brookings Institution, 97–133.

Caldeira, G. A., A. R. Clausen and S. C. Patterson, 1990. 'Partisan mobilisation and Electoral Participation', Electoral Studies, 9 (3), 191–204.

Cassel, C. A. 1999. 'Voluntary associations, churches, and social participation theories of turnout', Social Science Quarterly, 80 (3), 504–17.

Community Workers Co-operative (CWC). 2000. Partnership, Participation & Power: The Contribution of the Integrated Local Development Programme to the Development of Structures for Local Participation in Decision-Making. Galway: Community Workers Co-operative.

Fuchs, E. R., L. C. Minnitte and R. Y. Shapiro. 2000. 'Political capital and political participation', Paper presented at the Annual Meeting of the American Political Science Association, Washington DC, 30 August–3 September 2000.

Gallagher, M. and M. Marsh. 2002. Days of Blue Loyalty: The Politics of Membership of the Fine Gael Party. Dublin: PSAI Press.

Green, D. P. and A. S. Gerber. 2001. 'Do phone calls increase voter turnout?', in Public Opinion Quarterly, 65, 75–85.

Grofman, B., G. Owen and C. Collet. 1999. 'Rethinking the partisan effects of higher turnout', Public Choice, 99, 357–76.

Highton, B. and R. E. Wolfinger. 2001. 'The political implications of higher turnout', British Journal of Political Science, 31 (1), 179–223.

International IDEA. 1999. Youth Voter Participation: Involving Today's Young in Tomorrow's Democracy. Stockholm: International Institute for Democracy and Electoral Assistance.

Johnston, R. J. and C. Pattie. 2004. 'Electoral geography in electoral studies: Putting voters in their place' in C. Barnett and M. Low, (eds), Spaces of Democracy: Geographical Perspectives on Citizenship, Participation and Representation. London: Sage, 45–66.

Kavanagh, A. P. 2001. 'Voter turnout, social deprivation and political mobilisation', in S. Martin (ed.), Proceedings of the Academy of Marketing Fourth International Political Marketing Conference. Dublin: Dublin City University Business School, 155-76.

Kavanagh, A. P. 2002a. Unequal Participation – Unequal Influence: Voter Participation and Voter Education in Dublin's South West Inner City. Dublin: South West Inner City Network.

Kavanagh, A. P. 2002b. 'Social exclusion, political alienation and community empowerment' [Unpublished PhD Thesis, Department of Geography, NUI Maynooth].

Kavanagh, A. P. 2004. 'The 2004 Local election in the Republic of Ireland', Irish Political Studies, 19 (2), 64–84.

Kavanagh, A., Mills, G. and Sinnott, R. (2004) 'The geography of Irish voter turnout: A case study of the 2002 General Election', Irish Geography, 37(2), 177–186.

Key, V.O. 1949. Southern Politics in State and Nation. New York: Vintage Books.

Laver, M. 1986. 'Ireland: Politics with some social bases: An interpretation based on aggregate data', The Economic and Social Review, 17 (2), 107–31.

Lawless, J. L. and R. L. Fox, 2001. 'Political participation of the urban poor', Social Problems, 48 (3), 362–85.

Lijphart, A. 1997. 'Unequal participation: Democracy's unresolved dilemma', American Political Science Review, 91 (1), 1–14.

Lyons, P. and R. Sinnott, 2003. 'Voter turnout in 2002 and beyond', in M. Gallagher, M. Marsh and P. Mitchell, (eds.), How Ireland Voted 2002. New York: Palgrave Macmillan, 143–58.

Marsh, M., R. Sinnott, J. Garry and F. Kennedy. 2001. 'The Irish election study: Puzzles and priorities', Irish Political Studies, 16, 161–78.

Martinez, M. D. 1997.'Don't tax you, don't tax me, tax the fella behind the tree: Partisan and turnout effects on tax policy', Social Science Quarterly, 78 (4), 895–906.

Pacek, A. and B. Radcliff. 1995. 'Turnout and the vote for left-of-centre parties: A cross-national approach', British Journal of Political Studies, 25, 137–43.

Parker, A. J. 1982. 'The "friends and neighbours" effect in the Galway West constituency', *Political Geography Quarterly*, 1 (3), 243–62.

Piven, F. and Cloward, R. A. 1988. *Why Americans don't vote*. New York: Pantheon Books.

Putnam, R. D. 2000. *Bowling Alone: The Collapse and Revival of American Community*, New York: Simon & Schuster.

Rallings, C. and Thrasher, M. 1990. 'Turnout in English local elections – An aggregate analysis with electoral and contextual data', *Electoral Studies*, 9 (2), 79–90.

Rosenstone, S. J. and J. M. Hansen. 1993. *Mobilization, Participation, and Democracy in America*. New York: Macmillan.

Sinnott, R. 1995. *Irish Voters Decide: Voting Behaviour in Elections and Referendums since 1918*. Manchester: Manchester University Press.

Taylor, P. J. and R. J. Johnson. 1979. *Geography of Elections*. New York: Holmes and Meier.

Whyte, J. H. 1974. 'Ireland: politics without social bases', in R. Rose (ed.), *Electoral Behaviour: A Comparative Handbook*. New York: Free Press, 619–51.

9

Irish voting patterns: Dealignment or realignment?
Kenneth McKenzie

Irish society has undergone significant socio-political change over the course of the past twenty years (Girvin 1997, Hayward (this volume), O'Connell 2001). In acknowledging the unprecedented economic turnaround in Irish fortunes, it is important to try to provide a context for societal changes and how they might affect Irish voting patterns. There is a tendency in political science to understand with hindsight how the most recent election produced the results that it did (Dunleavy 1996), rather than by taking a longer-term view. In chasing the last election, academics may well be prone to attributing excessive importance to one-off confluences of circumstances at the expense of a clearer sight of what the long-run tells us. In the course of this chapter, attention will thus be paid to socio-political features that would seem to *predate* the Celtic Tiger phase. Moreover, the story of Irish politics is only partially told by voting patterns. A reasonably strong case could be made that the political landscape has not altered to the same extent as the social changes would lead one to believe. For example, the three main political parties for the past seventy years have been Fianna Fáil, Fine Gael, and Labour. As was the case for most of the twentieth century, only Fianna Fáil has the resources and the candidates to form a single-party government. With regard to the left/right divide, a European commonplace for the last ninety years, Ireland has always been, still is and is almost certain to remain exempt (see Sassoon 1997).

In order to address the question of qualitative change in Irish voting, this chapter tracks changes in the party and policy arenas as well. Using the theory of dealignment and realignment allows us to assess the weight of evidence for significant change. The chapter bottom of the same list of nineteen industrialised countries (even Northern Ireland, a region of the United Kingdom plagued by regime legitimacy problems, finishes ahead of the Republic). Against this picture, though, is Gilley's analysis (2006) of the legitimacy of states in the eyes of their publics. In a seventy-two-state sample, Ireland finishes fourteenth overall; for its 'Western Europe/Anglo-America' category, it ranks eleventh out of twenty.

Explaining change in voter behaviour

Political disengagement

How, then, are we to explain these disparate phenomena of current and contemporary Irish politics? The number of negative factors related to representative politics is plainly significant. In combining challenges to party function, administrative legitimacy and overall endorsement of politics as a worthwhile activity, it would seem that there is a diffuse discontentment with voting and its instrumentality (see the Democracy Commission report of 2005). Again, the time of onset of these voting (and ancillary political) indicators is vital. With many of them predating the years of rapid economic expansion, the challenge is to localise specified voting developments within a context of socio-economic transformation. The alternative is to deduce that the breakneck rate and extent of upheaval in arenas of Irish life as diverse as the Church and the media have not radically acted upon people's most symbolic and purposeful political act: voting.

An example of tracing the markers to further back than 1994[2] is to be found in Sinnott's (1995) authoritative work on voting history, *Irish Voters Decide*. He asserts that the waning partisanship trajectory had already been evident before the 1990s, with falls across all age-groups from the late 1970s (Sinnott 1995: 152). Evidently, all Irish parties have found it hard to retain a committed support. If one adds Fianna Fáil's lowest ever turnouts in the General Elections of 1992, 1997 and 2002 to general apathy in voter turnout, one has unquestionably the basic ingredients for long-term depoliticisation (which attracted much comment from the Democracy Commission of 2005). The announcement that there may be 800,000 inaccuracies in the electoral register (based on a preliminary analysis of the April 2006 census returns) is another sign that representative politics is far from healthy. After all, if people cared so much for their right to vote, would they not go to some length to ensure that they are correctly registered?

It could be argued that, although falling turnout strongly suggests people are less concerned with parliamentary politics and so feel less compelled to vote, people's political interests are still present but have transformed themselves. Instead of investing much value in first-order elections, they are resorting to other channels to express themselves politically, such as single issue protest groups (Gallagher 1997: 127). O'Connell (2001) argued to the contrary, pointing to a considerable dent in the number of people who try to persuade others of their own political thinking. There is a very visible tailing off in the corresponding *Eurobarometer* survey from the early 1990s through to 2000: a European trend is found in a heightened form in Ireland (O'Connell 2001: 101). If citizens' political disaffections and anti-status quo positions are indeed considered, then logically one should see an increase in proselytising as to the merits of pressure group politics, or even a complete opting-out of the political process. As O'Connell has shown, people are turning away from politics and not even bothering to debate this inclination in their conversations with friends.

All of the above may be taken as evidence of political disengagement, with voters becoming more frustrated and thus volatile, transferring votes from election to election, or going as far as to become non-voters. In the face of an altered political landscape and voter dissatisfaction, it is accepted practice to posit two related but different explanations.

Dealignment

Burnham (1970) was the first to try to conjoin weakened partisanship and rising electoral volatility (Dalton and Wattenberg 1993). His work drew on American presidential elections and introduced the concepts of 'electoral disaggregation' and 'party decomposition'. His ideas caught on, but not his terminology, which was superseded by Inglehart and Hochstein's construct of 'dealignment' (1972). Burnham had underlined the waning strength of the party machine to attract and retain voters, whereas Inglehart and Hochstein switched the focus onto the voter. In comparing the French legislative elections of 1968 with the US Presidential contest of 1972, they contended that it was the *voters'* evolving demands and subsequent party shifts that produced the novel outcomes in both states. Dealignment is viewed as the required first step for a prospective realignment; it entails moving from a structured political world with clearly located parties and voters, to a much more fluid structure. Referring to the classic survey data in *The American Voter* (1960), Inglehart (1977) acknowledged the durability and clarity of the cleavages structuring American voting. The 1972 American Presidential contest between the Republican incumbent, Richard Nixon, and the Democrat challenger, George McGovern, produced a seismic shift of the landscape. McGovern's pacifist ideals proved unpopular for a country still bogged down in Vietnam and the Democrats lost heavily – so heavily that the voter base they had relied on since Roosevelt's New Deal was eroded. In the case of the US, the old class and race cleavages were largely effaced: parties could no longer rely on drawing exclusively on these constituencies.

Realignment

The concept of 'realignment' is of a different ilk but, again, the progenitor of the idea is Inglehart. At its core, realignment is where an inveterate dividing line or political cleavage shifts to a new position. The new political axis of postmaterialism is exemplary of this rotation (see Dalton, Scarrow and Cain, 2004). For those voters socialised in the second half of the twentieth century, there has been a perceived security in the 'survival' politics (Castles 2000) that pivot on the welfare state, taxation, law and order and, to a lesser extent, foreign policy. As those cohorts who attained voting age from the 1960s on grew up not knowing the privations of war or prolonged deep depression, it was plausible to Inglehart that they would instead orient themselves to 'quality of life' issues (Dalton and Wattenberg 1993). Inglehart and Abramson (1999) argued that this evolution in political priorities is shown in the rising prominence of environmental and gender politics; inner city regeneration; a greater interest in civil liberties; increasing secularisation: and a desire to remove state involvement in questions of morality.

Inglehart and Abramson (1994) addressed the connection between dealignment and realignment in a co-authored article. They proposed that the electoral dealignment across much of the industrialised west since the late 1960s was due to parties' unresponsiveness to postmaterialist politics. As people opted out of politics, the symptoms of apathy and questioned legitimacy emerged. In cases where there has been a reasonably prolonged dealignment, there arises a series of political movements aiming to capitalise on the disaffected. Symptoms of a society moving away from discontentment towards a 'new politics' or realignment include:

- the formation of a new political axis, that of the 'new left' and 'new right';
- reduced turnout;
- the rolling back of the state on issues of private morality;
- growing participation in New Social Movements;
- ecological parties making their presence felt at elections;
- less interest in the politics of the economy;
- more liberal stances on freedom of speech and criminal justice policies.

All-or-nothing qualifying criteria may blunt the applicability of a theory even when a trend is apparent. Inglehartian realignment follows a strict checklist, but Niemi and Weisberg (1993) allude to the diversity of scholarly opinion concerning cleavage shifts. They proposed five contending candidates for cleavage shifts which are applicable to a European context:[3]

1 Simple switch in which party is in the majority;
2 Movement in levels of party support;
3 Alterations in which coalitions of voters or interests support which party;
4 Parties adopting new issue bases;
5 A new direction in public policy.

If one works within these frameworks, then the brief for realignment becomes admittedly more complicated, but also more informative (see Mayhew 2000 for difficulties with definitions of realignment).

The Irish case

The supply side of Irish politics does not tally with the changes in the demand function as demonstrated by changes in voting. First, Irish parties have been remarkably durable, both in their histories and in their rank (see Gallagher [1985] for an authoritative overview of

Irish parties and their origins). Secondly, there has not been a substantive shift in policy issues. The two major parties – Fianna Fáil and Fine Gael – both emerged from the Sinn Féin party of 1918–22. The split over the acceptability of the 1921 Treaty which established Ireland as a 'free state' was never resolved. Cumann na nGaedhael (the original name for Fine Gael), held office in 1922–32; hereafter, Fianna Fáil has held office, singly or in coalition, for fifty-nine years. Both Fianna Fáil and Fine Gael have much in common, in terms of policy convergence on the economy, Europe, foreign affairs and now (arguably) Northern Ireland, but history has served as a 'lock-in' in that they have never coalesced or contested a joint platform at elections.[3] Labour, the oldest Irish party, dates from 1912 and has been a perennial third-player, never succeeding in holding anything greater than the role of junior partner in coalitions (see Farrell, 1999). Apart from 1992–4, when the party formed a coalition with Fianna Fáil, they have always served as the smaller part in Fine Gael-led administrations. An oft-cited example of the illogic of the differences between the Fianna Fáil was the Tallaght Strategy pursued by Alan Dukes' Fine Gael opposition from 1987–9. In the aftermath of the inconclusive 1987 election, Fianna Fáil attained power due to the inability of the fragmented opposition to cobble together an alternative government. Ireland's economy was in a parlous state and Dukes felt he was acting in the national interest by pledging that his party would not oppose any substantive Fianna Fáil measures deemed necessary to right the economy on its feet (Marsh and Mitchell 1999: 50–4). The lack of palpable electoral reward for this act of 'magnanimity' fed growing restlessness within Fine Gael at the folly of an opposition party supporting their avowed rivals on a unilateral basis. Dukes' resignation cemented over the remains of the strategy. Although the main parties have similar views on Europe, Northern Ireland and social partnership, realignment in terms of cross-floor co-operation or grand coalition between the two big ones remains a perennial improbable.

Explanations for the lack of policy difference often include the argument that there has never been any substantive class-based cleavage in Irish politics (Carty 1981; Mair 1992; Whyte 1974). The canonical work on cleavages (Lipset and Rokkan 1967) pivoted on the rural/urban split. Again, this is difficult to graft onto a socio-historical analysis of Irish voting, as Ireland's status as an agricultural society for much of its life is unquestionable. The lack of a history conducive to strong social factors in voting is pointed out sharply by Mair (1992: 385), who writes of 'the striking electoral debility of class-based, left wing parties'. Mair asserts that the only real match to the Irish scenario is America, where a left wing is 'effectively non-existent'. This is not to say that a class-based account of Irish elections is entirely without explanatory power. In the three elections from 1987 to 1992, leftist parties recorded considerable gains as shown in Table 9.1:

Year	Labour Party	Workers Party	Democratic Left
1987	6.4	3.8	–
1989	9.5	5	–
1992	19.3	0.7	2.8

Table 9.1 Percentage of first preference votes obtained by leftist parties, Dáil elections, 1987–92.
Source: Coakley and Gallagher 1999: 367.

Although the Workers' Party vote did not bear up after the 1989 poll, the overall trend in rising leftist share was notable. Indeed, after the 1992 election, it would not have been an understatement to have proposed that a *party system alignment* was in the process of taking place, pitting Labour and Democratic Left on one side and the big two on the other. Labour's status as a salient was seemingly becoming attainable.

Referring back to Mair (1992), we see some erosion of the argument that the left wing is largely insignificant. However, in terms of Labour being the party capable of bringing about class voting, the 1992 election results did not advance the party's proprietorial claim to the working-class vote. Labour had attracted new votes from all classes, but particularly from the middle-class electorate. Exit polls for this election showed that Labour got twenty-two and a half per cent of the combined middle-class (upper and lower) vote. Whilst this tally falls considerably short of either Fianna Fáil's or Fine Gael's respective middle class shares, it is most interesting when compared with Labour's support from the working-classes (skilled and unskilled). At twenty-six and a half per cent of the votes cast by this group, it was evident that Labour's ability to recruit votes from this putatively loyal base was very much in doubt.

The 1997 election result further underlined the observation that the Labour Party's large gains in 1992 were not predominantly among working-class voters. Its sharp plummeting in seats can be taken as a vote of dissatisfaction from more Fine Gael-inclined floating voters who punished Labour for entering the 1992–4 coalition administration with Fianna Fáil. A close analysis of vote transfers in the previous election throws light on the roots of the floating voters' unease: where both Fine Gael and Fianna Fáil candidates were available to pick up Labour transfers, the latter were twice as successful at doing so (Mitchell 2000: 133). The Irish National Election Study (INES) of 2002 demonstrated that Labour got more of the non-manual vote (just under twelve per cent) than it did from the manual sector (just over nine and a half per cent) of the electorate (Marsh 2003). The same dataset showed that although the Greens, Progressive Democrats and Sinn Féin are socially distinctive in their support bases, the three large parties are not – a long-standing feature in both cases (Marsh 2003: 3).

The secular/religious dimension

An additional dividing line overlapping the Civil War split is Sinnott's secular/confessional dynamic (1995). One illustration of its growing prominence is the obvious factor of the referenda. There were six 'moral' (read abortion and divorce) amendment referenda in 1986–96, and another abortion referendum in 2002. Yet the impact of these divisive battles on electoral politics is massively attenuated; according to Sinnott (1995: 295), the 'moral' referendum acts as a pressure valve for secular/confessional clashes which the political parties do not feel comfortable to deal with through simple legislative procedures in parliament. A constitutional amendment is the battleground, rather than the general election hustings. To corroborate this claim, one notes that only 4 per cent of voters rated abortion as an electorally important issue in the 1992 contest (Marsh and Sinnott 1993). As for the electoral repercussions for a party that had backed a 'liberalising' referendum – due to a common platform, no one party could have been isolated from the others. Mud-slinging about the rival parties' and candidates' morals has been kept to a minimum, as all the players have remembered how vicious the 1983 abortion had been. Of the Independent TDs in the twenty-ninth Dáil, only Mildred Fox has claimed that she had been elected partly because the established parties had all backed a referendum that removed the 1983 pro-life amendment and so antiabortion TDs were nowhere to be found. Not one of the parties has presumed that it has a competitive electoral advantage due to its stance on the liberalising referenda. Collins (2001: 344) neatly packaged Fianna Fáil's attitude to the moral questions that veined Irish politics for much of the 1980s and 1990s:

> In the 1970s Fianna Fáil was against contraception, but for it in the 1980s. In the 1980s it was against divorce, but for it in the 1990s. In the 1980s it was against abortion in any circumstances, but became a little bit more flexible about it in the 1990s while still retaining links to the Pro-Life movement. In short, the party followed the voters rather than led them and by doing so managed to avoid alienating any significant segment of the electorate.

This 'escape clause' manoeuvre worked in Fine Gael's favour as well – they propitiated the conservative vote by putting the 1983 pro-life referendum before the voters and then offended the same constituency by trying to argue for the ratification of the 1986 divorce referendum. In no way could either of the big two be accused of consistency on the moral questions. The surface confusion in the parties' attitudes on these issues is a function of the rapid and erratic secularising process ongoing in Irish society – big drops in Church attendance and expressed confidence in the Catholic hierarchy have been paralleled by a stubbornly low number of people describing themselves as secular or of no religious belief. The process could hardly be described as pure secularisation (Hardiman and Whelan 1998), as the pace of the trend in disaffection is so great *and* it can be partially written off as a recoiling from scandal, rather than a patiently arrived at dismissal of Church involvement in the affairs of state.[4]

A 'new politics' split?

Again, it must be stressed that one of the representative features of Inglehart's realignment thesis, the 'new left' and 'new right', is not amenable to an Irish application, simply because Ireland has never had an old left or an old right. Sassoon (1997: xxv) specifically omits Ireland from his massive history of West European Left parties in the twentieth century because 'the Left does not play a leading role either in government or in opposition'. One can nevertheless acknowledge the emergence of a branch of the 'new politics' in the form of the Green Party since Roger Garland became their first TD in 1989, but what of the challenge of inserting environmental politics into a broader postmaterialist frame in Ireland? The evidence is not encouraging for Inglehart's theory of 'new values' realignment. Marsh et al. (2001) found some support for an environmental basis to Irish political attitudes, but they also found that such a minimal ecological ingredient to politics does not form part of a larger postmaterialist structure. It is far from certain that the emergence of the Greens will serve to shift the centre of gravity of Irish party politics, mainly because it is a classic niche party. The party is typical of its European counterparts in its emphases on environment, quality of life and political accountability, but the Greens are still small electorally (winning only six Dáil seats out of a total of 166 in 2002).

Lifestyle politics

The 'sexual politics' of the divorce and abortion referendums loaded onto a factor analysis in the preliminary Marsh et al. (2001) study.[5] The figures definitively put *religious moral conservatism* versus *secular moral libertarianism* on a line of partition in Irish political attitudes. This dimension explained more variance than any of the three others. Caution is advisable before any predictions can be made from this – total variance explained by the four factors was low, at less than 42 per cent (Marsh et al. 2001: 75), with the *'religious'* factor accounting for less than 14 per cent. Baker and Sinnott (2000) saw no reason to disagree with Sinnott, Walsh and Whelan's (1995) breakdown of Irish voters along the moral axis as being the following: *ultra-conservatives* 31 per cent, *pragmatists* 27 per cent and *liberals* 29 per cent. The 2002 abortion referendum's dichotomous aspect squeezed the three divisions into two; the very narrow margin betokens an even split when voters only have two options open to them. However, the impact on representative politics of this cleavage is insignificant: the INES study showed that a 'confessional' proxy in the shape of a question on abortion had little predictive power for general election vote choice in 2002 (Marsh 2003), arguably due to the lack of distinctiveness of all the parties on such lifestyle issues.

Extraparliamentary politics

One need only refer to O'Connell's (2001) datum on the lack of political conversations among the Irish (see above) to doubt the presence of any tendency to participate in New Social Movements. If the cause is worthy, surely it merits verbal comment on the part of that cause's proponent. If not, then one can only question the level of commitment to that issue, if it exists at all. A key concept in extraparliamentary politics is that of contention (Martin: 2002). The main criterion here is the absence of real friction in the relations between any new social groupings and how they operate at the legislative level to effect change. Forty-nine per cent of Irish citizens over eighteen are involved in some voluntary organisation (Murphy: 1998), yet it is arguable that this body of people has not interacted in an antagonistic way with the governments concerned. The vast majority of such involvement is in the offering of assistance in a charitable context with altruism as the motivating factor (Ruddle and Mulvihill 1999). The political content inherent in such acts is arguably nugatory.

No party realignment

It would appear to be the case that Irish politics has not undergone an Inglehartian realignment. This does not obviate the necessity to summate the departures from tradition observable in Irish voting in the last ten years. Fianna Fáil crossed a rubicon in 1989 when they coalesced for the first time in their history (with the Progressive Democrats). There has been no single party government since the end of the 1979–81 Fianna Fáil administration.

There is a subtle danger of raising the standard for realignment to too high a level and thus losing out on evidence of strong approximations. If evidence for a realignment is found to a considerable degree in industrialised nations generally (Inglehart and Abramson 1994), then one should further probe the Irish symptoms so that one may have a more conclusive assessment of the nature of any changes in voting behaviour.

A materialist alignment?

A materialist alignment would differ in one significant respect to a class alignment. Here, the *policy* divides voters rather than their socio-economic class. In the case of materialism, the policy is typically economic in kind. The outgoing Rainbow coalition of 1994–7 offered voters a gradual reform of taxation that was progressively geared. The rival Fianna Fáil/Progressive Democrats bloc proposed instead a simplified package of straight tax cuts that conversely favoured the better paid. Fianna Fáil's working-class support actually rose in opinion polls in 1997 (Table 9.2), which disconfirmed the notion that the Irish lower socio-economic classes would opt for progressiveness in a taxation system. This tax differentiation was taken by Murphy (1998) to mark the key distinction between the rival blocs in the 1997 election: the voters act with self-focused material interests at heart and with the more immediate pay-off of a straight tax cut.

Party	Year	Working-class
Fianna Fáil	1993	34
Fianna Fáil	1997	37

Table 9.2 Percentage of working-class electorate intending to vote Fianna Fáil at two successive General Elections, July 1993 and May 1997, according to MRBI opinion polls.
Source: Coakley and Gallagher 1999:373.

The materialism theory is potentially the most accurate of commentaries on the 1997 and 2002 elections. In contradistinction to the main differentiation of the last election, the Fianna Fáil/Progressive Democrat non-leftist pledge to cut taxes, Taoiseach Bertie Ahern declares:

> [Fianna Fáil's] advocacy of social partnership puts us in that regard well to the left of New Labour in Britain. I am glad the party is significantly more left than in the past and I am proud of that.[6]

More intriguingly, Fine Gael would appear to be in the process of recasting itself as a centre-left party; its 1997 promise to aim for a more progressive taxation set-up apart, the party's 2002 manifesto aimed to increase borrowing so as to maintain infrastructure investment *and* has the mission statement of making the Irish public services the envy of Europe within fifteen years. Coupled with a declaration to eliminate poverty within a five-year period and its negative stance towards the abortion amendment of 2002, the party would seem to be in the throes of facing towards a standard model of European social democracy. Suffering a large defeat at the polls in 2002 did not really alter the party's worldview – the sheer improbability of forming a coalition with the PDs was corroborated by Fine Gael's offer to Labour to present a joint platform. With Fine Gael classically assumed to be to the right of Fianna Fáil on economics (see Laver's 'policy spaces' model [1992]), there may well be an incentive to regraph Irish party coordinates on policy dimensions (see Benoit and Laver 2006).

Confirmation that materialism could well emerge even stronger in the coming years is obtainable from *Eurobarometer* surveys, which show that a composite index of materialism is steadily rising in Ireland from an early 1990s low (O'Connell 2001: 100).[7] Geraldine Kennedy (2002) wrote that the feeling among the electorate was that financially they had done quite well in the previous five years. An internal Labour Party post-mortem account of the election also attributed the Fianna Fáil/Progressive Democrats victory to the 'feelgood factor'.[8] Marsh et al. (2001) found no measure of postmaterialism as a structuring feature in Irish political attitudes; similarly, the follow-up INES report of 2002 did not consider postmaterialism as an explanatory factor. One awaits, probably for a very long time, an election where lifestyle issues are the impetus.

The outlook for Irish electoral politics

The Irish case may well prove to be an awkward fit for either dealigment or realignment. Dealignment entails 'people gradually moving away from all parties' (Dalton and Wattenberg 1993: 202). First, a solid cleavage must be present to begin with, and, for the vast bulk of industrialised nations, this cleavage was a class-antagonistic one. There must be a decline in class voting (Kriesi 1998) and, as noted above, Ireland's polity has not been organised on left/right lines. Dealignment in general entails moving from a structured political world, with clearly located parties and voters, to a much more fluid organisation. As for realignment, it is doubtful that the order of political change in Ireland has been of the magnitude of the reshaping of American voting patterns that occurred in 1972.

Pattie and Johnston (2001) affirmed that the closer an electoral contest is – on the basis of opinion polls and general impressions) in the run-up to a general election, the higher the turnout. Their case study was the 1997 UK election, where Labour was universally tipped to win a landslide. A British voter's impact is lessened in this case, as the tide has already turned, and so has the imperative to vote and possibly effect a change. Recent Irish elections have not had this 'walk-over' quality – the proportional representation voting system operating in Ireland tightens contests and increases the political power of smaller parties, theoretically motivating individual voters to have their say. Another explanation for the reduced turnout is required. Pattie and Johnston add another and seemingly crucial factor – the perceived policy differences. Where these are large, turnout increases and the converse happens when voters find it hard to identify party-defining stances. Overall, the layout is one of proximity and occasional overlap – there is not much of a gap between the Irish parties' loci on the key policy axes of fiscal and social policy. It would be harsh to use the 'Hobson's choice' analogy, but, as Pattie and Johnston attest (2001: 400) attest, 'constrained choice is an electoral turn-off'. Indeed, the run-up to the 2007 general election has been marked by echoes of the 1970s: Fianna Fáil in power for a sustained period (in coalition from 1997 onwards, but by itself in 1973), and a joint Fine Gael–Labour effort to unseat the incumbents.

In looking at the evidence of the activity of long-term processes of dealignment and realignment, one notes again Hayward's observation (in this volume) that the appearance of change is accompanied by a structural consistency. Most parties have implicitly or even explicitly agreed that, in the state's adaptation to what they see as new and rigid parameters, some hallmarks of Irish politics are absolute givens and are not open to any form of renegotiation or even fresh thinking. Four domains are marked by any substantive differentiation, at party level or indeed at the level of a seriously considered exchange of ideas in the Irish public sphere. First is the lack of debate around a binding social partnership, which removes any real space for fiscal manoeuvring. Secondly, there is the unquestioning acceptance of the EU, irrespective of its directions and purposes, with only Sinn Féin and the Greens voicing any serious concern about the Nice Treaty, for example. Thirdly, comes the operation of a tax regime on labour which is so entrenched that all parties label tinkering as restructuring. Fourthly, there is the lack of any real sense that, in drawing up our immigration policies, we may profit from vicarious learning. Only on the question of Europe would it seem that there is something akin to a national conversation taking place, with a noticeable rise in the level of disquiet concerning social dumping and militarisation – just to name two topics.

The presidency is illustrative of this structural consistency. On the face of it, it seems fair to argue that Mary Robinson re-invented the presidency: having mobilised previously under-represented political elements behind her, including the support of Labour and Democratic Left; as an educated woman; and as Ireland's first 'modern' president, Robinson was very much seen as a promoter of a new political outlook. Her victory had demonstrated that a successful tilt against the political duopoly of Fianna Fáil and Fine Gael could be made. Mair (1999: 142) went so far as to write that she brought about a new trend towards moderation in Irish political life, as Fianna Fáil migrated towards the modern centre. The transition to a new style of presidency has not been complete, however: the election of Mary McAleese in 1997 on the back of Fianna Fáil nomination and her return to office unopposed in 2004 indicate that the path towards postnational liberalism is not a straight one. Perhaps uncomfortably for a state that was taking pride in how much it had moved away from 'the national question', President McAleese has spoken much on the dark legacy of partition, to the point that she has been accused of irredentism by pundits in the Republic and unionist figures in Northern Ireland. The fractious discussions of 2006 around the appropriateness of marking the 1916 Rising (see chapter by Ni Éigeartaigh, this volume) also illustrated that the acceptability of the state and its past is contested by many. The inveterate questions of the limits and identity of the nation–state have been recycled in this 'postnational', post-confessional Republic. Indeed, history can seem to act as a very powerful 'lock-in' for contemporary Ireland. The consequences of past institutions and actors, of their actions and inactions reverberate in political and media debate. Four issues are seemingly timeless in their effects on Irish public life: the primacy of the Church; Northern Ireland; migration; and political corruption. The legacy of the pervasive power of the Catholic Church has caused significant disquiet with regard to the acceptance of the past, as reports and court cases on clerical sex and physical abuse continually expose a state and a Church which did not value the rights of children to any meaningful degree. The vexed issue of Northern Ireland has preoccupied Irish governments for many years, whether manifested by means of lip-service to a national ideal or in the form of serious political negotiations (Ferriter 2004). Migration has been a salient aspect for the last seventy years in Ireland – emigration for the first sixty, immigration more recently. Rumours of bribery in return for political favours trailed Fianna Fáil from the 1960s; since 1991, there has been an uninterrupted flow of tribunals investigating dubious and criminal practices of politicians. It is apposite that the theme of this volume is recycling, as these four factors alone lead one to think that much of Irish politics in the first decade of the twenty-first century merits the label of old wine in new bottles.

Acknowledgements

The author would like to extend his gratitude to Professor Robert Elgie of Dublin City University for his advice and to the Business School for funding the research on which this chapter is based.

NOTES

1   Mitchell's datum is ambiguous, as it conflates 'Independents' and 'others'.
2   Sweeney's book (1998) takes 1987 as the starting line of the strong Irish economic about turn. He himself notes that others date that turn at 1992.
3   A sixth one, concerning the operations of the Supreme Court, refers exclusively to the US.
4   A study of Fine Gael members reveals that one-third of them saw no discernible policy differences between their party and Fianna Fáil (Gallagher and Marsh 2002).
5   Unlike in France's history, for example, there has been no backlash against Church involvement in schools (Hazareesingh 1994).
6   Preliminary to INES 2002.
7   *The Irish Times*, Weekend supplement, 23 March 2002.
8   This index measure is derived from the number of people who prioritise the goals of monetary discipline and strong law and order policies in a four-item survey question.
9   Interview with Labour Party official on 17 July, 2004.

REFERENCES

Burnham, W. D. 1970. *Critical Elections and the Mainsprings of American Politics*. New York: Norton.
Baker, J. and R. Sinnott, 2000. 'Simulating multi-option referendums in Ireland: Neutrality and abortion', *Irish Political Studies*, 15, 105–25.
Benoit, K and M. Laver. 2006. *Party Policy in Modern Democracies*. London: Routledge.
Carty, R. K. 1981. *Party and Parish Pump: Electoral Politics in Ireland*. Waterloo; Ontario:

Wilfrid Laurier University Press.

Castles, F. G. 2000. 'Putting the economy first: or does postmodernization really matter?', *Political Studies*, 48, 38–50.

Coakley, J. and M. Gallagher. (eds). 1999. *Politics in the Republic of Ireland*. London: Routledge in association with PSAI Press.

Collins, S. 2001. *The Power Game – Ireland under Fianna Fáil*. Dublin: O'Brien Press.

Dalton, R. J. 1999. 'Political support in advanced industrial democracies', in P. Norris (ed.), *Critical Citizens: Global Support for Democratic Government*. Oxford: Oxford University Press, 57–77.

Dalton, R. J. and M. P. Wattenberg. 1993. 'The not so simple act of voting', in A. W. Finifter (ed.), *Political Science: The State of the Discipline II*. Washington, DC: The American Political Science Association, 193–218.

Dalton, R. J., S. E. Scarrow and B. E. Cain. 2004. 'Advanced democracies and the new politics', *Journal of Democracy*, 15, 124–38.

Democracy Commission of Ireland. 2005. Final Report. http://www.tascnet.ie/upload/Democratic%20Renewal%20final.pdf (accessed 19/11/05).

Dunleavy, P. 1996. 'Political behavior: Institutional and experiential approaches'. In R. E. Goodin and H. D. Klingemann (eds), *A New Handbook of Political Science*. Oxford: Oxford University Press.

Farrell, D. M. 1999. 'Ireland: A party system transformed', in D. Broughton and M. Donovan (eds), *Changing Party Systems in Western Europe*. London: Pinter, 30–47.

Ferriter, D. 2004. *The Transformation of Ireland, 1900-2000*. London: Profile.

Gallagher, M.1985. *Political Parties in the Republic of Ireland*. Dublin: Gill and Macmillan.

Gallagher, M. 1997. 'Electoral systems and voting behaviour', in M. Rhodes, P. Heywood and V. Wright (eds), *Developments in West European Politics*. Basingstoke: Macmillan, 114-130.

Gallagher, M. and M. Marsh. 2002. *Days of Blue Loyalty: The Politics of Membership of the Fine Gael Party*. Dublin: PSAI Press.

Gilley, B. 2006. 'The meaning and measure of state legitimacy: Results for 72 countries'. *European Journal of Political Research, 45*, 499–525.

Girvin, B. 1987. 'The campaign', in M. Laver, P. Mair and R. Sinnott (eds), *How Ireland Voted – the Irish General Election, 1987*. Dublin: Poolbeg Press, 9–29.

Girvin, B. 1997. 'Ireland', in R. Eatwell (ed.), *European Political Cultures: Conflict or Convergence?* London: Routledge, 122–38.

Hardiman, N. and C. Whelan. 1998. 'Changing values', in W. Crotty and D. E. Schmitt (eds), *Ireland and the Politics of Change*. London: Longman, 66–85.

Hazareesingh, S. 1994. *Political Traditions in Modern France*. Oxford: Oxford University Press.

Inglehart, R. 1977. *The Silent Revolution: Changing Values and Political Styles among Western Publics*. Princeton: Princeton University Press.

Inglehart, R. 1984. 'The changing structure of political cleavages in western society', in R. J. Dalton, S. C. Flanagan and P. A. Beck (eds), *Electoral Change in Advanced Industrial Democracies – Realignment or Dealignment?* Princeton: Princeton University Press, 25–69.

Inglehart, R. 1990. *Culture Shift in Advanced Industrial Society*. Princeton: Princeton University Press.

Inglehart, R. and P. Abramson. 1994. 'Economic security and value change', *American Political Science Review*, 88 (2), 336–54.

Inglehart, R. and Abramson, P. 1999. 'Measuring postmaterialism', *American Political Science Review*, Vol. 93, 665-677.

Inglehart, R. and A. Hochstein. 1972. 'Alignment and dealignment of the electorate in France and the United States', *Comparative Political Studies*, 5, 343–72.

Jones, J. 2001. *In Your Opinion: Social and Political Trends in Ireland through the Eyes of the Electorate*. Dublin: Townhouse.

Kennedy, G. (ed). 2002. *The Irish Times Nealon's Guide to the 29th Dáil & Seanad*. Dublin: Gill and MacMillan.

Kriesi, H. 1998. 'The transformation of cleavage politics – the 1997 Stein Rokkan lecture', *European Journal of Political Research*, 33, 165–85.

Laver, M. 1992. 'Are Irish Parties Peculiar?', in J. Goldthorpe and C. Whelan (eds), *The Development of Industrial Society in Ireland*. Oxford: Oxford University Press, 359–81.

Lipset, S. M. and S. Rokkan. 1967. 'Cleavage structures, party systems and voter alignments: An introduction', in S. M. Lipset and S. Rokkan (eds), *Party Systems and Voter Alignments*. New York: The Free Press, 1-64.

Mair, P. 1992. 'Explaining the absence of class politics in Ireland', *Proceedings of the British Academy*, 79, 383–410.

Mair, P. 1999. 'Party competition and the changing party system', in J. Coakley and M. Gallagher (eds), *Politics in the Republic of Ireland*. London: Routledge and PSAI Press, 127-152.

Marsh, M. 2003. 'Party identification and party choice in Ireland', Paper prepared for ECPR Joint Session 2003, Workshop 26: *Modelling Electoral Choice in Europe in the Twenty-First Century*, 28 March–2 April.

Marsh, M. and P. Mitchell. 1999. 'Office, votes, and then policy: hard choices for political parties in the Republic of Ireland', in W. C. Muller and K. Strom (eds), *Policy, Office, or Votes – How Political Parties in Western Europe Make Hard Decisions*. Cambridge: Cambridge University Press, 36–62.

Marsh, M. and R. Sinnott. 1993. 'The Voters: Stability and change', in M. Gallagher and M. Laver (eds), *How Ireland Voted 1992*. Dublin/Limerick: Folens/PSAI Press, 93–114.

Marsh, M. R. Sinnott, J. Garry and F. Kennedy. 2001. 'The Irish national election study', *Irish Political Studies*, 16, 161–78.

Martin, G. 2002. 'Conceptualizing cultural politics in subcultural and social movement studies', *Social Movement Studies*, 73–88.

Mayhew, D. R. 2000. 'Electoral realignments', *Annual Review of Political Science*, 3, 449–74.

Mitchell, P. 2000. 'Ireland – From single-party to coalition rule', in W. C. Muller and K. Strom (eds), *Coalition Governments in Western Europe*. Oxford: Oxford University Press, 126–57.

Mitchell, P. 2001. 'Divided Government in Ireland', in R. Elgie (ed.), *Divided Government in Comparative Perspective*. Oxford: Oxford University Press, 182–208.

Murphy, G. 1998. 'The 1997 General Election in the Republic of Ireland', *Irish Political Studies*, 13, 127–34.

Niemi, R. G. and H. F. Weisberg. 1993. *Controversies in Voting Behavior*. Washington, DC: CQ Press.

O'Connell, M. 2001. *Changed Utterly: Ireland and the New Irish Psyche*. Dublin: The Liffey Press.

O'Malley, E. 2001. 'Apathy or error? Questioning the Irish Register of Electors', *Irish Political Studies*, 16, 215–24.

Pattie, C. and R. Johnston. 2001. 'A low turnout landslide: Abstention at the British General Election of 1997', *Political Studies*, 49, 286–305.

Ruddle, H. and R. Mulvihill. 1999. *Reaching Out: Charitable Giving and Volunteering in the Republic of Ireland*. Dublin: National College of Ireland.

Sassoon, D. 1997. *One Hundred Years of Socialism: The West European Left in the Twentieth Century*. London: Fontana Press.

Sinnott, R. 1995. *Irish Voters Decide – Voting Behaviour in Elections and Referendums since 1918*. Manchester: Manchester University Press.

Sinnott, R., B. Walsh and B. J. Whelan. 1995. 'Conservatives, liberals, and pragmatists: Disaggregating the results of the Irish abortion referendums of 1992', *Economic and Social Review*, 26 (2), 207–19.

Sweeney, P. 1998. *The Celtic Tiger – Ireland's Economic Miracle Explained*. Dublin: Oak Tree Press.

Whyte, J. H. 1974. 'Ireland: Politics without Social Bases', in R. Rose (ed.), *Electoral Behavior: A Comparative Handbook*. New York: The Free Press, 619–51.

10

The recycling of political accountability
Muiris MacCarthaigh

The most fundamental element of a democratic system is the accountability of those elected to political power. Just as other chapters in this volume have identified important developments in contemporary Ireland, so too should our understanding of accountability, and particularly political accountability, be re-examined in the context of changing government–societal relations. Using the three concepts of definition, representation and participation, this chapter examines how the institutions and methods of policy-making in Ireland have evolved in recent years and what the consequences of this process are for democratic accountability today. Taking each concept in turn, the principal institutions and methods on which each is realised are considered, as well as the way each concept has been challenged by the 'recycling' of its own practice and the emergence of alternative institutions and practices of accountability. The practice of parliamentary accountability in Dáil Éireann is also examined. It is proposed that, while political accountability has become a more contested and multi-faceted doctrine in contemporary Ireland, it is one which remains essential to the functioning and legitimacy of the state. A discussion of accountability itself will be necessary first.

Accountability: An old concept in a new era

Traditionally, an accountability relationship implies a set of shared understandings between two actors, in which the task to be achieved and the sanctions for failure are mutually understood. However, all accountability relationships are context-specific, and the method through which accountability is pursued can vary substantially. Modern governance is accountable governance, and much political and bureaucratic reform has been justified on the basis of improving or increasing accountability (Mulgan 2000). As a consequence, the meaning of the term has expanded, as it is extensively employed in relation to issues of control, oversight, responsiveness, responsibility and stewardship.

Given its subjectivity, political accountability has always been one of the most contested among accountability relationships, and, as detailed below, its practice has become subject to competing interpretations in contemporary Ireland. At one extreme in the understanding of this concept, government, or rather the governing party or parties, are held accountable to the public via national elections based on a secret ballot. Strøm (1997) refers to this ability of voters to use the ballot box so as to reward or punish governments as 'retrospective voting', but also notes that the indeterminacy of election dates makes such *ex-post* electoral accountability inadequate (Strøm 2000: 274). Therefore a more sustained form of political accountability is required. In parliamentary democracies, parliament is given this task and must be equipped to oversee government work between elections in order to ensure that the executive is held to account for its actions (or inactions). Indeed, in addition to representing the people, producing legislation, controlling public expenditure and deliberating over policy, holding an elected government to account is one of the principal tasks legislatures perform in parliamentary democracies. In other words, political accountability requires institutions such as a parliament to vindicate and legitimise its practice.

As noted in Hayward's introductory chapter, the evolutionary trajectory of the modern Irish state is subject to competing interpretations. On the one hand, it is 'in retreat', as governments seek to redefine their role as 'steering' rather than 'rowing', and public sector reforms proclaim to demystify the bureaucracy and make the state more responsive to the needs of the public. On the other hand, the state increasingly encroaches on many aspects of public (and private) life as it is obliged to regulate and legislate in areas where it had little previous involvement.

A similar dichotomy of views surrounds the principal forum for political accountability in the State – Dáil Éireann, the lower House of the Irish Parliament or Oireachtas. It is through this chamber that the practice of parliamentary (and therefore political) accountability is principally manifested. Much has been made of its decline in the context of the supremacy of European Union law-making, the growth in power of the executive, social partnership agreements and general public disinterest in parliamentary politics (Ó Cinnéide 1999). Yet the Dáil is still the most important national institution in terms of law-making; it remains the focus of media attention and public protests; and, in the final analysis, general elections to Dáil Éireann remain the most important of political events. Furthermore, the workload of the Houses of the Oireachtas has continued to expand more or less unabated since independence. Frequent assertions that Dáil Éireann is irrelevant to policy-making betray the fact that, in the context of a recycled Ireland, parliamentary accountability continues, both formally and informally, to influence the activities of politicians and bureaucrats and to provide the foundation and principal forum for political accountability.

The 'decline of parliaments' thesis and, with it, the thesis of a decline in parliamentary accountability, have been prophesised since the start of the twentieth century and have occurred in tandem with the development of disciplined parliamentary parties. To some extent, the increase in partisanship and the professionalisation of party politics have indeed turned parliaments into fora where adversarial rather than parliamentary politics takes precedence. Yet, at the start of the twenty-first century, parliaments remain core public institutions, and, as the chapters by McKenzie and Kavanagh in this volume demonstrate, it is the political parties that find themselves under threat, not least from interest group agitation and general voter apathy.

As the only directly-elected national public institution in most democracies, legislatures are expected to ensure that the highest standards of political and administrative accountability are achieved. The growth of the executive state has made this role increasingly difficult to realise in most Western states, and has resulted in institutional innovations (such as committee systems) within legislatures for the purpose of increasing scrutiny and addressing informational asymmetry. However, there has also been an increased emphasis on creating alternative accountability mechanisms that provide information on the political and administrative spheres directly to the public (Mulgan 2003). The impact of these new accountability mechanisms on existing relationships has not been fully addressed in Ireland, and, as detailed below, may have unintended consequences for political accountability.

Defining political accountability

The Irish parliament has its structural and functional origins in its British equivalent at Westminster. In legislatures such as these, collectively referred to as 'Westminster-style' parliaments (Lijphart 1984), the system of accountability is frequently compared to, and explained through, the use of principal-agent theory (Figure 10.1). The chain of delegation in principal-agent theory is mirrored by a corresponding chain of accountability, but running in the opposite direction. Based on hierarchy and following an upward direction, the Westminster system, in theory, provides clearer lines of accountability than many other forms of government. In particular, it is a far cry from the grid-like system of checks and balances which make up presidential forms of government.

Public Service → *Minister* → *Government* → *Parliament* → *Electorate*

Figure 10.1 *Ideal-typical chain of accountability in Westminster parliamentary system where '→' means 'accountable to'.*

The channel of delegation moves through the various organisational grades in the civil service with the secretary-general of the various government departments ultimately answering to the relevant minister. From there the accountability chain passes upwards to the government, which is constitutionally responsible to Dáil Éireann, elected by the people.[1] Popular sovereignty implies that the citizens who elect parliament are the ultimate principals. At the heart of this system of accountability lies the complex doctrine of 'ministerial responsibility', which essentially posits that ministers shall be accountable to Dáil Éireann for their respective administrative departments.[2] In Westminster-style parliaments such as the Oireachtas, the college of ministers forms a government cabinet, each member of which is constitutionally bound to be collectively responsible for the decisions taken by the government.[3]

As the chain of accountability is only as strong as the weakest link in it, each one of these stages forms a unique part in our understanding of how decisions are made and acted upon. The link between parliament and government is the most crucial in the Westminster chain of accountability, and the fusion of the executive within the legislature in such parliamentary systems was famously referred to by Bagehot as 'the efficient secret' (2001 [1867]). This fusion remains at the heart of much of European politics and determines the activities of political parties who seek to assume power by controlling this relationship.

The political parties which compete to control the institutions of state in order to realise their view of how the state should function are as much an institution of Irish public life as the parliament and public administration. Conventionally, the nature of the Westminster system demanded that those ministers elected by Dáil Éireann took both the credit and the blame for the performance of their departments, and the politically neutral public administration accepted the minister as the public face of their work. The public service, and particularly the senior civil service, is expected to provide its political masters with policy options and faithfully implement the decisions of government, regardless of personal or political opinion. The quid pro quo of this process is that ministers defend their departments when responding to parliamentary questions concerning a department's work and during debates on issues within the department's remit. More importantly, where decisions fail to achieve desired outcomes, ministers and their political parties are expected to deal with the consequences by taking remedial action or even by resigning, and thus political accountability is secured.

While the traditional account of how political accountability is practised is easily made, defining it in the contemporary Irish state is a more complex task. This is due to institutional reforms, deepening complexity within the bureaucracy, greater democratic expectations and changes to the very nature of political engagement, which have eroded traditional understandings of political accountability.

The increased tendency within the political sphere to assign rather than accept (or at least share) blame for administrative failings has uncertain future consequences for the decision-making process, and it further challenges the conventional definition of political accountability. The media have also forced changes on this relationship, as television and newspaper journalists all clamour to 'unmask' the bureaucracy and to apportion blame rather than to attempt to understand the complexity of the issues faced by modern public administration. In this environment, Dáil Éireann finds itself responding to agendas set by the media rather than by its members.

Within the public administration, and the departmental civil service in particular, there have also been important changes instigated by 'new public management' style reforms. The 1997 Public Service Management Act has removed some of the powers and responsibilities of ministers in appointments, dismissals, performance and discipline and transferred them to the secretaries-general of government departments. Following on from this, the *Report of the Working Group on the Accountability of Secretaries-General and Accounting Officers* (otherwise known as the Mullarkey Report) considered the dual role played by secretaries-general as both senior civil servants and financial watchdogs. The report represented an attempt to clarify what exactly the most senior tier of the public administration could be reasonably expected to be accountable for.

Another challenge to the traditional definition of political accountability is the issue of 'agencification' within the Irish public administration, i.e. the creation of bodies outside of departments, to deal with issues such as regulation, implementation and commercial development. Of approximately 200 existing national agencies identified by McGauran et al. (2005), over half were established in the last fifteen years, which coincides with a period of public-sector reform designed to increase the efficiency of the public service. Significantly, a large percentage of the agencies examined in this study believed their role to be one of providing policy advice to government, a function traditionally fulfilled by the senior ranks of the civil service rather than by semi-autonomous agencies.

In terms of parliamentary accountability, agencies create difficulties as Ministers may view them and their operations as existing outside of their realm of responsibility to parliament (Democracy Commission 2005).[4] Indeed, the establishment in 2005 of the Health Service Executive as an implementation agency within the Department of Health was partially premised on the grounds that it would allow the Minister to develop overall health policy without being hindered by operational issues. Flinders (2006: 237) argues that the use of 'delegated public bodies' and public–private partnerships cuts the direct link between the ministers and elements of the bureaucracy. Similarly, the out-sourcing of functions to private-sector consultants and specialists is also problematic for political accountability.

In some cases, the creation of state agencies is part of a wider phenomenon of 'depoliticisation'. Depoliticisation posits that, under constant attack and subject to insatiable public demands, governments try to deflect accountability by portraying policy issues as being outside of their remit or control. Instead, the requirements of European Union membership, the necessity for professional expertise or even the demands of 'globalisation' are employed as explanations for particular policy actions or decisions. In many cases, state agencies as described above are created to undertake such policy actions as regulation, implementation or coordination.

Furthermore, the Irish administration has been undergoing a substantial overhaul of its modus operandi since the mid-1990s. The Public Service Modernisation Agenda[5] has introduced market-based reforms to the public service, in an attempt to improve the efficiency and responsiveness of the bureaucracy. This has involved new practices such as systems of performance measurement and management, more emphasis on strategic policy-making, and the creation of new mechanisms of what may be referred to as public accountability. Public accountability is concerned with directly providing consumers of services (citizens) with information about how those services operate and with helping them to make their decisions without the use of intermediary actors such as politicians. Indeed, one criticism of the public sector reform agenda is that, while it has placed considerable emphasis on the role and responsibilities of the public sector in order to match the growing complexity of policy formulation and implementation, the political dimension of decision-making has not received similar attention.

Finally, not without reason, the role of parliamentary accountability in Irish life has come in for considerable criticism in light of several corruption scandals in recent years. This has resulted in the establishment of several extra-parliamentary mechanisms of political and administrative scrutiny (see MacCarthaigh 2005). For example, quasi-judicial Tribunals of Inquiry, a new Standards in Public Office Commission and Freedom of Information legislation all exist to provide alternative avenues of information concerning the accountability of political actors, but in a non-political manner. However, the reasons for their establishment – a perceived lack of political accountability – do not of themselves address the issue of why this dearth in accountability arose in the first place.

The above examples demonstrate that the boundaries and relationships that defined the basis of political accountability in Ireland have experienced significant evolution in recent years. Almost every link in the chain that delineated the traditional parameters of political accountability has been subject to considerable strain. We turn here to consider the role of political actors and the changing nature of representation in the context of the recycled state.

Representation and Political Accountability

What is decided upon in a given polity will largely be determined by who is represented in the decision-making process. At local and national level in Ireland, the traditional representative actors have been political parties. While the activities of such parties are inherently difficult to predict and their motivations impossible to determine, each of them exists to intervene in the political process on behalf of their electorate, and is therefore accountable to that electorate. However, the nature of political engagement in Ireland has changed dramatically in recent years, with an increased emphasis on participatory as opposed to representative democracy – a phenomenon that has been identified as evidence of a shift from 'government' to 'governance' (Adshead and Quinn 1998). The issue of participation and its relationship with political accountability will be considered in greater detail below.

Political parties have been referred to as the 'main transmission belts' of Irish political life (Laffan 2001: 251). From a rational-choice point of view, they reduce transaction costs and solve collective action problems (Müller 2000). They offer parliamentarians and government a mechanism for achieving their goals and allow for large amounts of information to be processed and for decisions to be taken. Sartori (1976: 49) also draws attention to the value of political parties as channels of representation through the expression of public opinion. In Ireland, as with most other European States, parties are the principal actors of representation and compete to control the balance of power at local and national government. Political parties are therefore central to the exercise of political accountability.

The Irish electoral system of PR–STV (Proportional Representation by Single Transferable Vote) is based on multi-seat constituencies and ranking of preferences, and places particular emphasis on personal reputation (see Kavanagh in this volume). However, within parliament, the value of personal political reputation for most parliamentarians is secondary to that of membership of one's parliamentary party. This is because, in Westminster-type legislatures such as the Oireachtas, selecting and maintaining in office an executive who depends on parliamentary confidence requires high levels of party cohesion. Bloc voting along party lines is therefore a prominent feature in Irish parliamentary politics, and the major parties retain forms of sanction against members who vote against the party. Such high levels of party cohesion are also displayed at local level, where the large political parties similarly dominate city, county and town councils.

While the three main political parties today – Fianna Fáil, Fine Gael and the Labour Party – have dominated the political landscape since the 1930s, core party support has diminished, and this has forced the parties to move from their traditional ideological spaces to more centrist ones (Mair et al. 2004). Convergence on the centre on key political and economic issues has blunted ideological differences between parties and the succession of coalition governments since 1989 involving parties from various ends of the political spectrum bears witness to this. However, the tendency towards post-election bargaining creates an accountability deficit, particularly concerning the electoral process itself, as voters cannot be certain who their chosen party or parties may coalesce with in order to form a government.

At local and national level, those in the political sphere view their role as one of holding the administration to account on behalf of the people – as opposed to representing and defending the activities of that administration which they control. For example, county and city councillors tend to pursue issues with local authorities on behalf of their constituents rather than to support the authorities' decisions on unpopular issues to constituents. This break in the chain of accountability is also replicated at national level, where parliamentarians, as Chubb (1963) pointed out, traditionally viewed their role as 'persecuting civil servants'. The problem is further augmented by the desire of governments to be seen to respond to public demands which may or may not involve the optimal use of public resources. Thus the role of the public administration in ensuring the effective use of such resources is often undermined by short-term political necessity.

This dynamic confuses the nature of representative democracy and thus of political accountability as well. If those elected to office do not take responsibility for the work and failings of the bureaucracy, why are they there to begin with? Political accountability demands that the political sphere is responsive to the needs of citizens, but it carries with it the duty to ensure equity. If such distribution is perceived to be unequal, or action is not forthcoming on public demands, the situation raises opportunities for alternative avenues of representation.

Such alternatives include interest groups, and the increase in the number of interest groups attempting to win seats in Dáil Éireann bears evidence to this fact (Murphy 2005). For many decades, Ireland exhibited a pluralist model of interest-group competition for resources, where groups used their numbers and influence to gain concessions and to negotiate with the political parties and public administration as needs arose. However, the emergence of a more structured corporatist-style 'social partnership' process and an increased emphasis on 'network' governance means that interest groups now routinely seek to influence policy through more formal structures as well.

Since 1987, social partnership agreements have determined much of the framework for economic and, latterly, for social policy in Ireland. The original agreements were between umbrella organisations representing employers, workers and farmers' representative organisations. In more recent years, they have also included organisations representing what is collectively known as the 'community and voluntary' sector, that is, those charities and NGOs that lobby on behalf of those outside of the political mainstream. The social partnership process has provided for high levels of industrial stability and a platform for industrial development; yet, as a method of representative governance, it raises fundamental questions concerning accountability.

In the first instance, the claims of the social partners to represent various interests have never been tested – a fact which raises important legitimacy issues that have previously been viewed as secondary to the 'output legitimacy' generated by the processes' success (see Scharpf 1999). Also, governments claim to represent the taxpayer in the process, and do not seek approval of parliament in advance of finalising any agreements. While the opposition parties may make their views publicly known, they have no possibility of preventing an agreement which bounds an ever-increasing portion of the policy-making agenda across a range of policy areas. Social partnership has also spawned a dense network of review, oversight and evaluation bodies that are largely opaque to those outside of the process itself.

A final issue concerning representation and political accountability relates to the comparatively recent phenomenon of political lobbyists as a feature of Irish political life. Unlike political parties and interest groups who exist to represent collective demands, lobbyists are paid for their attempts to influence decision-making by intervening with the existing powers on behalf of individuals or companies (or, occasionally, interest groups). While no official register of lobbyists exists in Ireland, there have been many unsavoury revelations at Tribunals of Inquiry[6] concerning the activities of lobbyists at national and local level. In the absence of legislation or regulation of the sector, the lack of accountability for the work of lobbyists fuels speculation concerning the integrity of the decision-making process.

As the limits of representative democracy are exposed in the context of the changing nature of government, alternatives for involving those affected by public policy in the decision-making process have emerged. Such alternative modes of governing and political involvement involve the recycling of traditional conceptions of representation through new modes of participation. We turn here to consider developments in participative democracy and what it means for political accountability in Ireland.

Participation and political accountability

One of the most influential works to emerge in the social sciences in recent years is Robert Putnam's *Making Democracy Work* (1994). Based on monitoring the birth and development of regional government in Italy over twenty-five years, Putnam coined the now familiar phrases 'civic community' and 'social capital' to describe two of the most important features underpinning a successful democracy. The former refers to a society in which there is active citizen involvement in public affairs; rights and obligations are shared equally; and there are high levels of trust between citizens and the institutions of government. The latter is defined as consisting of 'features of social organisation, such as trust, norms, and networks, that can improve the efficiency of society by facilitating coordinated actions'. Putnam argues that the key to a successful democracy is not economic success or institutional design, but the development of a civic community and the fostering of social capital. A strong 'civil society' is identified as underpinning greater levels of social harmony and higher levels of trust in the political system. Indeed, he argues that 'the practical performance of institutions ... is shaped by the social context in which they operate'. In other words, where opportunities for citizen involvement are maximised, the likelihood of stable government is greater.

Developing and encouraging civic engagement is viewed as central to increasing levels of confidence and democratic participation in modern states. It also provides for greater legitimacy and accountability in the democratic process. However, citizens are traditionally more likely to participate in public life when a problem arises that concerns them directly, and it is more difficult to maintain such levels of participation when problems are solved. In order to stimulate and sustain engagement, formal networks of participation in the governing process are a key component of political and administrative reform programmes in Western democracies. The demand for what Majone (1994: 4) terms 'better focused and more flexible forms of public intervention' has played a part in the development of institutions removed from political interference across much of western Europe.

This coincides with a fundamentally important trend, identified by Mair (2005), which sees not only the movement by citizens away from political engagement, but also a movement by political parties away from an increasingly volatile electorate towards the state itself. Political parties, he argues, increasingly draw their legitimacy from public institutions, as the traditional terrain of political interaction where parties and voters met is being evacuated. Take, for example, the funding of political parties not by their membership but by the state, as well as the fact that political parties are no longer private and voluntary entities but are increasingly subject to the regulations bounding the activities of public organisations. This has the effect of binding them closer to the state apparatus.

In Ireland, declining voter turnouts and dissatisfaction with traditional methods of government have resulted in new mechanisms of participation in the democratic process being established. In fact, alternative forms of societal involvement in the governing process are not new; arguably, they are as old as the state itself. To counteract executive dominance and the pervasive effects of organised political parties, two provisions were made in the 1922 Irish Free State Constitution for direct popular participation in legislation. The use of referenda, as well as popular initiative whereby as issue would be debated by parliament once a critical mass of signatures was collected (followed by decision on the matter by a referendum), were provided for in order to encourage a more participatory form of democratic government. While the provision for popular initiative was removed in 1927, the referendum procedure was reasserted in the 1937 Constitution and remains a core decision-making instrument.

Challenges to electoral legitimacy by other means, professional or popular, are therefore not uncommon and the Irish state has tried to reconcile these competing legitimacies in a formal manner. As reconstituted under the 1937 Constitution, the purpose of the Seanad (Upper House of the Oireachtas) was to ensure that various professions or 'vocations' not otherwise represented in Dáil Éireann would be able to participate in the democratic process and to be subject to political accountability. However, while the five vocational panels[7] still exist today, they are dominated by political parties rather than by professional interests.

The use of 'policy networks' involving combinations of political (state) and non-political (societal) actors is routinely advocated as holding the key to problem-solving, by bringing together individuals from different backgrounds who nevertheless share common concerns. Thus formal methods of harnessing such networks and of providing direct citizen participation in the decision-making process have re-emerged. They include public consultations on issues of national concern and the use of web-based surveys and question-naires to gauge public opinion. Similarly, in order to achieve greater responsiveness, many EU member-states (including Ireland) are attempting to mainstream procedures so as to increase public consultations for draft legislation.

At the local level, there have been several institutional innovations with the aim of reconciling the increasingly complex demands of society with the principle of efficiency and democratic legitimacy (see also Callanan in this volume). Examples of such innovations include Strategic Policy Committees and City and County Development Boards. However, as at the national level, the idea of having such participatory bodies is technically not new. Established methods of public consultation at local level include public notices concerning planning developments. Also, the Local Government Acts of 1941 and 1955 provided for the creation of 'approved local councils' as circumstances demanded. However, unlike the contemporary participatory fora, little came of these developments.

While mechanisms of participatory democracy are portrayed as supplementing rather than supplanting representative democracy, they carry certain inherent limitations. In the first instance, the participation of non-elected actors in decision-making does not guarantee that the demands or ideas of such actors will be factored into a policy. Also, as noted above in relation to social partnership, the issue arises as to whether or not those who avail themselves of mechanisms of participation are in fact representative. Are such mechanisms simply providing an even louder voice to organised interests, and how can they be certain of achieving inputs from marginalised or invisible groups in society? The relationship between elected representatives and such participative bodies is also an uncertain one, particularly in the context of competition for popular approval.

Recycling political accountability?

As noted above, issues of participation, representation and definition are closely intertwined and fundamental to the legitimacy of government in any state. While there has been significant institutional reform across developed democracies, including Ireland, in order to meet changing societal expectations and to address declining levels of public trust in government institutions, the resilience of governing institutions dictates that parliaments, governments and even political parties remain central actors in modern governance. In this context, political accountability is crucial to our understanding of power relationships in the 'recycled' state.

While the *definition* of political accountability has often been context-specific and subject to much interpretation, it is a core principle of democratic politics. What is important is that what governments have been prepared to be accountable for has certainly shifted in recent years. Coinciding with significant public-sector reform, the public administration in Ireland finds itself increasingly under public and media scrutiny. The proliferation of state agencies, the depoliticisation of issues of public concern, as well as the varying interpretations of what government can be expected to be held to account for – all create new challenges in a system based on a simple but effective design.

Nonetheless, the core doctrines of parliamentary – and thus political – accountability remain ministerial and collective responsibility, and governments remain ultimately accountable for administrative and policy failures. In other words, while the performance of duties may be 'out-sourced' or devolved, corresponding accountability cannot similarly be delegated. Also, attempts to remove an issue from political scrutiny through depoliticisation can in fact have unintended consequences, and, as the analysis by Hogwood et al. (2000) has identified, instead of deflecting attention, agencies involved in politically sensitive issues tend to attract above-average notice.

New understandings and modes of interaction in Irish political life have emerged, but it may be argued that 'governance' is not a new form of governing per se but represents a change in the way government engages with other actors. In other words, the 'shadow of hierarchy' that defined much of Irish policy-making during the twentieth century continues to inform political and administrative life, and, likewise, new conceptions of accountability must take cognisance of more established accountability relationships. While alternative methods of problem-solving are currently in vogue, ministers are always ready to intervene and exert their influence on processes which might run counter to their party or electoral platforms.

With respect to *representation*, the emergence of alternative methods of political expression and decision-making fora has created a more complex decision-making process, but one that largely remains informed by the ideals of representative democracy. The responsiveness of the political system to public demands has consequences for the efficiency of that system, and better modes of participation (below) may yet prove to be essential supports to representative politics.

Existing inherited institutions of representation, such as local authority council chambers and the national parliament, remain crucial venues for the legitimisation of binding political decisions. If anything, it is the methods through which they organise their business and take decisions that are mostly in need of reform, rather than the existence of the institutions themselves. In spite of the challenges posed by the alternative modes of political representation discussed above, elected chambers are particularly durable and continue to inform the nature of political interaction and decision taking.

With respect to *participation*, by definition, political accountability must reside in political bodies, and hence alternative avenues of political involvement cannot replace those public bodies constitutionally or legally empowered to take decisions. Also, the institutions of participative democracy are not designed to resolve conflict in the manner that legislatures and council chambers are. Furthermore, the rules and methods for accessing these institutions are known, and, as long as access to the levers of power is open to all, they will be as effective at making decisions as other forms of governance are (Peters and Pierre 2006: 217).

The emphasis in western democracies on alternative forms of governance and on administrative reforms based on market principles, which characterised much of the 1980s and 1990s, is slowly giving way to a recognition of the need for stronger political input in decision-making. In many cases, this includes a 'recentralisation' of government functions and a strengthening of core state institutions. Most notably, parliaments have responded to this challenge through a range of institutional reforms.

Political accountability and parliament

Improving accountability has become so widespread a justification for political and public sector reforms that criticism of the concept is uncommon. In fact, as noted above, there are multiple forms of accountability and types of accountability relationship, and the proliferation of such relationships can cause confusion as to who exactly is responsible for what. As demonstrated here, the traditional understanding of political accountability has been challenged by its redefinition in the context of public management reforms, as well as by the emergence of alternative avenues of representation and participation. However, as Peters and Pierre indicate, 'the ultimate responsibility for accountability must reside with public institutions' (2006: 216). As the principal representative institution in most democratic states, parliament is uniquely charged with ensuring the accountability of both the political and the administrative spheres, simultaneously.

The ability of parliaments to effectively hold executives to account is dependent on a variety of factors. Institutional design is the primary one; whether or not a parliament has a second chamber, strong rules for protecting the rights of the non-government members, and even adequate sitting times can also have an important bearing on parliamentary accountability. The nature of political engagement is another factor, and this is influenced by the opportunities available for opposition parties to involve themselves in the political process.

In Ireland, while a second chamber exists, its exclusion from the process of electing the executive means that Dáil Éireann is principally charged with the responsibility of holding government to account in-between elections. As with other legislatures in parliamentary democracies, one of the key functions of the Dáil is to provide consent for the political system, so that the power exercised by those in control may be accepted as democratically legitimate. In order to do so, meaningful processes and mechanisms of engagement with the executive are necessary: these ensure that the requirements of democratic accountability are fulfilled.

Traditionally, the accountability of the core executive has been pursued through parliamentary questions and parliamentary debate over motions and legislation. More recently, parliamentary committees have emerged as a permanent feature of the parliamentary infrastructure in the Oireachtas (below). However, as party political considerations dictate the modus operandi of the House, so too have these mechanisms and processes become embroiled in party politics. The partisan nature of political engagement undermines the effectiveness of oversight and scrutiny mechanisms, and political parties increasingly rely on the media to present their positions on issues of public policy.

The reasons for the relative weakness of parliamentary accountability in Ireland are related to a combination of institutional design, the nature of political engagement, and decisions taken at certain critical junctures in the development of the lower House (MacCarthaigh 2005: 97–184). Governments in Westminster systems are 'power hungry' (Webb and O'Brien 1991: 343), and, where such systems exist, the twentieth century has witnessed a decline in the role of the legislature, as the executive and judicial pillars of state have accumulated influence. In Ireland, the post-independence Civil War ensured that parliamentary politics quickly became a zero-sum game, in which the rights of the opposition parties were gradually eroded by successive governments.

The refusal of Fianna Fáil to engage in coalition governments for several decades after Independence ensured that Irish politics operated around two major party blocs, in which a 'winner-takes-all' form of parliamentary engagement developed. Such an environment was inimical to the successful operation of parliamentary accountability, as governments saw no need to negotiate with the opposition. In particular, the standing orders of Dáil Éireann, which governed everything from sitting times to the order of questions, were amended during the twentieth century in a manner that increasingly secured the government's grip on the parliamentary agenda. Indeed, it remains the case today that the control wielded by Irish governments over the business of the Chamber is practically unrivalled anywhere else in western Europe (Döring 1995; Döring and Hallerberg 2004: 149). Opposition parties have limited opportunities to propose legislation, ask questions and discuss matters of their choosing, and what time is made available to them is usually spent trying to embarrass the government.

For their part, Irish governments have often viewed the practice of parliamentary accountability as an obstacle to the implementation of their work rather than as a fundamental part of the democratic process. The most elementary tool in the practice of parliamentary accountability is the parliamentary question, whereby a member of the House is accorded the right to ask a member of government a question concerning a matter within his or her remit. The sheer volume of questions (around 30,000 in 2005) makes it impossible to receive oral answers to each and, in general, replies tend adopt a *de minimis* interpretation of the question asked. Naturally, government departments will want to present their efforts in the best possible light, and, given the adversarial nature of parliament and media attention, ministers will not be inclined to admit weaknesses or failures within their bailiwick. Similarly, parliamentary debates on legislation or motions are restricted by timetabling rules and 'guillotines' which governments can employ to their advantage.

It is clear, therefore, that the executive holds significant agenda-setting powers within Dáil Éireann and that the parliamentary opposition is afforded little opportunity to prevent the executive from pursuing its prerogative. In the adversarial environment of Dáil Éireann, the effectiveness of political accountability is limited and has been the source of much criticism. The Oireachtas has not been unresponsive to greater public expectations of accountability, and, though limited, there have been some developments within the legislature which offer new opportunities for more effective political accountability.

The phenomenon of successive coalition governments since 1992 has resulted in some corresponding developments within Dáil Éireann in respect of parliamentary accountability. In particular, there have been some innovations in order to allow for more topical questions to be asked,[8] as well as for discussions on pressing issues of public importance (MacCarthaigh 2005: 85–93). The most important development of all concerns parliamentary committees and their integration into the work of the Oireachtas.

For many scholars of parliaments, the development of a strong committee system is the hallmark of an effective legislature. As with most political institutions, however, there is a wide range of variation concerning the design and functioning of parliamentary committees (Strøm 1995, 1998). A common theme in much of the literature on parliamentary committees has been the importance of committee reform in reversing the decline of parliament thesis (Olson and Mezey 1991; Copeland and Patterson 1994; Longley and Ágh 1997). The general view is that legislatures have re-established themselves in the face of threats from other forms of political engagement, and have done so primarily through the effective use of committees. The increasing influence of committees within the legislature and the benefits achieved for the legislative branch raises the potential of a re-assertion of the legislative influence over the executive. After all, parliamentary committees offer several benefits to legislatures and legislators alike (Mattson and Strøm 1995; Longley and Davidson 1998). For example, as they work in parallel, committees can help to process parliamentary work more efficiently than a single plenary chamber. They also provide party leaders with structures to control their party members, and members can develop their expertise in different policy areas.

In Ireland, the development of the parliamentary committee system is comparatively recent.[9] Committees today routinely hear evidence from public officials who would traditionally have been protected by the doctrine of ministerial responsibility. Committees also act as venues for interest groups, to inform parliamentarians of their concerns. They also fulfil the valuable function of involving backbenchers in the policy-making process, something which, as previous generations of Irish parliamentarians complained, used to be the preserve of party leaderships. The experience with parliamentary committees has been so successful that new buildings have been created to facilitate their work.

Another important development has been the establishment through legislation, in 2003, of the Houses of the Oireachtas Commission. Traditionally, the Oireachtas was underfunded (Houses of the Oireachtas Commission 2005: 7) and had to apply for funding from the Department of Finance on an annual basis, a position which undermined the constitutional separation of powers. In 2004, the Houses assumed control over their finances, and an 11-member body (albeit with a government majority) now decides on the disbursement of funds on a rolling three-year basis. As a consequence, the resources and facilities at the disposal of parliamentarians are now vastly improved, and full-time researchers have been appointed to help non-government members develop their policy-making capacity. The commission is obliged to present an annual statement to the Houses, which provides the Oireachtas with an opportunity for a debate on its finances.

While these are important steps in allowing for a more open parliamentary environment, democratic accountability remains only partially realised in Dáil Éireann due to the continuing control of the agenda by government and to the strength of parliamentary party discipline. As in other Westminster-style jurisdictions (Flinders 2001: 309–38; Mulgan 2003: 75–114), a consequence of this has been the search for political and administrative accountability in Ireland through other means, including Freedom of Information legislation and legal mechanisms such as judicial inquiries. However, such mechanisms can only ever supplement rather than supplant the established forum for political accountability. In spite of its shortcomings outlined above, Dáil Éireann remains central to the process of democratic accountability in Ireland; in the context of a 'recycled' state, it is not an institution to be ignored.

Conclusion

Political accountability is the most fundamental principle of democratic government. However, defining it in the context of alternative governing arrangements, modes of representation and avenues of participation is problematic. In this chapter, the challenges faced by traditional accountability relationships and by the institution of parliament have been described. The pursuit of accountability remains central to institutional reform in contemporary Ireland, but, as with 'good governance', identifying the ideal accountability relationship remains elusive.

As Dubnick (2005) points out, a paradox exists in that more accountability does not necessarily mean better government. In fact, the point where diminishing returns begin may soon approach in the search for alternative accountability and reporting relationships. In such a scenario, the importance of robust core accountability relationships between the executive and the legislature are essential. Other forms of administrative and political accountability cannot have the democratic imprimatur necessary for public trust and accountability for political decisions cannot be transferred to non-elected bodies. In the final analysis only government, through the medium of parliament, can bestow legitimacy on political power. In a 'recycled' state, we should not lose sight of the established mechanisms of political accountability or the role of parliament itself.

NOTES

1   Article 28.4.1 of Bunreacht na hÉireann states that 'The Government shall be responsible to Dáil Éireann'. However, the Irish version of the Constitution (and, technically, the official version) uses the term '*freagrach*', the literal translation of which is 'answerable'.
2   This principle, that the administrative system should be subordinate to the administrative one, is statutorily provided for in the Ministers and Secretaries Act, 1924.
3   Article 28.4.2: 'The Government shall meet and act as a collective authority, and shall be collectively responsible for the Departments of State administered by the members of the Government'.
4   This Report also identified that 'there is little evidence that non-departmental public bodies are adequately accountable to the Dáil or Seanad' (p.75).
5   Formerly known as the Strategic Management Initiative.
6   In particular, the Flood/Mahon Tribunal has revealed extensive political lobbying over the issue of land rezoning.
7   These panels are Cultural and Education, Agriculture, Labour, Industry and Commerce, and Administration.
8   Routine parliamentary questions must be submitted at least three days in advance.
9   The current sectoral committee system has only been maintained by successive governments since 1992, far later than other European parliaments.

REFERENCES

Adshead, M. and Quinn, B. 1998. 'The move from government to governance: Irish development policy's paradigm shift', *Policy and Politics* 26 (2), 209–225.
Bagehot, W. 2001 [1867]). *The English Constitution*. Cambridge: Cambridge University Press.
Bunreacht na hÉireann/The Constitution of Ireland. 2004. Dublin: Stationery Office.
Chubb, B. 1963. 'Going about persecuting civil servants: The role of the Irish parliamentary representative', *Political Studies* 10 (3), 272–86.
Copeland, Gary W. and Samuel C. Patterson, (eds), 1994. *Parliaments in the Modern World: Changing Institutions*. Michigan: University of Michigan Press.
Döring, H. 1995. 'Time as a scarce resource: Government control of the agenda', in H. Döring (ed.) *Parliaments and Majority Rule in Western Europe*. New York: St Martin's Press, 223–48.
Döring, H. and Hallerberg, M. (eds) 2004. *Patterns of Parliamentary Behaviour*. (Alshershot: Ashgate.
Dubnick, M. 2005. 'Accountability and the promise of performance', *Public Performance & Management Review*, 28 (3), 376–417.
Flinders, M. 2001. *The Politics of Accountability in the Modern State*. Aldershot: Ashgate.
Flinders, M. 2006. 'Public/private: The boundaries of the state', in C. Hay, M. Lister and D. Marsh (eds), *The State: Theories and Issues*. Basingstoke: Palgrave Macmillan, 223–247.
Harris, C. (ed.) 2005. The Report of the Democracy Commission – Engaging Citizens: The Case for Democratic Renewal in Ireland. Dublin: New Island Press.
Hogwood, B., D. Judge and M. McVicar, 2000. 'Agencies and accountability', in Rhodes, R. (ed.), *Transforming British Government: Volume I: Changing Institutions*. Basingstoke: Macmillan, 195–222.
Houses of the Oireachtas Commission 2005. *Annual Report*. Dublin: Stationery Office.
Laffan, B. 2001. 'The parliament of Ireland: A passive adapter coming in from the cold', in A. Maurer and W. Wessels (eds), *National Parliaments on their Ways to Europe: Losers or Latecomers?* Baden-Baden, Germany: Nomos, 251–68.

Lijphart, A. 1984. *Democracies*. New Haven, CT: Yale University Press.

Lijphart, A. 1999. *Patterns of Democracy: Government Forms and Performance in Thirty-Six Countries*. New Haven, CT: Yale University Press.

Longley, L. D. and R. H. Davidson. 1998. 'Parliamentary committees: Changing perspectives on changing institutions', in L. D. Longley and R. H. Davidson (eds), *The New Roles of Parliamentary Committees*. London: Frank Cass, 1–20.

Longley, L. D. and A. Ágh, 1997. 'On the changing nature of parliamentary committees', in L. D. Longley and A. Ágh (eds), *The Changing Roles of Parliamentary Committees*. Research Committee of Legislative Specialists: Working Paper II.

MacCarthaigh, M. 2005. *Accountability in Irish Parliamentary Politics*. Dublin: Institute of Public Administration.

Mair, P. 2005. *Democracy Beyond Parties*. Paper 05/06: Center for the Study of Democracy, University of California Irvine.

Mair, P., W. C. Müller and F. Plasser (eds), 2004. *Political Parties and Electoral Change: Party Responses to Electoral Markets*. London: Sage.

Majone, G. 1994. 'Independence vs. accountability? Non-majoritarian institutions and democratic government in Europe', EUI Working Papers in Political and Social Sciences. Florence: European University Institute.

Mattson, I. and K. Strøm, 1995. 'Parliamentary committees' in H. Döring (ed.), *Parliaments and Majority Rule in Western Europe*. New York: St Martin's Press, 249–307

McGauran, A-M., K. Verhoest and P. C. Humphreys, 2005. *The Corporate Governance of Agencies in Ireland: Non-Commercial Public Sector Bodies*. Dublin: Institute of Public Administration.

Mulgan, R. 2000. 'Accountability: An ever-expanding concept?', *Public Administration*, 78 (3), 555–73.

Mulgan, R. 2003. *Holding Power to Account: Accountability in Modern Democracies*. Basingstoke: Palgrave Macmillan.

Müller, W. 2000. 'Political parties in parliamentary democracies: Making delegation and accountability work', *European Journal of Political Research*, 37 (3), 309–33.

Murphy, G. 2005. 'Interest groups in the policy-making process', in J. Coakley and M. Gallagher (eds), *Politics in the Republic of Ireland*. London: Routledge, 352–83.

Ó Cinnéide, S. 1999. 'Democracy and the Constitution', *Administration* 46 (4), 41–58.

Olson, D. and M. Mezey, 1991. 'Introduction', in D. M. Olson and M. L. Mezey (eds), *Legislatures in the policy process*. Cambridge: Cambridge University Press.

Peters, B. G. and J. Pierre, 2006. 'Governance, government and the state', in C. Hay, M. Lister and D. Marsh (eds), *The State: Theories and Issues*. Basingstoke: Palgrave Macmillan.

Putnam, R. 1994. *Making Democracy Work*. Chichester: Princeton University Press.

Sartori, G. 1976. *Parties and Party Systems*. Cambridge: Cambridge University Press.

Scharpf, F. W. 1999. *Governing in Europe: Effective and Democratic?* Oxford: Oxford University Press.

Strøm, K. 1995. 'Parliamentary government and legislative organisation', in H. Döring (ed.), *Parliaments and Majority Rule in Western Europe*. New York: St Martin's Press, 51–82.

Strøm, K. 1997. 'Democracy, accountability and coalition bargaining', *European Journal of Political Research*, 31(1), 47–62.

Strøm, K. 1998. 'Parliamentary committees in european democracies', in L. D. Longley and R. H. Davidson (eds), 21–59.

Strøm, K. 2000. 'Delegation and accountability in parliamentary democracies', *European Journal of Political Research*, 37 (3), 261–86.

Webb, M. and P. O'Brien 1991. 'The ghost in the system', in P. O'Brien and M. Webb (eds), *The Executive State: WA Inc. and the Constitution*. Perth, Australia: Constitutional Press, 341–52.

11

Conclusions:
The recycled state

Muiris MacCarthaigh
and Katy Hayward

Recent developments across a range of policy fields, new forms of political engagement and changing identities in modern Ireland do not necessarily represent breaks with the past. The Celtic Tiger years have resulted in every aspect of Irish life being subject to pressures of 'globalisation', including expansions in individual liberties, demands for transparency, and conformity to international norms. However, the strength of the underlying dynamics and historical forces which combine to make Irish social and political culture unique remains undimmed. The present book contends that, especially during the last two decades, Ireland has experienced a 'recycling' of many of its political values and practices. As its chapters have demonstrated, this has occurred through the maintenance of a certain degree of continuity in the definition of, representation by, and participation in the state across a range of policy areas. The legacy of the state's brief history is not only preserved and cherished in much of the contemporary Irish state but serves, to a large measure to plot its future trajectory.

The recycling model

In the introductory chapter, Hayward presents the theoretical basis for this volume. Identifying competing interpretations of how best to understand the development of the modern nation–state, she notes that the constant interaction between the state and the forces of change is one of competition and antagonism. It is the inherently adaptative and resilient nature of the state that ensures its endurance, and, recognising this, political elites seek to marry modern goals with the persistent requirements of statehood. While there is considerable emphasis on the institutions and structures of the state, the processes of interaction between competing ideologies are fundamental in the explanation of the modern state's constant renewal. Therefore a 'recycling' of the state in which history, present and future are merged in ideal and pragmatic terms is a defining feature of modern states.

Developing the theme of 'recycling', Hayward identifies three dimensions of political adaptation to contemporary change – definition, representation and participation of, and in, the state – and the interplay between their dynamics. The definition of the state can vary depending on the function in question, one such function being to uphold the distinction between 'insiders' and 'outsiders' in a political community, as embodied in conflicts over citizenship. This relates to the second point, namely representation by the state, which connects the majority of people to the activity of the governing power. The failure to develop and embed radical new forms of political representation in response to significant changes in other areas (such as technological development) is clear evidence of a certain traditionalism in this field – a matter which is criticised in detail in a number of chapters in this volume. Channels of representation are closely connected to levels of political participation, which is the final element of the 'recycling' trend examined in this volume. It is clear that the participation of individuals in politics is not merely a matter of citizens' choice or motivation but relates to the structural conditions of statehood, which do not adjust with the times so much as maintain certain lines of exclusion. In this concluding chapter, we briefly highlight and compare evidence provided in the contributing chapters for the illumination of such trends.

Definition

The definition of the Irish state and, thereby, of its polity reflects the unsettled nature of 'Irishness', both within and beyond the territory of the Irish state. The definition of statehood is intrinsically connected to the definition of national identity; it is shaped by nationalism to give the political institutions of the state a cultural significance and an historical context. Recent re-examinations (and revisions) of the early years of the state's independence demonstrate the unsettled nature and meaning of Irish history, as well as a prevalent desire in Irish politics to link current and past events in order to justify planned political activity or direction. Ni Éigeartaigh's chapter uses the tools of literary analysis to highlight the role of historical myth and discourse in the definition of the modern state. Beginning from Anderson's model of nationhood as a unifying idealised set of values and beliefs (1983), Ni Éigeartaigh illuminates the role of nationalist myths in underpinning the definition of the Irish state, from its conception to the present day. The 'nation' provides a sense of belonging and nationalist myths of heroes and martyrdom are used to underpin and construct a dominant definition of the Irish state. Iconography and ideology were popularly utilised to this end as they were easy to incorporate into the new state. Moreover, as Ni Éigeartaigh notes, the focus on mythology helped the state elite to avoid engaging with the conflicts deep-rooted in its foundation.

Ni Éigeartaigh illuminates the central role of mythology in linking the state to its past and the latter's implications for the way the state develops. She argues that de Valera was able to remodel heroes of the past in order to address needs of the present, and that he used the 1935 commemoration of the 1916 Rising to delimit those who could claim to be inheritors of the Irish nationalist legacy (and, in doing so, marginalise those who didn't fit this narrative). If de Valera is shown to be a master of using nationalist ideology to address the needs of the present, Ni Éigeartaigh demonstrates that the same tactics is very much in use in contemporary Ireland. She shows the 2006 official commemoration of the Easter Rising to be a clear attempt to wrest back control over the narratives of Irish nationalist heroes from the contemporary opponents of Fianna Fáil, specifically Sinn Féin. In affirming the Irish state's right to celebrate its 'origins' in the Rising, the commemoration was a perfect illustration of how nationalist mythology not only is continually recycled but has now been successfully subsumed into the narrative of the Irish state.

Focusing on the influence of the 'border' in the definition of the Irish state and of Northern Ireland, McCall notes the persistence of some all-Ireland activity despite partition. Yet, whereas unionists may have seen some value in co-operating with the Irish state, ambiguity about the definition of the limits of the Irish polity made them reluctant to engage in an activity so heavily-laden with symbolism.

McCall documents the failed attempts at developing enhanced cross-border co-operation and contrasts this failure with the success of the North/South bodies established under the Good Friday Agreement. In particular, he considers the Agreement's redefinition of the Northern Ireland conflict in East/West as well as North/South terms, and the re-establishment of the idea of the border as a bridge. This has all been achieved within the context of the European Union, which has assisted the redefinition of British–Irish relations in both economic and diplomatic terms. Ultimately North/South institutions, he argues, are key to progress on redefining the nature of the Irish border in a European context.

Articles 2 & 3

A substantial element and a consequence of the Good Friday Agreement of 1998 was the change to Articles 2 and 3 (which define the Irish nation and its territory) of Bunreacht na hÉireann following a constitutional referendum. It is notable that three chapters in this volume identify the amendments to Articles 2 and 3 in the constitution as of major importance in the definition of the contemporary state, albeit for different reasons. McCall notes that such a clarification of the bounds of the Irish state was a necessary condition for positive political cooperation between North and South. Yet the rewriting of Articles 2 and 3, and redefinition of the Irish state in general, has not been an exercise directed at engagement with Northern Ireland alone, a point illuminated by both Ni Éigeartaigh's and Howard's chapters. The original Articles 2 and 3 defined the Irish 'nation' in a way that included individuals beyond the territorial jurisdiction of the state; their revision following the 1998 Agreement sought to depoliticise this claim in relation to Northern Ireland by including recognition of the Irish diaspora in the broadest terms. Yet, as Howard shows, this has given rise to more contradictions and problems for practical issues of contemporary Irish citizenship, as second- and third- generation Irish people are caught between Ireland's relatively generous citizenship regime and its closed procedures for political representation.

Citizenship

The definition of the Irish state's identity is integrally related to the evolution of the concept of Irish citizenship. Because citizenship 'mediates the relationship between civil society and the state', citizenship regimes epitomise the values and assumptions upheld in the definition of the state (Faulks 1999: 127). Howard reveals that one response of the Irish state to integration in the context of globalisation has been the redefinition of Irish citizens abroad as 'transnational diasporans' instead of 'rmigrants'. In his study, Howard not only traces the historical ambiguities and tensions in the definition of the external Irish but shows how traditional ideals and present pragmatism continue to be merged in Irish official policy towards its citizens. This is evident in the government-supported strategy at the turn of the twenty-first century to encourage those of Irish descent around the world to 'come home' to feed the Celtic Tiger economy (see also Hayward and Howard 2007).

McKenzie identifies the impact of the Celtic Tiger – in terms of modernisation, population growth, European integration and affluence – on the definition of the Irish polity from day to day. Thus the new definition of the state sees the recycling of traditional principles (ethnic Irishness, all-island grounds for Irish identity, Irish cultural values, and so on) in adaptation to the new context (significance of global links, recognition of the border in order to cross it, and so on). The significance of this definition is reflected in the legislation of the state, which is shaped by certain social, economic and cultural values. Crowley shows how changing values, norms and discourse in Irish politics have had practical consequences for Travellers as a minority group in Ireland. Not only does the exclusive nature of citizenship and political practice contribute to the stigmatisation of minority groups in civil society, it also leads to their effective exclusion from traditional processes of political representation.

Representation

The necessary exclusion of the mass of people from daily decision-making in the affairs of the modern state means that democratic elections on the basis of territorial constituencies has become the standard means of representation in, and by, the state. The scope and effectiveness of political representation in Ireland is under pressure from a variety of directions. This process has two dimensions: first, the inability of the system to adjust to, and reflect, significant change in political identification; and, secondly, the disengagement of Irish citizens from the representative process. In relation to the first point, as Kavanagh and MacKenzie note, the Irish state is very much in line with its contemporaries in facing issues of declining partisanship and voter turnout. Weakening identification with political parties (particularly the larger mainstream parties) has seen a corresponding growth in the influence of other factors at the polling booth, for example socio-economic background and local constituency issues. This undermines the representative system and can only produce greater distortion in terms of the gap between state and society. This gap, MacCarthaigh shows, is further exacerbated by the weak mechanisms of account-ability in the Irish Parliament, which allow for a breakdown in trust between those represented and their representatives. Decline in the representative system is perpetuating problems of low voter confidence. This is borne out by the fact that those traditionally on the margins of Irish civil society, whether because of their physical location, economic position or social condition, continue to be so. In the case of the Irish diaspora, as outlined by Howard, the pressure for some form of representation of its diaspora by the kin-state has necessitated the creation of institutionalised linkages in varying degrees and forms (for instance, the Díon funds for Irish charities in Britain). However, the Irish state's recognition of a symbolic and even economic obligation to Irish citizens abroad has not extended to facilitating their political representation in state affairs.

MacKenzie's chapter on political parties draws attention to the challenges faced by political parties in the context of a more volatile electorate; yet Irish politics still revolves around two familiar blocs that continue to defy compatibility with other European party systems. Kavanagh demonstrates, that in spite of Ireland's convergence with international downward trends in voting turnout, linkages between turnout, partisanship and patterns of support and representation remain particularly strong. In other words, interpersonal engagement continues to be a defining characteristic of Irish political life in spite of the emergence of alternative routes of representation. Developing this point, MacCarthaigh argues that, while alternative forms of administrative and political accountability have emerged in contemporary Ireland, they cannot assume the democratic legitimacy of public institutions such as parliament and locally elected councils. In the recycled state, responsibility for accountability must reside in public institutions in order that basic requirements of democratic representation may be fulfilled.

Local governance

Turning to the often neglected issue of local governance in Ireland, the chapter by Callanan links the issues of representation and participation through an analysis of administrative and managerial reforms in Irish local authorities. Noting the importance of local government as an arena for representing issues of identity and community through participation in democratic structures, he notes the enduring nature of the traditional power imbalance between central and local government. This is in spite of the democratic mandate of the latter, and in spite of the fact that it predates the existence of the central state. Callanan identifies the administrative overhaul within the local government system in recent years, which has included the out-sourcing of services and the rationalisation of staffing structures. More importantly for this volume, he identifies reforms aimed at increasing the policy-making capacity of local authorities and the direct involvement of citizens and interest groups in policy formulation. While these new participative structures are undoubtedly innovative, in the absence of revenue-raising ability and real devolution of power, they are simply a recycling of the status quo. The volte-face taken by government on the concept of directly elected mayors, for example, reveals a view of local government as, primarily, a form of local administration rather than of popular participation and representation. It also shows the enduring nature of national foundations and traditions within political systems.

Staying with the theme of local representation, Kavanagh's chapter on political behaviour demonstrates the enduring strong link between representation through the medium of political parties and voter turnout levels in Ireland. In the face of downward trends in voting turnout and growing political disconnection, interpersonal engagement continues to be a defining characteristic of Irish political life. Using sub-constituency data, he draws attention to the importance of local influences on political mobilisation and turnout and challenges conventional wisdom that modern Irish politics is without social bases. Kavanagh proposes a virtuous circle whereby increases in politicisation can lead to improved turnouts and hence to better representation of the concerns and views of the sub-constituencies. For this to occur, sustained and community-based mobilisation of the electorate is required.

MacCarthaigh also notes the changing nature of political engagement and documents the reforms that have challenged traditional understandings of political accountability. He suggests that the Irish representative system has been slow to evolve and Irish politicians are reluctant to adjust the instruments for representation and executive oversight. Institutional stasis in the central state and voter apathy in relation to national forms of representation have therefore involved a readjustment of participation in politics in Ireland.

Participation

Participation in the state may be defined as the actions of private citizens, aimed at influencing the constitution and the activity of government. The chapters in this volume have not been concerned so much with the nature of such actions but rather the ways in which they have been encouraged, confined and mobilised by the strictures of the contemporary state. The phenomena of declining voter turnout and partisanship, as well as the weakening bonds of between political parties and citizens, contrast with the enduring mould of Irish political participation. The crucial factor of territory – in terms of constituency boundaries and conditions of citizenship, for example – remains absolute, as demonstrated in the chapters by Howard and Crowley in relation to quite different contexts.

Howard shows that participation in the state for Irish people (even those with full Irish citizenship) who physically reside outside the state is highly restrictive. Political rights and voice for Irish citizens is here shown to be dependent on territorial location. Even the citizenship granted to those born outside the state (such as those in Northern Ireland) may be termed 'of second order', in that the full rights of citizenship (including voting) cannot be exercised from outside the state's jurisdiction. Crowley's analysis gives perhaps greater cause for concern when it becomes clear that some citizens within the territorial confines of the state are marginalised in such a way as to be excluded from participation in the modern state, not to mention from representation by it and from its definition. Crowley notes how contemporary discourses of inclusion and 'active citizenship' betray the reality of exclusiveness and restriction, thus demonstrating how they represent a recycling of discourses from earlier generations. In particular, she challenges the popular notion of inclusion as a positive dynamics, by questioning its underpinnings in concepts of place, locality and spatial fixity as well as in the rejection of other ways of being. If anything, active citizenship discourse demonstrates the continuing significance of long-held values and policies of the state in relation to its citizens. Fundamental to such values – as in Howard's case study – is the continued importance (and subsequent restrictions) of territory among the means available to participate in the state. Traveller issues, Crowley argues, continue to be considered in the context of an exclusionary model of citizenship, with an emphasis on territory that disregards the values and desires of nomadic Travellers.

Whilst, as Howard, Crowley and McCall concur, the state can decide the limits of participation in the traditional forms of national politics, new channels for political expression and new outlets for political activity reflect shifts in the nature of participation in contemporary Ireland. All the chapters examine, from their own particular point of focus, the scope of these developments, their implications and their limitations. What is undeniable, however, is that the effects of the dynamics between these political forcesare not confined simply to the structures of the Irish state; they also have a significant impact upon the state's processes of adaptation. The politics of this adaptation in contemporary Ireland centre upon a continual recycling of the definition of the Irish state, its fields of representation, and avenues for participation. Kavanagh and McKenzie identify weakening party support amongst voters which, they suggest, is producing new forms of political mobilisation, based on community activity and voluntary organisations. However, the low levels of political activism and the continuing link between party affiliation and the individuals' political engagement in Ireland make both authors stop short of defining these changes in terms of new social movements. The anti-statism associated with new social movements is weak in Ireland, not least because the Irish state remains at the heart of the definition of politics. Crowley illustrates this through the example of active citizenship discourse, which shows the continuing significance of the values and policies of the state in relation to its citizens.

Social policy

Following on from Crowley, Fanning and MacVeigh also look at the recycling of the way the Irish state serves to support its citizens – but this time in terms of the development of the welfare provision. Starting from the recent publication of the *Developmental Welfare State*, they compare it to earlier attempts to establish a framework for dealing with challenges faced by contemporary Irish social policy, but which fail to address the issues of comprehensive wealth redistribution and equality. In proposing that there has never truly been a 'welfare state' in the Republic of Ireland, they draw attention to the traditional involvement of voluntary, market and state sectors in the implementation of social policy.

Rather than a break with the past, they argue that the *Developmental Welfare State* has its roots in the nation-building project that replaced previous post-colonial isolationism. In this, they draw comparisons with plans for wider provision of secondary education in the mid-1960s and with the emphasis on mercantile rather than human-capital needs. They argue that, just as *Investment in Education* (1965) ultimately favoured the middle classes and those in a position to take advantage of the extension of public goods, so too does the *Developmental Welfare State* (2005) place much of the developmental emphasis on relatively advantaged groups. New developments in welfare provision do not overhaul a system that has emerged incrementally, but they represent a social policy response to the challenges of globalisation and to the subsequent re-branding of all welfare goods and services as having developmental functions.

Conclusions

Despite fresh attempts to define the nation-state, the creation of new multi-level avenues for political representation and embryonic forms of participative citizenship, the elementary tenets of Irish statehood remain consistent. For example, as preceding chapters have demonstrated, the political community stays territorially-based, many social policies are rebranded but not reconstructed, and political discourse relies heavily on images from the past in justifying future trajectories. While mainstream political parties claim an inheritance from the crucible of revolution, their influence on politics necessarily serves to keep fundamental adjustment to a minimum. This is seen in the fact that, as the Irish citizenry becomes more diverse and 'globalized', the conceptualization of Irish citizenship is more conservative than ever. In the rapidly-changing environment initiated by the 'Celtic Tiger' economy, adaptation in Irish politics is characterized by ambiguity and contradiction. And so, we conclude, the process of recycling looks set to remain an essential element of the 'new Ireland'.

REFERENCES

Anderson, B. 1983. *Imagined Communities*. London: Verso.

Faulks, R. 1999. *Political Sociology: A critical introduction*. Edinburgh: Edinburgh University Press.

Hayward, K. and Howard, K. 2007. 'Cherry-picking the diaspora', in B. Fanning (ed.) *Immigration and social change in Ireland*. Manchester: Manchester University Press, 47–62.

OECD/Government in Ireland. 1965. *Investment in Education*. Dublin: Stationery Office.

National Economic and Social Council. 2005. *The Developmental Welfare State*. Report No. 113. Dublin: Stationery Office.

Index

242

RECYCLING THE STATE

O'Sullivan, Denis, 111,
118–19, 121
O'Sullivan, Gerry, 77–8
Owen, G., 166, 167
Özkirimli, U., 7

P
Pacek, A., 166
Painter, J., 105
Paisley, Revd. Ian,
49–50, 53
Palma, G.D., 13
Panayi, P., 69
Parekh, B., 71
parliamentary
committees, 204, 218,
219–20
parliamentary questions,
218, 219
participation, political,
xv, 9, 11, 12–13, 202,
226, 232–4
accountability and,
209, 212–15, 216
adaptation and, 235
community activity,
154–5, 175–6, 233
continuity and, 225,
235
dealignment, theory of,
180, 184–6, 194,
195
hierarchy of
involvement, 12–13,
67, 84–5, 216
innovations, 213–15
Irish diaspora and, 66,
67, 77–81, 83–5
local government and,
133, 141–2, 231
'policy networks' and,
214
realignment, theory of,
180, 185–6, 190–1,
192, 194, 195
voluntary
organisations,
154–5, 175–6, 233
see also elections,
Irish; referenda,
Irish; turnout,
electoral

partition, xiii, 44–50, 67,
196
see also border, Irish
Patterson, Henry, 54
Patterson, Samuel C.,
220
Pattie, C., 176, 195
Payne, D., xv, 57
PEACE II programme
(EU), 57
Pearse, Pádraig, 27, 31,
32, 33
poetry of, 21–3, 29, 30
Peillon, M., 118
Peters, B.G., 216, 217
Philo, C., 105
Pierre, J., 216, 217
Pilet, J.B., 150
Pitkin, H.F., 11
Piven, F., 165–6
Plamenatz, J., 8
Plunkett, Sir Horace, 46
pluralism, 6, 33, 38, 59,
88, 106, 211
poetry, 21–3, 29, 30,
32–3
Poggi, G., 43
'policy networks', 214
political parties, 204,
206, 209, 210, 213
campaigning
methods, 159–60,
163–4, 175
cohesion and
discipline, 209–10,
221
continuity, xiii, 186–7,
195–6
local government and,
139, 210, 231
membership, 13, 160
moral issues and,
189–91
political mobilisation
and, 159–65, 231,
233
representation and, 11,
230, 231–2
voter identification
with, 166, 167, 182,
183–5, 230, 232
political sociology, 6, 10

Pollak, A., 57
postmaterialism, 185–6,
191, 194
postmodernity, 4, 5
'postnationalism', 4–5
poverty, 2, 97, 98, 117,
122, 124, 194
Powell, F., 97, 106
power-sharing Executive,
Northern Ireland, 45,
50
presidential elections,
Irish, 156
press, the, 38, 51, 95–6,
106, 206
Irish Times, 35, 38,
46, 51, 59, 95, 101
pressure group politics,
13, 184, 204, 210–11,
220
Prevention of Cruelty to
Children Act (1908),
90
principal-agent theory,
205
private sector, 4, 113,
123, 125, 127–8, 138,
141, 207
Procacci, G., 93, 98–9
Programme for
Economic Expansion
(1958), 115
Progressive Democrats,
xiii, 80, 81, 164, 170,
182, 192, 194
electoral support, 189,
193
electoral turnout and,
167, 169, 173
Prohibition of Incitement
to Hatred Act (1991),
97
property taxes, local,
145–6
Protestantism in Ireland,
88, 92
Provisional Government,
Irish, 43, 44, 47
public administration,
206–7, 210
depoliticisation,
207–8, 215